Call Me LUMPY

My Leave It to Beaver Days and Other Wild Hollywood Life

by Frank Bank

with Gib Twyman

Foreword by Kenny Osmond

ADDAX
PUBLISHING
GROUP

Published by Addax Publishing Group
Copyright © 1997 by Frank Bank

Designed by Randy Breeden
Cover Design by Jerry Hirt

ISBN: 1-886110-29-8
Distributed to the trade by Andrews McMeel
4520 Main Street
Kansas City, MO 64111

Library of Congress Catalog Card Number
Printed in the United States of America
1 3 5 7 9 10 8 6 4 2

Library of Congress Cataloging-in-Publication Data

Bank, Frank, 1942-
        Call me Lumpy : my Leave it to Beaver days and other
Hollywood
    life / by Frank Bank with Gib Twyman.
            p.   cm.
        ISBN 1-886110-29-8
        1. Bank, Frank, 1941-   . 2. Television actors and actresses-
    -United States—Biography. 3. Leave it to Beaver (Television
    program) I. Twyman, Gib. II. Title.
    PN2287.B165A3   1997
    791.45′028′092—dc21
    [B]   97-41563
                                                        CIP

Dedication

To my Beeky and the girls—*Michelle, Julie, Joanne and Kelly*
— F. B.

To the guys I grew up with in the Cleaver years, my own little
Beavers, my brothers, Tom, Greg, Geoff and Mark.
— G. T.

SUPERFRIENDS...Tony, Jerry, Kenny and I share a moment in the
locker room before Super Bowl XXI in Pasadena in 1987. That's 30
years after the debut of the original "Leave It To Beaver," but I still
regard these guys as family. I love seeing them whenever I can. I
always will.

Table of Contents

Foreword

By Kenny Osmond

J tell you, Frank Bank gives the impression when you first meet him that he is Lumpy Rutherford. That is, he's "Big Dumpy Lumpy."

And he's not.

The guy is particularly sharp.

He's got some working brain cells. They just don't show when you first meet him.

I have no idea why.

He's an extrovert. He's very social.

And yet, maybe right at first, he's a little guarded and reiterates into his old character for just an instant.

All I know is, the Frank Bank inside, all that is a guy, I consider a really good friend.

And I guess the thing I find most interesting about Frank and me is that we are good friends—even though we don't have a great deal in common.

His music and mine are different. His politics and mine are different. His social activities and mine are different.

I'm a hard-core country music guy. Country and bluegrass.

Allison Krause. Union Station. That type of stuff. Frank wouldn't even know these names. Frank is kind of contemporary. Pop. That type of thing.

I'm a hard-core conservative. He's on the conservative side, but not as opinionated as I am. I was a Goldwaterite long before he was a Reaganite.

I'm more of a down-home type. I would go to a nightclub that has sawdust on the floor. He would prefer to go to someplace in Beverly Hills that has crystal glasses and linens on the tables.

But in spite of that, he's a good friend.

I don't know. We just click.

Even though we're totally different in other areas.

I'm a mechanical person. He's not.

He just moved into a house a couple months ago. I was out there the day he was just starting to get moved in. He had a washer-dryer there and he didn't know how to hook 'em up.

So I said. "Get me a pair of pliers."

And he said, "What's a pair of pliers?"

I hooked up his washer-dryer for him.

I became a policeman in L.A.—and I hope none of you ever has to know what it is to be a policeman. You just don't want to know. I got shot a couple of times.

Frank went off and became a stock broker.

He wears clean clothes and a tie when he goes to work.

I don't. I renovate houses now. So I put on cut-off Levis and I go and play with my houses.

And yet I love the guy.

We just get along.

You know, there are people that you just don't want to be with.

You're sociable with them. You have to be. They're there at a function, so you're sociable with them.

And there's other people that you prefer to be with. I definitely prefer to be with Frank.

We can go out after we've done an appearance or something and have a drink together and sit and chit-chat.

I always feel respect and affection from Frank. I feel that same respect and affection for him.

Like I say, he's sharp.

I would trust him totally with money. If I had $50,000 and I wanted to put it someplace to make some money, he's the first guy I'd call.

I have a couple of Franklin accounts and he's done them for me. And they've been great. I mean, I'm not making a million dollars on 'em. But they've been consistently profitable.

So I appreciate his abilities professionally. He definitely knows what he's doing with a dollar.

And yet, it's interesting...I know when we did "The New Leave It To Beaver" series, Frank would actually lose money. He'd take off work and drive to Florida to do an episode. And it would cost him—the amount he'd make on the show versus being away from his brokerage business.

But he'd do it anyway just because he loved it.

I understand it. It's good for your ego. Why not?

If he were working at the poverty line and losing money, I'd say, "No, that's dumb, Frank. Don't do that."

But this is not the case.

Still, this is another difference between us.

Frank loves the limelight.

I can't say that I do.

I mean, I certainly hope "Beaver" is always in my life.

It's a major part of my income. Personal appearances. Endorsements. That sort of thing.

But people don't "Eddie" me so much in Los Angeles these days and I think that's fine.

First off, I don't look the same here. Because I renovate houses for the most part, I'm usually in cut-offs and a dirty T-shirt, and really raunchy tennis shoes with my hair's askew. And I'm grubby because I've just been snakin' out a sewer or reroofing a house, or whatever.

So they don't see me.

That, and the people in L.A. are very complacent. They just don't care.

If I get decent-looking and go to Cacumonga, Iowa, yes. They do make over Eddie.

But generally, I don't really miss it.

I think Frank always will.

I'll tell you, if Frank and I are out someplace and I am cleaned up, people will come up and ask if I'm Eddie. Now, to me it's a fan and I'll do what I can to please 'em and all.

And then I'll point across the table and go, "And right here is Lumpy."

And they'll go, "Yeah! Lumpy!"

And I can see that Frank still eats this up. He absolutely thrives on it.

When it happens, he lights up like a birthday cake.

Fortunately for both of us, there are 40 candles now on "Beaver's" birthday cake and people still respond to the show.

I know both of us are grateful for our fans and their long-standing devotion to "Beaver" over all these years.

When all is said and done, "Beaver" is a kind of foundation in both our lives. Frank and I share that. And that is a bond that won't ever break.

Kenny Osmond
aka "Eddie"
September, 1997

Introduction

'm just sittin' here thinkin' about all of my lunatic friends and the crazy times we had, which went into writing this book.

I have reached one conclusion.

My friends are better than any Damon Runyon characters ever were.

Because of them, I can only say one thing.

Doing this book has been a blast.

I mean, you know, when we first started the project, I'm goin', "What the heck am I gonna say for even 25 pages?"

But then all of a sudden, we got into it. And more stuff kept coming up, and coming up, and coming up.

I guess this type of thing brings up another fact that has come to me after reading my own book.

Maybe my family has had more to put up with than I originally thought, now that I look back.

I probably have been a heavy load at times.

But my heart was always in the right place.

I don't apologize for anything I did in my life.

I never hurt anybody.

I helped 'em, if anything.

I mean, Marlene, the wife I left after six days...I suppose you could say I did her dirty and I shouldn't have done it. You may well be right.

But it wasn't malicious. It only lasted for a little while.

From the time I met her, married her and divorced her, it was less than a month, all told.

It still was probably for the best that we split.

Marlene was very nice. I'd love to see her again.

I hope she's had a good life.

I hope everyone that I've ever come in contact with has had as good a life as I have.

I didn't want to offend anybody by the sexploitations in Chapter 4, but that certainly was a part of my life.

I can't deny it.

It was a fact.

But that was only a couple of years out of my life.

It was just like, I was this normal guy in, like, '58.

And then came the sexual revolution. I was at the very center of it.

All it was, was havin' fun.

That was so for both sides, boys and girls.

If anyone thinks I'm a sex maniac, I swear I'm not.

I took advantage of the time that existed in the country, especially in Southern and Northern California, and I went with it.

Everybody else across the country started doing the same thing.

Maybe just not as much.

I was hoggin' it up.

And, oh, God, did I have fun.

I was a guy who always was looking for adventure.

Like the Steppenwolf song, I guess, I was born to be wild.

I loved being out among 'em.

But I don't just talk about my sex life in this book.

The more I talked about my big heart attack in Chapter 10, the more I realized that it was basically as funny as hell.

You know how sometimes you'll lie in your bed and think about dying and you're scared to death. At those points, I was scared.

When this life-and-death experience was actually happening, I wasn't scared.

I don't know, I didn't think I was that brave. I was ignorant.

I was shocked at myself, the way I took it.

I guess this kind of self-examination is why some people say that doing a book about their lives is therapeutic.

They're right.

It has been for me.

And you know, what? It's just given me a thirst to do more things.

I was sittin' here now thinkin', "My gosh, look at all the things I missed."

Now I gotta go cover a lotta bases.

I'm gonna be very, very busy.

I have to see more things first hand. Things I've heard about.

I've gotta do some traveling. That's very important.

The Far East.

I think Becka and I could have a ball there.

I like the food. The people. I think everything is just so interesting there.

I would like to go to Nepal.

I would like to go to Tibet.

I would love to talk with the Dalai Lama.

I'd love to sit down and break yeast-cakes with that man.

Maybe split an insect with him.

Whatever they eat.

I understand yak's milk is pink.

I want to go to Tibet and find out for myself.

I got some people that I want to see that I haven't seen forever.

Like a couple guys I've never brought up that were good friends of mine. Guy named Bobby Gorman and a guy named Bobby Workeiser.

And then my best friend in grammar school was a guy named Bobby Weiss. I haven't seen hide nor hair of him in 40 years.

I'm gonna try and look up some of these old people, with whom I shared some of my greatest achievements.

But what I did get to in the book, I'm very happy with it.

I want to thank my moron buddy, Gib, for collaborating on this book with me.

Of course, I've got to thank my wife, Rebecca. She encouraged me to write this book. I don't think I ever would have done this unless she said, "You know, your life is really interesting."

I'd go, "Really?"

She'd say, "Just start talking. You'll see what I mean."

So Rebecca is the No. 1 person I want to thank.

I'm glad she inspired and encouraged me.

I may have missed a lot of people this time around. Honest to God, there are probably 75 or 80 people I shoulda talked about.

But this is a big manuscript as it is.

So we'll just have to do it again sometime.

My old man, Leonard-the-Sport, used to take me, as a kid, to Gilmore Park to watch the Hollywood Stars minor league baseball team, and we'd sit by Al Jolson.

Al Jolson used to have one remark.

I'd hear him say it all the time.

It counts right now.

"You ain't seen nuthin' yet."

He was right.

See you in the next book.

It truly is an amazing time to be alive.

We've all still got a long way to go.

Frank J. Bank
aka "Lumpy"
September, 1997
Calabassas, California

Introduction

I knew Lumpy.

Just like you did.

I grew up watching "Leave It To Beaver" and I was hooked, the same as millions of other Americans.

That idyllic charm. The simple lines. Pure. Elegant.

Like sitting by the gentle foam of an eddying ocean, watching "Beaver" was playful and pacifying.

It put a smile on your face. It made you feel good inside.

And part of that feeling was Frank Bank, who played Lumpy Rutherford.

While he wasn't the big star, he blended. Added just the right touch. Think of him as a plump cherry on top.

During our time together Frank and I shared endless sports insanities.

And as Yogi Berra once put it so well, you can see a lot just by observing. I saw a lot more of Frank when we visited his old haunts in L.A. Everywhere we'd go, there was a piece of Frank flotsam floating in the air, a Frank jetsam jogging memories.

Such as Knights Beach where his high school crew hung out, a couple blocks from the Santa Monica pier.

Such as Peter Lawford's house on the Pacific Coast Highway near Sunset where Frank's buddy, Chuck, used to drive Marilyn Monroe for assignations with JFK.

The little city park where Marilyn is buried. Joe DiMaggio promised to send fresh flowers every day to her burial vault.

Sure enough, we saw an orchid there. Of greater historical significance, one of Frank's old pals is buried in the vault right over Marilyn.

"He insisted that he be placed face-down," says Frank.

"The guys I grew up with were lunatics—every one of them," he adds fondly.

My special thanks go out to Bob Snodgrass, and his wife, Sharon for their belief and commitment to this project. Darcie Kidson for undying patience and cheeriness as my editor at Addax. Steve Cameron, my fellow time-traveler through the sometimes wild terrain of authorship, for always encouraging and inspiring me. Sherry White for her completely faithful friendship and enthusiasm, as well as literary suggestions. Dana Fries Miller for her caring, support and love as well as her humor and intelligence. And I want to thank you, Frank and Rebecca, for friendship, help, love and many laughs and good times.

The Roughriders never made better music together.

Gib Twyman
1997
Kansas City

Introduction

Chapter One

Gee I'm With the Beav

arlon Brando was on the next set.

We'd heard what a giant pain in the ass he was.

We didn't mean to be breaking his balls or interrupting his scene.

So Tony Dow, Jerry Mathers, Kenny Osmond, Pat Curtis and I were creeping in, trying to be as quiet as five kids could possibly be.

Besides, we were all professional actors and we knew what it cost to keep a full crew shooting, especially during daylight hours.

I mean, Tony and Jerry played Wally and Beaver Cleaver, as you probably know.

I am Frank Bank, and I played Clarence "Lumpy" Rutherford for over 300 episodes with Tony and Jerry on "Leave It to Beaver" and "The New Leave It to Beaver," which you may or may not know. But which you are about to find out a lot in the next couple hundred pages or so.

Kenny, of course, played every parent's nightmare, Eddie Haskell.

Pat was Tony's stand-in and sometimes my stand-in.

So it wasn't exactly like we were five Gomers from Iowa who barged into a sound stage, going, "Is this the men's room? Ain't that the T-shirt concession over there?"

No.

We did "Beaver" every day on Stage 17 at Universal Studios—matter of fact we owned Universal.

We were one of the top shows in America.

We were it.

And all we wanted to do was go next door to Stage 16 for a little while and watch them film "The Ugly American."

Starring Brando.

The bastard.

Talk about typecasting. I didn't know an uglier American than Brando.

Heck, we weren't doing anything that didn't happen to us all the time on

"Beaver." Every day we had people—average people from all over—stopping by to watch us film an episode and we were cool about it.

We could have been stuck up.

I mean, we were like gods on "Beaver."

But we were really nice.

We were family.

We treated others like family.

People would come onto our set and we'd stop and give autographs. Say hello.

"So you're from Pangwich, Utah. Neat. Good to meet you."

"Florida, huh? Great state. Have a nice vacation."

We took time.

We believed that's how you acted toward people.

So now we were taking a break from "Beaver" and we got tired of throwing the football around back of the set. And we said, "Hey, let's walk next door and check out 'The Ugly American' set."

Because of Brando?

Forget Brando.

Just cuz. No big deal.

We didn't care about Brando.

I mean, the only movie star that ever impressed me was Cary Grant.

That's the only guy I ever stopped and looked at him and I went, "Wow!"

The only guy.

We saw 'em all there at Universal. I had lunch with 'em all. The Jimmy Stewarts, the Gary Coopers. Jimmy was cool. I liked him. But Cary Grant took my breath away.

I mean, I used to see Rock Hudson almost every day. He was a real nice guy. He was so shy, it was terrible. He was gay as a goose, and all his buddies who surrounded him were gay as geese. But you know what? I didn't have to sleep with him. So when he said, "Hi. How are ya?" I said, "Hey, how are you?"

He'd be in the commissary and he'd go, "Hey, I saw the show last night. Really cute show. I liked the one part where this happened or that happened."

And we'd go, "Great, Rock. What are you working on?"

And he'd say, "Oh, 'Lover Come Back.'"

Whatever.

The point is, he was just a really nice guy.

Tony Randall was sweet as sugar.

Alfred Hitchcock was kind of a fussy old coot. But almost all the rest of these guys—the Stewarts, the Coopers, the Duke Waynes...no matter who you were, they'd treat you decently.

Brando?

He was the consummate creep.

As we're about to find out in person.

As Tony and Jerry and Eddie and Pat and I are walking onto the set of "Ugly American," we see the "Closed Set" sign up, but that's pretty typical. We know the drill about being super-quiet. We don't say a word. We are very respectful.

We are just going to walk onto the set and sorta look around and stand in the wings.

We're watching this one shot, which of course Brando didn't know his dialogue. He wasn't even close.

The director yells, "Cut!"

And Brando specifically looks at Tony Dow, because Tony was standing nearer to him than the rest of us. He looks Tony right in the eye.

He yells, "Get those fuckin' kids outta here. What the hell do you think you're doing? Can't you kids read?"

That's when Tony turns to him and calmly hollers, "Up yours, asshole!"

We turned deliberately and slowly walked out.

I never was prouder of being part of "Beaver" than that moment.

I mean, hey, Wally was never better as the big brother. He stuck up for The Beav. He stuck up for Eddie. Me. Pat. For us all. Just like a real family.

Which we were. That was the cool thing about being on the show. We actually were like family to each other. Hugh Beaumont and Barbara Billingsley, who played Ward and June Cleaver, were like second moms and dads to us.

I mean, I'm sure they wouldn't have appreciated the language we used— make that I know they wouldn't have approved. I never once heard Hugh Beaumont swear or say a mean word to anyone. And Barbara was a flat-out saint, the most fantastic woman I had met in the world, next to my own mom, Sylvia.

Hugh and Barbara would have sat us down and given us a good lecture and made us go to our rooms for talking like we did to Brando, the fat freak. Maybe they'd have made us apologize to the great man.

"Gee, Mr. Brando, we're sorry you're a big fat, bitter blob, who doesn't like himself or anyone else. And we're really, really sorry you think you're God's gift to the entertainment industry, so you can come onto a set, not do your homework, blow your lines all over the place and blame it on some kids, who are not saying a word, just standing there watching you mess up a multi-million dollar production all by your big, fat blowhard self.

"We're sorry, Fatso, you're such a sleazebag.

"Sorry. We mean Mr. Fatso sleazebag."

Chapter One

OK. Hugh and Barbara would never have put up with such a thing as that. They were too good and decent.

They'd have washed our mouths out with soap, but good. Several times. And we probably couldn't have ridden our bikes or get any ice cream for a week.

(Hey, to bag back on Brando, it would have been worth it.)

But in a way, our visit to "The Ugly American" set was like a "Beaver" episode, a Wally-and-Beav caper, a just-kids escapade gone awry.

Just a slightly more carnal version of a Beaver episode. Perhaps a slightly more realistic one.

But the thing that the Brando incident reminds me of is this: Life on "Beaver" was never dull.

Life on "Beaver" was always the opposite of dull. It was the absolute best. Better than the best, it was epic entertainment.

"Leave It to Beaver" was one of those rare moments in time when the dream-weavers and wordmeisters and the cutthroat studio machinery combined in some cosmic, almost mystical way, to get it right.

America cleaved to the Cleavers.

Not once. Not twice. But always.

The original "Leave It to Beaver" ran more than 200 episodes. "The New Leave It to Beaver," the reprise of the show, ran more than 100 episodes. That makes both of them among the relatively small handful of shows ever to make 100, and "Beaver" was a Top Ten show in both cases.

Clearly, Cleaverdom stuck with us.

It is the only show with two episodes in the Television Hall of Fame. The made-for-TV "Beaver" movie received wonderful, healthy ratings.

And in 1997, the 40th anniversary of the birth of the Beav, Universal released "Leave It to Beaver, the Movie" in theaters nationwide.

I am proud to have been a small part of it. I am blessed to have been among the Beaver family. They remain a true, second family to me to this day and I love them all dearly.

That is why I am happy that the name, "Lumpy," stuck with me all these years.

On the show, whenever anyone called Clarence Rutherford by his nickname, he always replied, irritably, in that whiny voice of his:

"Don't call me Lumpy."

But I say:

"Call me Lumpy."

I say it proudly.

Call me Lumpy all you want.

Call me Lumpy any time at all.

I am the luckiest man alive.

I am not Lou Gehrig.

I am not dying.

(Well, I guess I am, but, like everyone else, I just don't know when it will happen—although everyone thought I might when I had that heart attack awhile back. More on that later.)

But I have always seriously felt this way about myself.

I am just...so lucky.

I just happened.

I happened to come along at the right time, at the right moment, for the best possible things to happen in the best possible way to take the most joy and happiness from the situations I was placed in.

Whoever's pulling the strings up there, I am one of his favorite puppets.

Whoever's pushing buttons on the time machine always has punched me up at the absolute perfect moment for the perfect things to take place in my life.

Like getting into show business.

Like getting on "Leave It to Beaver."

Classic examples of what I'm talking about.

It was at the end of second grade when I made a friend with a guy named Whitey Haupt.

He's the reason I'm an actor.

He just didn't know it.

The foundation was laid by his mother, actually. The Haupts lived seven houses from us in West Los Angeles.

Her kid was in the movies.

And I thought Mrs. Haupt's kid was kinda cool because he was in "The Babe Ruth Story" with William Bendix. Babe Ruth was a big hero of mine, because he was left-handed like me. So I thought this kid being in "The Babe" was way cool.

You've seen Whitey a million times. He was in a hundred movies. He was that blond kid with the long hair back in the '40s when Bobby Driscoll and Margaret O'Brien were stars.

Whitey wasn't a star.

Whitey was a second-banana kind of guy.

But he always had a couple of important lines in the show. So you always knew who Whitey was.

Anyhow, this one day, Whitey's mother comes over to our house and says, "Whitey has an interview at the Ben Hecht Studios this afternoon, Sylvia."

Ben Hecht is the guy who is the subject of the movie, "Gaily, Gaily"—one of the great writers and producers of the first half of the 20th Century.

Chapter One

So Whitey is going over to his studios and his mom says to Sylvia, "Could you take us over for the interview? It's 2:30 or so."

And my mom says, "I would love to, but what am I gonna do with Frankie?"

My mom is one of the few people to call me Frankie. I am Frankie to her because of Frank Sinatra. My mom loved Frank Sinatra. So did I until I found out what a nasty man he is. My grandfather was named Frank Bank and he was a bootlegger, a really cool bootlegger, although not a very successful one, and I'd have rather been named after him, actually, than a jerkoff like Sinatra.

But anyhow, Sylvia says what-to-do-with-Frankie.

And Mrs. Haupt says to my mom, "Just bring Frank along."

So we go.

Over to the Ben Hecht Studios on Cahuenga.

The four of us are sitting in the little reception room—Whitey, Mrs. Haupt, Mom and me. And a guy comes walking through the door toward the office and sorta looks around, then looks at me.

Then he says to me, not my mom, or anyone else, but to me: "What are you doing here?"

And I was kinda scared.

I'll never forget, they have at this time, Wheaties boxes where they put masks of, like, bears and rabbits and chipmunks on the back of the cereal packages.

And I had this mask, this racoon mask—you took a string on each side and put a hole in there and tie the string, and you put the mask on your face.

I sorta had the mask in my lap, but when this guy looks at me, I draw the mask up close to my face, because I was a little bit scared and a little bit shy.

And the guy looks at me some more and goes, "I said, 'What are you doing here today?'"

I didn't answer, but my mom says, "Well, we're here to have Whitey talk to Mr. Hecht."

And the guy points to me and says to my mother, "Bring him back tomorrow. He's not supposed to be here 'til tomorrow."

Tomorrow?

Hey, I was never supposed to be there.

So I said something like, "I'm not an actor."

He looked right back at me and said, "You are now."

And I was.

That's how it happened for so many kids those days in the movies, when you got right down to it. There was no factory somewhere, spitting out child actors and actresses. There weren't tons of schools you sent kids to, to be actors. No insightful institute where they scoured the countryside for talent and collected it and groomed it in some careful, calibrated way.

Shoot, they just found us schlumped over on a chair somewhere.

Next thing you knew, you were in the movies.

Like I say. Luck. Timing. It doesn't happen that way so much today, but it did back then.

You were in the neighborhood. They latched onto some neighborhood kids.

Was some tyke in Tallahassee or some prodigy in Pittsburgh more talented than we were?

Could well have been.

Probably was.

But they were putzes out there in the middle of nowhere, halfway across the country. We were putzes who happened to be handy.

We were accidents of birth and geography and the time period of the entertainment industry.

We were in.

You weren't.

So there.

So anyway, we do go back the next day and, sure enough, I get a job in a movie called "Cargo to Capetown" with Broderick Crawford and Mercedes McCambridge.

I got washed overboard in the first scene. That was it for me.

All you saw was me with some water and then the next thing, I wasn't there. I was history.

That was OK.

It took one day for me to make this movie.

I made 150 bucks for that.

It was more'n my old man made in a week.

My mother made me put it in the bank and I was so mad. We always had this sign up over the kitchen sink in our house and it said, "Waste Not, Want Not." Believe me, no family ever lived by those words more than we did.

Mom wouldn't let me have the money. It was like a "Beaver" episode: "Son, you better let us take care of this until you're old enough."

Gee thanks, Ma.

I got nothing. Wait. I remember I got a chance to go over to Ralph's Five and Ten Cents Store and I bought a dollar, maybe two dollars, worth of stuff. Maybe some Hopalong Cassidy junk—which, by the way, I should have kept. I was a big Hopalong Cassidy fan in those days. I loved Hoppy. Topper was cool, too—his horse.

Anyway, about a week or two later, the phone starts ringing. It's Bill McClain from the Screen Children's Guild, and he wants me to join. Here's the kicker. Joining is free. But he wanted me to have some pictures made.

Chapter One

Now, my old man, Leonard, didn't exactly throw dollar bills around, as indicated by the sign in the kitchen. We were truly lower-middle class in those days.

But I didn't really put it together, what a strain they were under. Brat that I was, I went, "Ma, I want the pictures!"

Whiney and all that kind of stuff. I was an obnoxious little twerp.

So we went over to this guy, John Reed. I blew 60 bucks of the $150 at the John Reed Photography Studio. Man, that was a car, in those days. We're talking 60 bucks in 1949. Sixty bucks.

I threw my tantrum and I was in the Screen Children's Guild.

But I got my clock cleaned.

I guess I should have listened to Leonard and Sylvia. I didn't and paid a price.

But then, I couldn't have felt too bad. I mean, it turns out ever since that first transaction, I have pretty much made my own decisions in my career.

I can thank Sylvia and Len for allowing me to fall on my face and make my own choices, however stupid they might have been sometimes.

Besides, I guess they appreciated the fact that I have been gainfully employed since I was 8 years old.

I have not had a day off since I was 8. 'Scuse me. Two months off when I had the bypass surgery—the longest I ever had off.

From the beginning I loved work, really. It started with my paper corner, at La Cienega and Cadillac. After school, I was out there in the middle of the street with the *Herald-Examiner* and the *LA Mirror*.

"Getcha papuh right he-ah."

I was really good. I had my little skirt on with the change in there, ya know? S'great. Get my customers coming home from work, 4 to 6 o'clock.

After that I had Hebrew school.

I was a busy little bee.

Hebrew school was for religious instruction, all that good stuff. Patch it up with God for, you know, overcharging on a newspaper once in awhile. (Ward and June would have gotten me for that one, too, huh? And been right in doing so.)

Anyway, I'm in the Screen Children's Guild along about now and they have this little catalogue. The next thing you know, someone has looked me up in the catalogue and I get a phone call from Columbia Studios.

And I'm on the initial go-round of a series called Ford Theater. I do a show with Will Rogers, Jr., Margeruite Chapman and a guy named John Archer called "Life, Liberty and Orren Dooley."

I spent a week with Will Rogers, Jr., out at "the ranch." It was on Riverside Drive, over by the Burbank Airport. It was called the Columbia Ranch. It was kind of plowed-up ground, out by nowhere.

But I'm out in the middle of nowhere with Will Rogers, Jr., for a week. Will Rogers.

He taught me to twirl a rope, he sure did. I was a rope-twirlin' fool. I could get that big loop going. You think Monty Montana was good in the "Rose Parade?" I could do everything Monty Montana could do. I could step into it. I could twirl it around, step out of it.

I could lift it up over my head and then I could getcha with it.

Absolutely. Thanks to Will.

Will was a nice, nice guy. The joke was, ironically, I wound up playing Will Rogers as a kid in the "Will Rogers Story," for Warner Brothers, not that long after. Four years later. I had a line or two. No big deal.

But Will loved his dad. He listened to everything Will Rogers told him to do. He thinks everything he was as an adult was because of his dad. It was a pleasure to be around him.

After that, I had a little hiatus as an actor. The whole thing kicked back up again right at the beginning of 1952. It was Washington's Birthday. I was 10 years old.

That's when I got on the "Jack Benny Radio Program."

Jack Benny had this club called the Beverly Hills Beavers (again with the Beavers, huh? Beavers have always been good to me, in more ways than one).

The Beverly Hills Beavers was a kid's club that Jack Benny sponsored on radio.

What it was, was an imitation of Benny's own show with kids. He thought it would be cute to have kids play the parts of all the regular people on his show, and play it out over the radio.

I wound up getting the part of Don Wilson, the announcer. Could it have been the silhouette? Gee, I wonder.

Don was the fat guy on the Benny show. I was a fat little kid. Even though the show was on radio, and they couldn't see me, Jack Benny was such a perfectionist, he had us completely in character, right down to our appearances.

He had this little Irish kid, Stuffy Singer, who I knew pretty well. Stuffy had a voice like an angel until it changed. He played Dennis Day, because Dennis Day sang tenor on the show, and Stuffy brought that Irish trill.

Rosemary and Patty Ianone were the girls. They played Mary Livingston, Jack's wife. And they had this other kid, a funny little black kid, who did Rochester. He was nervous as all-get-out and the only one of us who didn't sound professional on the air, because he was so scared.

Somewhat understandable, since we did the show in front of a live audience, and live listening audience, coast-to-coast, on Sunday afternoon, on CBS Radio.

Television City was not built yet. The CBS Radio studio was on Sunset and Gower. It was right next door to the Paladium.

It was real impressive because on Sunday, in comes Jack Benny. He sits us all down. There were six or seven kids. He says, "You kids are professionals. I know you're gonna do a great job. Ta-da, ta-da, ta-da."

We ran through the show twice and then we did it, just like you see in the movies. We stood up to a microphone with a script. You hear the theme music. And then the announcer, Don Wilson, who is actually me, comes on. And Dennis Day, aka Stuffy Singer, is singing.

And I said to myself when I was doing it, standing there at the microphone, I couldn't believe where I was.

I'm sitting there with Jack Benny. The guy I listened to from my house. That was really Jack Benny. That was really Rochester. And Don Wilson and all these people, and I'm going, "Wow!"

I mean, Will Rogers didn't impress me. He was a nice guy. I had done this show on CBS television, "The Allen Young Show." Allen Young didn't impress me. He was a nice guy, too.

But Jack Benny impressed the hell out of me.

I couldn't believe it.

I mean, Jack was nice, too.

Nice?

He was a god.

He was, oh man, he was Jack Benny.

Burns and Allen, Jack Benny, Fibber McGee and Molly, Amos and Andy. That was my life, man.

Jack Benny. He was bigger than Crusader Rabbit.

I did four or five Jack Benny radio shows.

It was big scoots to me, too. I made 200 bucks a show. That was cool. Hey, man, I had like $1,000 before I was 10 years old.

I went out and bought myself a bicycle.

"Want not," my foot.

I wanted. I got.

Actually, it was not my first bicycle, though. I got my first bike, a Schwinn-some-kinda-master, from Captain Jet. Captain Jet was on TV and he used to put his finger around his eye and he used to go, "Zooooom!"

And then he'd go, "And for you big kids, Moooooz!"

Hey, Captain Jet was cool, man. When you were in LA, you watched either Uncle Archie or Captain Jet. Uncle Archie, it turned out when you met him, was a drunken old sot and he was mean. But Captain Jet, while he was slightly loony, he was cool. So I watched Captain Jet.

And somehow, Captain Jet picked my name on a postcard one time and I got to be his co-pilot for a day.

And for that I got this Schwinn bicycle. It was beautiful and it was chrome and blue. What a gorgeous bike. It had streamers and I put a baseball card, you know, in the back wheel with a clothes pin, so it could make that motor noise.

Yeah, it was a cool bike.

I keep telling you—I am the luckiest guy alive.

Now I'm 10. I'm rollin' in bucks.

I am about to get luckier.

Enter Lola Moore.

Lola Moore was the consummate kid's agent in Hollywood.

Anybody who was anybody—or ever pretended to be anybody—had to have Lola Moore for an agent.

God, who didn't have Lola Moore?

Tommy Rettig, Billy Gray and lots of the Mousketeers had Lola Moore. There was a ton of Corcorans—Kevin Corcoran and eight or nine in all, I want to say. They all had Lola.

The Kirks—Tommy Kirk and all the other Kirks—had Lola as an agent, too.

Now I get a call from Lola Moore and I have a chance to have her as my agent. So I joined the Lola Moore Agency. Funny to say, this was pretty much all my decision. My mom has always said to trust my instincts. I don't know how smart she was to have told me that, because I've had some pretty stupid instincts. But for awhile, I guess I must have been pretty sharp as a kid.

I go with Lola and the next thing I know, I'm doin' all kinds of stuff. I'm working, geez, on "Playhouse 90."

I remember it was directed by Fielder Cook, who was a big-time director. Nina Foch was in it. Wendell Corey was in it.

My role? Oh, some punk kid, as usual. I had a couple of scenes. I was never an extra, though. I always had speaking lines. Whether it be as a bit player or co-star or feature player.

I was usually just the wise guy or the troublemaker or the bully. I was never like a warm son, because I was always bigger.

I was 13 and I wasn't really that fat. I was chunky. In high school, I thinned out. I was doing a lot of athletics, so I had lost weight. I got to the point, I used to think I was a leading-man type.

Now everyone has to have a good vision of themselves, you know— shoulda-woulda-coulda.

But I guess I was kidding myself about the leading man thing. I was always a little bit of a pork chop. If there was a part for a fat kid...it was me.

Me or another kid, whose name escapes me right now. He wasn't any-thing next to me. I was it. I really was. When it came to playing fat punks, no one did it better.

You had to decide what you could do best. I remember the Aker boys, Lee and Dee Aker. They were twins. Lee Aker was a kid with a husky voice, and

Chapter One

whenever you needed a husky-voiced kid, you called Lee. He was Corporal Rusty on "Rin Tin Tin." And it was always kinda sad because Dee was probably every bit as good as Lee, but Dee didn't get the roles and Lee did. And Dee's probably walking around muttering to himself and Lee just kept rolling along.

They were both nice guys, but somehow Lee knew what his niche was and he was good at it.

Same thing happened to me, pretty much. I wasn't really looking for fame. It just sort of happened.

My niche kind of started to solidify when I was 13 on "Peck's Bad Girl." Patty McCormick starred in this series. It was a good show. It was live. We didn't have drugs or prostitution or AIDS as big topics at the time, so the plots were pretty simple and similar. The plot always called for Patty, this young blonde girl, to get led astray in some small way, but she'd find the right path by the end of the show.

I usually played the heavy...because I was heavy in more ways than one. I guess the fat person's lobby—if there was such a thing—could get really steamed, because fat guys are tired of being the bad guys. There aren't that many fat people who were the good guys. I mean, Sydney Greenstreet, Edward Arnold, Peter Lorre, Victor Buono. All these guys, from time immemorial, were fat guys who played bad guys.

Well, guess what? I know a lot of fat guys and they're nice guys. But in television and the movies, you were bad guys. Or played dullards or guys who weren't too hip.

It was stereotyping. Typecasting. It still exists today, though it's lessened somewhat. John Goodman is a great example of a guy who can play any role. He can play a smart guy, he can play a stupid guy, a rich guy, a poor guy, a sloth, a classy guy—whatever it might be.

But it's changed.

I was around in the day of the Rocks and Tabs and Troys and all those funny first names. It was a different time. Henry Winkler never would have been allowed to use "Henry Winkler" on screen. He would have been Edward Bennett. Or he would have been Rush Gladstone. Weird names or ethnic names were not used.

Unfortunately. I mean, what was wrong with Marion Morrison? Nothing. Except some turkey said, "We have to use John Wayne instead."

What was wrong with Archie Leach? I think Archie Leach is a pretty cool name. But wrong. He had to become Cary Grant. Bernie Schwartz today could have been Bernie Schwartz, instead of Tony Curtis. Think about Arnold Swarzenegger. It's over the top. It's a dynamite name. Like the kid, David Schwimmer from "Friends." Great name. But he never would have been allowed to be David Schwimmer way back when. He would have been

David Brown, you know, or David Strong.

Me? Frank Bank was my original name. Frank Bank was a cool name. Leonard and Sylvia did all right there.

I got lucky on that score.

They weren't going to mess with Frank Bank as my name.

And the name fit all these kinds of punks and dimwits and heavies I was playing anyway, I guess.

Lola had me making out like a bandit.

I'm making all kinds of movies. I am in all kinds of television shows. I had been on "Wagon Train." "GE Theater." "Alfred Hitchcock Presents." "Cimarron City." "Father Knows Best." "Bachelor Father." "87th Precinct."

And along about the time I had put in two or three hectic years doing these shows, I got it.

The Call.

It's November of 1957. Lola Moore's office calls. More specifically, I get a call from none other than Mrs. Osmond. That's all I knew her by. She is Kenny Osmond's mom and, lo and behold, she is Lola Moore's right-hand lady in the agency.

She calls me and says, "Frank, go out to Review Studios, out to George Gobel's office."

Remember George Gobel? Most people do and think of him as a great comedian, which he was.

But George Gobel also was the original owner of "Leave It to Beaver."

I tell Mrs. Osmond, "OK, I'll go over to Gobel's."

I was only 15 at the time. I didn't drive yet. Kenny didn't drive either. His brother, Dayton, drives him back and forth.

So my mom takes me out there.

I walk in and there is Joe Connelly and Bob Mosher. Joe Connelly and Bob Mosher were the guys who wrote "Amos and Andy."

The minute I saw their names, I knew who they were.

When I walked in, I went, "Whoaa. A-how do ya do, de-ah, Andy?" doing my best to sound like Kingfish from the "Amos and Andy Show."

They cracked up. So did the guys who played Kingfish and Andy on the radio. They were Freeman Gosden and Charles Carrell. They were also connected to Connelly and Mosher.

Matter of fact, Connelly and Mosher had their hands in several hits. They had "Life of Riley." They wrote "Amos and Andy." Their last show was "The Munsters."

Pretty good parlay, huh?

So I walk in, I see these guys. They had seen my work. They said they were going to do this new show, "Leave It to Beaver."

Chapter One

They said, "We've got the part of this little loudmouthed fat kid."

And I looked at them and I went, "Well you know that's me."

And I remember Bob Mosher—he was the quiet one—he looked at me and he sorta smiles and nods his head.

Joe Connelly says, "Let's hear you read a coupla lines." I read the lines. Joe Connelly had a smile that could light up the moon. He gives me this big Irish grin and he goes, "I think you'll do."

And I felt really good, because I knew I had the job. They told me about their new show, but I had seen it the week before. It had premiered on CBS, I believe, on a Thursday or Friday night. It was sponsored by the Remington-Rand typewriter company. Or Ralston Purina.

I remembered the kids on the show walking down the sidewalk, with hopscotch chalk drawn on it. And the words that were scrawled there said, "Leave It to Beaver." And I thought at the time, "Well, this is kind of a cute show."

They were doing the one-foot-on-the-curb thing. Beaver stuff.

I said, "This is a nice and pleasant show."

A week later, I'm over at the old Republic Studios shooting that show. They send me a script at the ripe price of 150 bucks a day. That was pretty much the going rate at the time.

I did my usual bad-guy routine in the episode.

I wouldn't let Beaver and Wally come home from school because they were crossing "my turf." And they had to walk around the block. They decided they were going to get even with me.

They set up these barrel hoops in my driveway and they start screaming, "Lumpy, Lumpy, dumb as an ox!" I was supposed to run out and these barrel hoops would fly up and hit me in the shins, you know, and all that stuff.

Only, when they start shouting, instead of me coming out, my father, Richard Deacon, comes out. Who happens to be working with their father, Hugh Beaumont, at the office. And that was Fred Rutherford and Ward Cleaver. They were buddies and social friends and all that.

Where Beaver and Wally got the idea for the barrel hoops was Ward telling an old story at the dinner table about the hoops. Well, the next time the Cleavers and the Rutherfords are playing bridge, Fred Rutherford starts talking about these "young hooligans" who came over and put these barrel hoops in his driveway.

Ward looked at June. June looked at Ward. The next thing you see is Ward talking to the boys, Wally and Beav.

"Boys, did you do this?" he says.

They fessed up. They went over and apologized.

Of course, being "Leave It to Beaver," bad doesn't triumph. I get my comeuppance by the end of the half hour.

Well, I guess some magic happened. It was only supposed to be one episode, and one espisode only. But, remember, I always said I was in the right place at the right time my whole life.

This was the sixth episode of "Beaver." If I must say so myself, I was really good at the part. And you know what? I enjoyed it.

I went home and my dad asked me, "What was the name of the show you did today?"

"It's called 'Leave It to Beaver,'" I said. "You know what, I think it's going to be a really good show. These people are neat."

My dad goes, "Neat?"

I had never used the word before like that. But there were certain words that started to be associated with "Beaver." I had heard this word, "neat," a dozen times on the set that day. Wally. Beaver. Norman Tokar, the director. A couple of times it was in the script.

"Neat" and "neat-o" became part of the personality of "Leave It to Beaver."

I felt good using the word.

I felt even better about a week later. Usually I would get my paycheck on Wednesday in the mail. The day before my paycheck was to have arrived, I got a phone call from Gomalco Productions—named after Gobel and a guy named David P. O'Malley.

Was I available for another "Beaver" next week?

Is there hair on a gorilla?

Of course I was.

I was going to be a regular on the show.

My dad's reaction?

Not exactly neat-o.

My dad wanted me to have a "legitimate" job. To him, I was just hanging around with a bunch of no-account actors. My dad was pretty much a two-feet-on-the-ground kind of guy. My dad was not an idealist and he was not a dreamer.

I'm kind of a dreamer in some respects, but I'm also very pragmatic. When I got this call to do more "Beavers," it also seemed like a sound thing to do.

I went down to do the second show and this time when I walked in, it was like I was a long-lost relative.

"Hiya, Norman, how are you?" I said to Norman Tokar, the director.

"Fine, Frank, how are you?"

"Hey, where's Tony and Jerry?" I asked.

"Oh, they're in school."

I met Kenny on this show. He had been in one or two of the first six episodes. I was in the sixth and seventh.

Chapter One

I also met Tiger Fafara, who played Tooey. And I met Buddy Hart, who played Chester. Judy Hensler was the girl with the pigtails who drove Beaver crazy. She was really obnoxious and good in her role.

Larry Mondello showed up about this time. Buddy Hart left pretty quickly and became one of the greatest stunt men in Hollywood. Then Tiger disappeared.

It was down to me and Kenny as the regulars.

Kenny and I were so thoroughly obnoxious that not only did we not disappear, we were workin' fools. Our entire show turned into Aesop's Fables. The show inevitably started off and the bad guys, Eddie and I, would lead Beaver and Wally astray. Beaver and Wally would find their way after talking to Ward and June. Eddie and I would be foiled and the good guys would win again.

Every week, Kenny and I, dutiful to our roles, totally screwed up Beaver, totally fucked up Wally.

That was our lot in life to booger them up and lead them down the wrong path. To illustrate the wrong way of doing things.

We were absolute idiots, morons.

And the bigger idiots and morons we became, the more we were drawn into the "Beaver" family.

I love these guys all dearly to this day.

To this day, I consider Barbara my second mother. She is the most wonderful, caring, thoughtful, kind, considerate person. She is America's mother.

This woman is more than she's cracked up to be.

Sometimes you'd hear people say, "Oh, she's so phony on the show...I mean, June and her pearls, nothing out of place, always perfect and all that."

She was just as she was depicted on the show. Only better.

First of all, she was flat-out gorgeous. Anyone who denies that needs a German Shepherd. Secondly, better than being flat-out gorgeous, she had a heart of gold.

She cared about everybody. She was so courteous it was sickening.

If we ever screwed up or did anything wrong around her, we felt so guilty. It was like doing something bad in front of the Pope. You didn't mess around in front of Barbara. You respected her.

You were just happy she's there.

If Kenny and I were spouting off, with our usual bad verbiage, she would go, "Boys. Boys."

That was it.

That's all she had to say.

If you flubbed a line—well, to tell the truth, we were pretty darn good and didn't flub many— she was so good to you.

If there was a stranger who came in, who didn't know what he was doing, Barbara was kind and considerate, and tried to help them. If we had a strange director—we didn't have many—Barbara tried to help them.

She cared so much about our crew, about her neighbors, about her family, about everyone.

I'm telling you right now, this woman's a friggin' saint.

I love her.

I actually went to school with her son, Glenn. He was a friend of mine in high school. He was a great guy. A year younger than I was. Big tall blond dude. Good athlete. Barbara was married at the time to Glenn Billingsley, who owned a chain of Golden Bull steakhouses. Later on, she married Dr. Mortenson. I know she was crazy about the guy.

We were just kids, but we knew Barbara was always there for us. If we had any problem, we felt like we could actually talk to her just like our real moms.

Hugh was the same way.

I respected Hugh Beaumont a lot. Hugh was a very, very good director. I thought Hugh was a nice, nice man. I never had any run-ins with him.

Now, Jerry and Hugh were not the best of friends. Really, I think there was just a lot of difference in personality between the two. Water and oil. Jerry was young. Hugh was older. Hugh was sterner. And I don't think Jerry liked that. I believe Jerry didn't like somebody who was that strict.

When the script called for friction between father and son, they weren't exactly always acting.

I knew there was no long lost love there between them. But it wasn't open dislike or warfare, either. You didn't do things that way back then too often. It was more just beneath the surface.

But for me, I can honestly say that Hugh was always a good guy. We never sat down and told jokes a lot, but we would be sitting there and Hugh would go, "So Frank, what's goin' on today? How're you doing? School going OK?" Something like that.

We had nice little chats, if not long ones.

Hugh was always a perfect gentleman. He had been in the ministry and he was the perfect counterpart to Barbara on and off the screen. He never used coarse language. Never.

That was reserved for me and Kenny and Pat Curtis. Pat, as I said, was a stand-in for Tony and me. But this was hardly his claim to fame.

Not by a long shot.

Not by two long shots.

He was the guy who was married to Raquel Welch.

We thought he must be some kind of god if he had Raquel.

But basically, it turned out, he was just a good guy. Pat was our friend. When we went to lunch, Pat used to come with us. Pat was older than we were by, oh, maybe five years.

By now, we're all driving. I'm driving a Corvette, a cool, '58 custom-colored, metallic turquoise little number. Tony was driving the salmon T-Bird that his mom had always driven.

Jerry, of course, wasn't driving, though.

Kenny? Let's go to Kenny.

Do you remember what a Renault-Dauphine looked like? Kenny had a Renault-Dauphine with an antenna coming off the back bumper that stretched over, and he used to tie it down on the front bumper.

And he wore a crash helmet.

Now, if you ever in life could have known a more consummate nerd, it was Kenny.

We loved him. We used to tease him to no end.

Always. I mean, when we used to see him driving onto the lot, we couldn't understand how he could have figured a way to do anything nerdier.

Actually, there was no word, "nerd," at the time. We used to call him putz. Schmuck. Peckerhead. Whatever derogatory words we could.

But we all loved him. Kenny was a good guy. But Kenny could not figure out "cool." Kenny was great, because when Kenny did it, you didn't want to do it.

The crash helmet was hysterical. The Renault. The antenna. If someone had taken dork lessons and graduated at the head of the class, Kenny was it.

Even Jerry bagged on him and Jerry was a little punk kid. Jerry is five or six years younger. All the time we were on the show, Jerry was in grammar school a lot, while we were in high school.

Jerry was a neat kid. He never got a really big head. I think at least some of that had to do with Hugh, even if they didn't get along incredibly well.

But Jerry just naturally wasn't the kind to go ego-crazy.

And Joe Connelly and Bob Mosher. They never put anyone on a pedestal.

"Kids," they would say, "There's no horsing around on the set. If you're gonna play ball, you go outside and play ball. You don't throw the football on the sound stage."

Luckily, he did not say we couldn't go over to Stage 16 and yell, "Up yours" at Brando.

So we didn't disobey a direct order there.

But we had father figures up the ying-yang.

We were flush with father figures and basically we did not putz around too much at the studios.

We did all go out to lunch sometimes, and when we did it was mostly to hit Bob's Big Boy in Toluca Lake. Now, imagine, here we come into Bob's Big Boy, all of us at once. We didn't think anything of it, but the people at Bob's in Toluca Lake did.

They'd see the whole cast come rumblin' in to order a Big Boy Combination Plate and a lemonade and we'd say, "Make it snappy. We gotta get back to work."

This would be Tony, me, Osmond—oh, no, not Beav. He usually did not come. I told you. He was a squirt. Just like Eddie Haskell called him on the show. Sometimes, we'd give Jerry a thrill and let him ride in my Corvette with us and go for burgers. Pat would come with us, too.

We didn't have to go looking for girls. Girls found us. Everywhere. Wherever we went. It wasn't too bad, believe me. Not too bad at all.

Understand something. Arguably speaking, Tony might have been the biggest teenage heartthrobe in the country at the time. It was real close between him and Ricky Nelson.

I always thought Tony was better than Ricky. Ricky seemed a little hung-up or something.

Tony was always a shy guy, but believe me, he had his share. He had a girlfriend for a long time. Not really from the cast.

Mary Ellen Rogers? Well, Cheryl Holdridge, who first played Mary Ellen, turned out getting married real young. She married some poor slob from the backwoods.

His name was Lance Reventlow. He was the heir to Revlon.

He was a race-car driver and he got killed. Guess who inherited it all? Girl named Cheryl.

But Cheryl was a doll. I loved Cheryl. We all did. She was a good kid. And she wasn't stuck up either. She was good people.

Everyone was good people on the show.

As a fellow bad-lad on the show, I asked Kenny Osmond what he thought about the "Leave It to Beaver" years. What he thought of the cast, the way the show developed, our different personalities, pranks we played.

I find it pretty interesting after all these years to get Kenny's take on things.

Here's what he had to say.

About me:

"Frank was an older kid and even back then he was a sharp dresser. God, it seemed like he changed cars like underwear. They were always nice cars. Brand new. Usually a convertible, bright red, some other bright color. Always a nice car. He looked like he was enjoying life. That was impressive.

"I know it was neat having a guy with a driver's license and a fancy convertible to shoot over to Bob's Big Boy.

"I don't know if 'admired' was the word I'd use for him at the time. I was raised considerably different, I guess. He was definitely flashier than my

Chapter One

tastes. God, my first car, my brother and I got from selling illicit firecrackers. We always spent our summers in Oklahoma and there you can buy fireworks over the counter. Every time we came back, we'd bring a trunk-load. A dollar a pack here, a dollar a pack there. We were able to buy this old car.

"It was a 1950 Mercury. Not much of a car.

"I don't think I resented Frank's flashy ways. No. It was just different than what I was accustomed to and I had no idea how he could afford such things. I was making the same money he was and I couldn't."

About others in the cast:

"We played basketball on a hoop outside the soundstage. I've never really been into sports. It was not my thing. But Tony was a jock from the get-go. Whoever was on Tony's team won. It was a lot of fun, even if I couldn't play worth a crap."

Best prank ever on the set:

"There was this time when Frank went around whip-creaming everybody. He'd sneak up and get it in your hair. Squirt it in your face. Down your neck. Down your pants.

"We made up our minds to get even.

"We'd gone camping according to this one script on 'The New Leave It to Beaver.' Everyone except Lumpy went on the trip. The storyline called for us to get jammed out in the rain, with no tents or anything. The scene called for every last one of us to be lounging around in the mud trying to get some sleep.

"We were really crudded up and terrible.

"Frank was inside this humongous motor home, meanwhile, with this microwave and color TV and everything. And he never got a drop of mud on him.

"But we just kind of worked behind his back and kept the cameras rolling at the end of our camping scene. As we reached the end of the scene, we grabbed Frank and dragged him out into the mud.

"Oh yeah, he saw it coming the instant before we grabbed him. He tried to escape, but he didn't make it. There was a whole bunch of us on him. The crew was in on it, too.

"We plopped him in this big mudhole that was created by the artificial rain, not far from his motor home. We got him good and muddy. He looked like a mummy wrapped in mud.

"Matter of fact, we got him so good, the cameras were rolling when we dragged him in the mud and they kept it on tape and used it in the show."

About Hugh and Barbara:

"They were Mom and Dad. When I still see Barbara today, I call her 'Mom.' I love Barbara dearly. She is everybody's mom. We miss Hugh terribly since his death."

About the fact Jerry Mathers once said Kenny and I had the toughest roles on the show:

"It's very flattering to hear Jerry say that. I thank him for it. I don't think it's so much a matter of how we made our characters work. It's more the types of characters Jerry and Tony had. The characters of Wally and the Beaver don't lend themselves to raw energy and playing with the characters.

"I'd been to every acting class available before 'Beaver' came along. So I had a lot of professional training prior to that. Before they turned the cameras on, I'd really try and be Eddie.

"As far as Lumpy Rutherford, he started out as a guy stuck in one episode. Dumpy Lumpy, dumb as an ox. Instead of one or two episodes, Frank stuck around. The reason? He was perfect for Lumpy. Both physically and, if you watch him, you can see it in his face. He is Lumpy for X-period of minutes. Big Dumpy Lumpy."

About why the show has endured in the hearts of its fans:

"Believe me, I've heard this question a lot, so I've given it a great deal of thought.

"First off, film-making back then was an art. Today it's no longer so much of an art. Today it's a matter of 'let's put this together real quick and make some money on it.' It's not about quality.

"Another major thing is that 'Leave It to Beaver' was totally different in that it didn't have funny lines. It had funny situations. That's totally different from any sitcom you watch today.

"Today, it's setup...setup...joke. I think the thing that made 'Beaver' fly so well is that every show, every plot, was something that you as a child went through yourself. So you could relate to it.

"Remember the time that you lost your haircut money? Are you gonna tell your mom? The time you ordered something from a catalogue without mom and dad's permission? Just silly things like that.

"It's good, clean entertainment. When you get home after a hard day at the office, you want to escape someplace. That's what television is all about.

"Do you want to escape to Miami and chase drug-dealers? No. I tell you, Mayfield's a nice place to escape to.

"Another thing that helped the longevity is that you can go back for years and years and years, through all the supermarket tabloids—you will not find any crap associated with anyone on our show.

"Nobody robbed a liquor store. Nobody has been strung out on drugs. Nobody went into prostitution. I mean, not just the cast, but the crewmembers, and everyone, were family people.

"I think most people watching the show felt that way, too.

"We were just part of their family."

Chapter One

Finally, I ought to be shot—shouldn't I?—if I got out of this chapter without hearing from The Man, himself.

Jerry Mathers.

The Beav.

He was, after all, the reason there was a Beaver to leave it to.

I was asking him about the show and these are some of the things he said.

About paling with Tony and Eddie and me:

Every once in a while if I was lucky—because I was kind of the tagalong as the youngest one—we would go to lunch at Bob's Big Boy. Frank always had a really neat car. Being the youngest kid and very impressionable, cars became very important to me.

But in a way it was kind of a favor if they would even bother to take me along.

Did we treat him like "The Squirt," as Eddie called him?

Not really. That really wasn't part of their persona. We were all working together, so it was really the kind of thing where everybody wanted, honestly, to make Tony and me happy. If for some reason—and this never happened—we'd had some huge blowout, it would not have been good for the show. So everybody tried to keep everybody else happy.

His recollections of me:

I remember Frank over the series of the show, but not so much at first. Especially in the first few months of the show, there were all sorts of people who would come and go.

Only the good ones stayed.

When I met Frank, he was a very nice guy. But because there was a big age difference between us (7 years), I didn't really know Frank until the "New Leave It to Beaver" years.

When you're in your teens and early 20s and a guy is a few years older than you, it's a lot...but when you're in your 30s and 40s, that age difference pretty much evaporates.

When I started my business career and had more money to invest—and Frank had then gone into the investment field—that's when Frank and I really became friends, when he started managing some of my accounts.

Frank is very articulate. A very smart business person. A very good friend. That's the Frank I know today. I don't hesitate to trust a lot of my assets with him. And I definitely go to him for advice, any time there's a turn in the market, or for some reason I either come into or have to get ahold of some of my money and I want to know what to do with it, Frank's always the one I call. He has a very good insight into the market.

Obviously, he's honest.

He's somebody I care very very much and deeply about.

One that I'll always care and worry about.

Gee J'm With the Beav

Frank, Kenny, Tony and and I were all very much good friends and we all remained good friends. You know, I went to Frank's weddings and over the years, whenever anybody would have babies, or even today when Ken Osmond's son got married and things like that.

You don't find many people like that. I've worked in a lot of different businesses and most of those people, while you're working with them, they're business acqaintances. And that's pretty much it.

But I go to personal events in Frank's and Kenny's and Tony's lives and when things happen in my life, I definitely tell them about it.

Why the Lumpy character endured:

Well, you know, all the characters on "Leave It to Beaver" are all very endearing because people know people like that. Everyone knows an Eddie Haskell, who's the guy that stabs you in the back. Everyone knows a Lumpy, who's dominated by their father and in some ways is kind of the bully, because their father dominates them so much they're frustrated.

Because the characters are so well-written, there are general things about them, so that everyone can find some of their characteristics in people they know.

Frank is definitely a fine actor. He had a hard part to play, in a lot of ways. The bully is fairly easy, and almost every character actor could do that. But it's demeaning to have to play a bully who's also a browbeaten coward. That's a hard part for a young vibrant man to play a lot of times. And Frank took that part on, even though it's very far-flung from his own nature;

I mean, for me it was very easy, because the Beaver character is an every-man character.

But the Eddie Haskell character and the Lumpy character are harder to play, because when people see them they tend to think that the way they were like on the show, that's their true personality.

I mean, I'm sure Frank took a lot of guff for being Lumpy.

And yet, a lot of people identify with Lumpy. It may not be your parent, but you may have to knuckle under to your boss, or to maybe a wife, or some authority figure in your life. And that's what the Lumpy character does. He's the person who, you know, goes along...but the sad part about the Lumpy character, he takes it out on everyone else around him.

He's so frustrated, he vents all the stuff that's lingering in him. And the Beaver is the low man on the totem pole, so he gets the brunt of the frustration a lot of times.

Best athlete on the show:

Tony Dow. Tony almost in a way was a professional athlete. When he got the show, he was training for the Olympics in swimming and diving.

Ken Osmond was a fair athlete, but he was always kind of a skinny person, so he wasn't as athletic as Tony.

Chapter One

Frank was fairly athletic. Baseball was more his sport, but there was no real place to play baseball. With baseball, all we basically could do was catch.

With basketball we could play half-court right on the sound stage, 2-on-2 or 3-on-3, depending on how many people were there.

Hugh Beaumont would play with us. He was very good. In fact, he taught me how to shoot one-handed shots and jump shots, all that stuff.

Whether I got to play basketball would depend on whether there was another kid there my age. Larry Mondello, Rusty Stevens would work. But otherwise, I wouldn't play just because when they divvied up the teams, there was no one close to my age or my prowess at the sport, because I was so much smaller.

When they're 13 or 15 and you're 8, you really don't play with them that much.

But anyway, what a lot of people don't understand, it was really almost a total work environment. We were on a very tight schedule. There really wasn't a whole lot of time for fooling around.

About Hugh Beaumont

I've been an actor since I was 2. And I knew Hugh before "Leave It to Beaver." Hugh actually was a very very close friend of my family. So I knew him not only on the set, but off the set. He would come over and my father and he would play golf and things like that. Aside from being someone I worked with, Hugh was like a Dutch Uncle maybe.

Why the show endured:

I think the first thing is the writing. Joe Connelly and Bob Mosher were both excellent writers. All of the shows from the original "Leave It to Beaver" came from real life.

They had quite a few kids of their own...11. And then Richard Currell, who played Richard Rickover on the show...a lot of the "Beaver" character was based on things he and his friends did. And on things my friends and I did.

What Joe and Bob would do, when their kids came home from school, or Richard or I told them about things that had happened, they would pick little parts out that were universal, that happened to all kids.

Each show, I'm not saying happened to one kid. It's a conglomerate that happened in a similar vein to hundreds of kids. But because they really did happen to kids, things that really happened in the '50s or early '60s, could have happened in the '20s or '30s—and still could happen in the '90s. And I think that's why so many people could relate to them.

In fact, one of the things I found peculiar, they just did a big demographic view of "Leave It to Beaver" and the No. 1 audience group for "Leave It to Beaver"...what would you think it would be?

You might think men in their 50s or 40s, right?

Actually, the No.1 demographic group for watching the show is women 18-to-35.

So it just shows "Beaver" is not just things happening to two brothers growing up in the '50s.

It's stuff everybody can relate to. It's things that happen to kids. It's gender-neutral. It's things that happen to two children growing up. And it's not two kids growing up in the '50s. It's not two kids growing up in the '80s or '90s or whatever 2000s there are.

Any drawbacks to the show:

Actually the biggest problem with the show—if there is a problem—is that a lot of people don't understand that it's situation comedy and all the problems are cleared up in 23 minutes.

And then they live their own life and go, "My life is the pits because this is going wrong and that's going wrong."

Well, it's television and it's comedy. It's not a documentary of those times.

I do a lot of personal appearances. People always say, "If my life could be like the Cleavers, it would be perfect."

I tell them, "No one's life was like that."

This is comedy. This is not real life.

But a lot of people in our society today—especially homes where there are less than two parents, or are dysfunctional—they tend to glom onto the TV and say, "This is the perfect life. If only my life had been like this."

The thing is, there's no family in America that has the "Leave It to Beaver" life. There's always things that go wrong that can't be fixed in 23 minutes. A lot of them go over a lifetime and what people have to learn to do is take those things that are wrong with their family and in some ways cope with them and rise above them.

And that's part of living.

Would he have changed being The Beav?

The way I always tell people is this: knowing what I know now, if when I went on the interview for "Leave It to Beaver," would I still go on it and still accept the job? Very definitely. As an actors, we're part of the golden age of television. We're part of one of the great shows. We'll go down as part of television history.

I got very lucky to be picked as The Beaver and be part of that phenomenon.

Well, we all got very lucky. Jerry, Kenny, Tony and I.

No question about that.

I can't imagine any of us would change the chance we had to be part of the Cleaver family. No way.

And, in fact, I don't think I could have put any of this any better than my

Chapter One

buddies, Kenny and Jerry.

Especially the part about my being such a brilliant actor.

Just kidding.

But the "wholesome" thing?

Well, maybe for everyone else, that's the way their lives went off-camera. Mine?

I can't honestly say it was squeaky clean.

In fact, some of it was as far away from your average "Beaver" espisode as the other side of the moon.

I probably was fortunate I was in the public limelight when the tabloids were a lot less active.

I told you I was always lucky. Right place. Right time.

Because it's probably for the best that all of my life wasn't known during my acting days.

Behind the Lumpy and Beaver and innocent Mayfield facade was a wild child inside me about to get out.

And the more I passed from being a child, the wilder he got.

Leonard, Sylvia and Scarface

e should have known something unusual was happening because my poor mother was trying to make it to Cedars of Lebanon Hospital.

I was on the way with her, trying to wait to be born.

And not doing a very good job of it, I might add.

Sylvia—that's my mom—is doing her best to wait for my dad, Leonard. But that also is proving a difficult thing to do.

Remember the movie, "1941," Spielberg's big bomb?

Honest to God, they really did have air-raid warnings in Los Angeles back in the early '40s. Because my old man was an air-raid warden. We're in the middle of World War II and Leonard and Sylvia live in Huntington Park at the time. Huntington Park is down in the southern part of Los Angeles, not far from Long Beach.

So Leonard is the air-raid warden for our block and Sylvia is so pregnant she's about to burst. And it takes awhile for Leonard to get home from air-raid-wardening and all like that. And things are moving right along for Sylvia by now, and there's no Hollywood Freeway. There's no Harbor Freeway. And to get to Cedars from Huntington must have taken an hour.

It's 15 minutes by freeway now. But it was an hour or more back then.

Anyhow, we're all on the way to Cedars, even if I don't exactly know it so far, and I start showing up.

So Leonard takes a sharp turn into Hollywood Presbyterian Hospital instead of Cedars and it turns out to be a pretty darn brilliant maneuver by pop.

I am born in the ambulance entrance of Hollywood Presbyterian Hospital.

I mean, I came sliding into first base before they could get me into the hospital. I was born in the wrong hospital.

Right then and there, I was mucking things up.

I popped right out and went, "I'm outta here. What's happenin'?"

I can just imagine the ride before we all got there. Hollywood Presbyterian is only maybe a mile, mile-and-a-half from Cedars, but the five miles before they stopped at Hollywood, I'm sure my mom is going, "Len. Len. Something is happening here."

My old man was really funny. I can just hear him going, "Sylvia, shaddup. I'm goin' as fast as I can."

My mom told me he pulled right up into the parking lot at Hollywood Pres and ran up to the ambulance entrance. I never made it to the delivery room. I didn't make it to the reception desk either. I poked out in the car.

That was April 12, 1942.

And, you know what? I feel like I've always been right on time.

Part of the joy of my life, in my estimation, has been timing. It's just that I seemed to have been at the right place at the most perfect time.

Even if I didn't know it was the most perfect time in a lot of instances.

And so much of my perfect times in life begin with my parents. They were good people. I was so lucky. My whole life, you could call me "Lucky" instead of "Lumpy."

Because I have been.

I had the greatest childhood anyone could ever want.

The greatest adolescence.

I've lived like nobody ever lived and it all started with Sylvia and Leonard.

My father was the consummate male chauvinist pig. My father was the pre-eminent Archie Bunker and chauvinist pig all rolled up into one, with a heart of gold, and he was the biggest pussycat that ever lived.

That was my old man. I loved him dearly. He was a diamond in the rough. My dad used to walk around with a stogie, swore like a sailor. But he was the biggest, mushiest pushover you ever saw in your life.

We were strictly a middle-class family. My dad was a butcher. He had his own business, the Leonard Meat Co.

My mother was the Minnesota state typing champion when she was 18 and she was a knockout. My mother was flat-out gorgeous. She was queen of the Mardis Gras. Sylvia was so beautiful.

My mother went to work for Remington-Rand when she was 18. My mother had a job during the Depression, when my dad didn't for seven years. She supported the family as a secretary for Remington-Rand while my dad couldn't find a job.

They were "victims," if you called it that, of the Depression. But they refused to stay down. They always got back up. They always fought on. Moved forward. Prevailed. They couldn't be stopped with elephant guns.

My parents had a great romance.

My mother was from Northfield, Minn., about 100 miles north of

Minneapolis. Northfield is where Jesse James had the great Minnesota raid. OK? The Daltons were killed there and Frank James was shot there.

Do you know who shot Frank James?

A 14-year-old deputy sheriff who was hiding behind a watering trough because they had no sidewalks. His name was Tom Anderson.

That was my grandfather. My mother's maiden name was Anderson. I am half-Norwegian. My mother was a heavy-duty Lutheran before converting to Judaism.

And it was Sylvia's father, Tom, who shot Frank James. Only he didn't know it was Frank James.

He was hiding behind the watering trough because he knew it was the James Gang. He was scared out of his gourd and he was aiming over the watering trough and he hit some guy in the leg.

The guy fell off the horse.

All these other guys come running out of everyplace with pitchforks and shovels and all that and started beating the living daylights out of the guys on the ground.

Jesse made it out of town.

But Frank didn't.

Frank spent 20 years in the Minnesota State Reformatory, courtesy of Grandpa Tom.

Fact. And the movies about Frank and Jesse are total baloney, because they have them riding all over the friggin' place doing different bank jobs. Meanwhile, Frank is hanging out back in the cooler, because Grandpa Tom put him there.

Even if Grandpa Tom didn't know what the hell he was doing at the time. So what?

Andersons and Banks were always right on time.

They were always right on top of everything.

My dad was a great athlete in Minneapolis. He played high school football with a guy named Pudge Heffelfinger, whom you might have heard of, if you are a dyed-in-the-wool sports nut. Pudge was greater than Bronko Nagurski. Better than Red Grange. One of the first guys elected to the Pro Football Hall of Fame. They were fond of calling him the greatest football player who ever lived that we don't know about.

Well, my old man was just as good. Leonard was the greatest athlete in the history of North High School in Minneapolis. My dad was an all-city tackle.

They didn't have numbers on their uniforms in those days.

He was known only by one name—Vicious Bank.

Honest to God.

Chapter Two

I saw a class yearbook that said, "And here's Vicious Bank, all-city tackle."

He played both ways, 60 minutes a game. Nobody screwed with Leonard Bank.

From what I've been told by his brothers, he was the meanest, nastiest dude in Minneapolis. He was big for the time. Leonard was 6-feet, 190. He was fast and strong as a bull. He threw the shot and the javelin on the track team and was all-city in the shotput.

It was some ridiculously short distance he threw when you look back at it. The techniques were so different and I gave him static about it all the time.

I'd look in his yearbook and I'd go, "Dad, you're telling me that you were all-city?"

He goes, "Here, take a look."

Like I haven't already taken a look a few trillion times.

I'd read in there, "Vicious Bank, City Trackman of the Year, Minneapolis, 1919."

I remember it was 1919, because it was the same year as the Black Sox Scandal.

And I'd go, "Dad, how far'd you put the shot?"

He'd mumble something.

And I'd go, "Dad, I'm not even on the track team. The guy at our school puts the shot 55 or 56 feet. It says here you put it 48 feet. Dad, I can do 48 feet."

And he goes, "Screw you."

So anyway, this majorly athletic, studly, better-than-Pudge-Heffelfinger, football-track star from North High, the Jewish section of Minneapolis, meets this blonde beauty queen from Lutheran-as-anything Northfield, Minnesota.

And they fall in love.

My dad is managing a bowling alley at the time and he sees this great-lookin' chick walk in. And, being a Bank, he figures he will cruise over and sweep this beauty off her feet.

Being a Bank, he does.

So my dad marries my mother and they have to run off because my mother isn't Jewish and my dad had this real Orthodox family that said, "You're taking out a girl that's not Jewish?"

It was true. My mother had a Minnesota accent, like in the movie "Fargo." I got such a kick out of it. It's a great movie. And I remember my mother's family talking like that. I used to go, "They sure talk funny, Mom." And she'd go, "What are you talking aboot?"

My aunts and uncles used to talk this Fargo stuff and I'd laugh at them. Like them, I was totally blond growing up. My hair didn't darken until I was about 12. As a teenager, my hair went from blond to sandy to brown. Lumpy

Leonard, Sylvia and Scarface

on the show was kind of a sandy guy. He wasn't dark, but he wasn't blond either. Gettin' dark.

So now Leonard brings home this Fargo-talking, blonde, Lutheran Norwegian shiksa from someplace called Northfield, and his family is not exactly wildly enthusiastic.

I mean, later on, when my mom converted, she took the 999-yard plunge. She became a zealot. But back then, she was still an infidel, as far as Leonard's folks were concerned.

That would not fly. So Leonard and Sylvia took off. I don't think you could exactly say they eloped. They didn't have enough bread for an official elopement. They just were married by a justice of the peace and ran away.

This was in 1926.

Now, when they run away, my dad, in order to get something going so they could eat...he starts off on a thing people called "walkathons."

Or marathon dances.

They made a movie about it: "They Shoot Horses, Don't They?" Jane Fonda. Gig Young. Fantastic movie.

The movie could have been about Leonard and Sylvia, in many ways.

My dad was the promoter and he was the emcee of these marathon dances.

He was the "Yowsa-yowsa" man.

He was doing OK at it, but to show you he wasn't always the sharpest pencil in the box, one of his favorite stories is how he turned down Red Skelton for a job in the walkathons.

When he told me that, I said, "You what?"

And he said, "I didn't think he was funny."

I said, "Dad, that's why you didn't make it in the walkathon business. Red Skelton is a riot. I mean, Clem Kaddiddlhopper, Heathcliffe and Gertrude...all that stuff? C'mon."

Red Skelton was a sweet man. A wonderful comic. I'd tell my dad this. He'd shrug.

"So shoot me...I didn't think so," his expression said.

In spite of brilliant moves like rejecting Red Skelton, my dad and mom are doing pretty well at the walkathons. They are going around the Midwest. They're staying in all these halfway decent places. They're starting to save up some money. And now they're taking their act westward.

That's where it all ended for them, in Ogden, Utah.

They're in a hotel room in Ogden, Utah, with my brother, Doug, who is 15 years older than I am, sleeping in a dresser drawer.

Someone knocks at the door.

My dad thinks it's room service.

He opens the door.

It is not room service.

It is bad news knocking.

Leonard is looking at Al Capone.

Looking him straight in the Scarface.

May God strike me dead.

Al Capone walks into the room with a couple of his muscle guys and informs my dad and my mom that they are hereby formerly out of the walkathon business.

Dad told me it was a scene right out of "The Untouchables." Big Al is wearing this huge cashmere trenchcoat, a wide fedora hat, and he's got this 5-mile long stogie with the ashes falling all over the place.

My mom takes one look and immediately hightails it across the room to where Doug, who is about 1, is sleeping in the drawer. She slams the drawer shut.

No gangster is getting her baby, not matter how tough he thinks he is.

But Scarface definitely gets what he came for.

Eighty-sixing Leonard and Sylvia from the marathons.

His first words are something to the effect, "Youse are outta here."

Now, my dad may have been known as Vicious Bank back in Minnesota, but he was not also known as Bonehead Bank.

He did not question Al Capone's authority in the matter. I guess that should go without saying from the movies we've seen about him and all.

But back then there were no movies to go by. Just reputation. And in those times, the worlds of the jocks, the bootleggers, the gangsters and entertainers kind of flowed together (come to think of it, not much has really changed nowadays, has it?).

My dad knew enough that a visit from Big Al—a personal visit, at that— was more cue than he needed to exit, stage right, from the walkathons.

You know how in the gangster movies, one of the bad guys says, "He took sick" and that's why so-and-so didn't show up for some gangster gathering?

Well, Leonard and Sylvia just took sick. They are no longer showing up for the marathons.

I guess Capone didn't already have enough going with the booze and prostitution and other stuff, so Big Al needed to corner the walkathon racket, too.

I mean, you never see it on "The Untouchables," guys rat-tat-tatting the Tommy-guns out of those old black cars while the announcer goes: "Meanwhile, Ness speeds over to Nitti's hideout on the way to busting up Capone's walkathon joints."

But even though it wasn't talked about in the movies, the Mob did take over the walkathons.

It actually was Al Capone at my dad's door.

This was in 1928. Ogden, Utah.

What was Al Capone doing in Ogden, Utah, in 1928, you say?

He was chasing my old man out of the walkathon business, that's what. Other than that, I don't have a clue.

I think that visit from Scarface took some of the starch out of my old man's shorts. That started the seven-year period when he didn't work and my mother supported the family.

My mom was a dish. But she was very pragmatic. She was a go-getter and a hustler. She worked hard.

Times were tough. There was a year, my brother lived on sardines. My brother would never eat sardines as an adult because he ate them every day of his life. They were a nickel a can or something. I mean, that's what they could afford.

I know it was killin' my dad, though, that he wasn't working. This was still before I came along, in the late '30s. Because of my mom's jobs, they somehow scraped enough credit together, and borrowed from friends, to open a little store. And they lived behind the store.

It was just a corner grocery store. They had one ice box that they kept milk and soda pop in—whatever. They had one meat case. Some shelves with bread and canned goods.

It was a tiny mom-and-pop store. It was called Bank's Grocery.

It was on Santa Fe in Huntington Park. That's in the middle of the barrio now, but back then it was a major Jewish section.

Now the store is going OK. Things are sort of on an even keel and I come along. I told you I was a master of timing. No daily freakin' sardines for me. Uh-uh. I come along and life is pretty decent. Leonard and Sylvia are on their feet. They're not rich or anything. Not even close. But they are doing all right.

And I was lucky because my dad was by then in a position to be a great father to me.

You know all this hype about the country going down the tubes because of the lack of a father figure...it's true.

I saw my father's weaknesses. I wasn't blind. But I saw his virtues more than his weaknesses.

His main virtue was that he was my best friend.

We talked sports, morning, noon and night. He took me to every ball game that I could possibly go to. He took me to the Rams-Browns championship at the L.A. Coliseum in 1951. The Rams won the championship, and I got to see it with my dad.

He used to take me to Gilmore Field in the late '40s to watch the Hollywood Stars minor-league baseball team.

Chapter Two

He used to sit right behind Al Jolson and became friends with Jolie.

Jolson would bring a big basket to the ball game. And that basket was filled with salamis and rye bread and pickles and all this other stuff. It wouldn't be a small salami either—it'd be one of those 5-pounders which would stick way out of the basket. He'd have a big pot of potato salad in there, too.

See, the Stars ballpark was just one block from the Borscht Belt, with all the delicatessens along in there.

You'd see guys bringing in these big strings of knockwurst, all linked together. They didn't have anything but waxed paper to carry it in at the time, so it got all greasy and slimy.

They'd have this stick they'd dip into this big old jar of mustard and they'd slather it all over the wursts and the salami.

Jolie had this block of about 50 seats—it only cost a quarter apiece to get in—which he'd picked for himself and his cronies.

These seats were behind the Stars dugout and you'd see Jolie and his crew down there in their straw hats and fedoras and suspenders with no jacket, no tie.

Leonard-the-Sport was one of those guys.

He wasn't really tight with Jolson or anything. More like a second-banana.

But he was a guy Jolson knew.

He'd give a wave, "Hi, Len, how are ya?"

Jolson joked with everybody.

And yet, this was pretty much kiss-my-ring stuff, with everybody kind of catering to Jolson. Guys would go get him beers and stuff. They wanted to be around him.

That's where I came in.

Every now and then, Jolson would kind of bark, "Hey kid, go get some sodas."

I wasn't sure what kid he meant, but, what the heck, I was only maybe 5, 6 years old at the time. I was pretty excited to go run some errands for Mr. Jolson.

And, not incidentally, I was also able to turn this experience into my first profit as an entrepeneur.

I'd go up and buy a whole case of sodas, and when you did that, they'd give you a discount and sell 'em to you for a nickel apiece. I'd turn around and peddle 'em for 7 cents.

So my time among Jolie and his gang was fairly memorable.

So was some of his byplay with the players. He used to keep up a running commentary and critique of the players. Frankie Kelleher, guys like that—Jolie was always on 'em.

Leonard, Sylvia and Scarface

And they'd be back at him.

Once this guy from the Stars—I don't remember who it was, but it was a guy Jolson had been ridin' pretty good—hit a home run. And when he comes across the plate, he takes about two or three steps and slides down onto one knee like Jolson did in his act.

You know:

"Mammy!"

The guy spreads his hands out at Jolson, like: Take that, wiseguy.

Jolson cracked up.

Everybody did.

Moments like that were the reasons my old man loved to hang around jocks.

He loved rubbing elbows with the fighters. He was kind of a street guy. One of his buds was Benny Leonard. Benny Leonard held three world boxing championships at one time. Of course, my father told me Benny was much better than Joe Louis.

"Better than any Schwartzer," Leonard used to say. Which is to say a black guy.

I mean, Benny was Jewish and there ain't an Irish guy or a black guy alive can lick this Jew, right?

My dad was friends with Slapsie Maxie Rosenbloom, the fighter. And then there was this one guy my dad said was the greatest fighter you never heard of. His name was King Lavinsky. King Lavinsky was a big-time fighter in the '30s. Dad said he packed a right cross that was just the greatest.

This was my dad. He ran his little meat business—with Sylvia's help. My dad never drank. He didn't carouse. Because he loved my mother. But he loved to be with the guys.

There are some guys...they're...out with the guys. That was my dad. Even when I was growing up, my dad had a night out with the boys. He was either playing poker or they were going to Hollywood Park for the ponies.

So that was our family, Leonard and Sylvia and me and Doug and Teddy the dog. He was a Spitz. Teddy was a cool, cool dog.

And Doug was pretty cool in his own way. There were 15 years between us, so we never got close as we might have otherwise. In fact, we never really got along because he had a drinking problem.

It used to burn my butt because I didn't like to see him that way, and I also didn't like the strain that his alcoholism put on Mom and Dad.

But Doug was a very talented, very bright guy. He lived his own fascinating life.

He was named Doug after Douglas Fairbanks, because my mother had the hots for Douglas Fairbanks.

Doug was the valedictorian of his graduating class at the University of

Chapter Two

Southern California. This was 1950.

My brother was a pipe dreamer. His intentions were good, but he wasn't practical. He dreamt of everything being Utopian. My brother was a terrific writer. He wrote this one show called "The Preacher," which made them revive "Elmer Gantry."

It was voted the best play of 1958 in Beverly Hills.

Doug owned a theater called the Beverly Hills Playhouse, and he had a lot of big stars who actually did small theater in Los Angeles in those days.

Leonard Nimoy was always hanging around, and Marvin Kaplan was one of Doug's best buddies. I mean, these guys had a bunch called "The Group." The Group used to meet over on Sunset at this little hamburger stand named The Hamburger Hamlet.

In those days it was a little hash house on Sunset, near Doheny, one block up from the current Whiskey-a-Go-Go.

The cook was a guy named Harry Lewis. The waitress was a lady named Marilyn Lewis. You might know her now as Cardinale, the designer. Because that's what she wound up doing.

Harry and Marilyn Lewis started up the chain of Hamburger Hamlets that I knew when I was growing up and all through my young adult days. Hamburger Hamlet was probably the best coffee shop in Southern California. McDonald's started in the '50s and the Hamlets started in the '40s, and the Hamlets ruled, with the best burgers anywhere in the world.

Anyhow, my brother's buddies, Nimoy, Peter Leeds—one of the best character actors in Hollywood—a guy named Stanley Adams and a guy named Nick Adams, who played Johnny Yuma on the TV western series, "The Rebel"...these guys all met with my brother, Doug, in The Group.

Leonard Nimoy was probably the least talented of those guys, but "Star Trek" and Spock turned him into the biggest star. Although I think Marvin Kaplan is still one of the greatest character actors I've ever seen. I loved him. He played Topcat in the cartoon. He was Meek Millie's boyfriend.

Every time you saw a nebbish in the movies back then it was Marvin Kaplan. He was a better nebbish than Arnold Stang.

Through all this, my brother was writing and acting. My dad always said, "Doug, when you gonna get a job?"

Maybe this fell back to the dad who didn't work for seven years. He sees this kid graduate with honors from USC and not go get "gainful employment." He's just hanging out with a bunch of shiftless actors.

My brother was in a ton of movies. A ton of movies. Most of them were bit parts, but he was in them all the same.

I betcha Doug had a hundred movie credits, all like two-day wonders. Couple lines here, couple lines there. Nothing big, but he was in a lotta movies just the same.

Leonard, Sylvia and Scarface

One of my brother's real close buddies was Ira.

Only you knew him by the name of Jeff Chandler, one of the major leading men of the '40s and '50s.

All I knew was, he was Ira.

Ira used to come over to our house. He was this big galloot with an Adam's apple that stuck way out.

I remember I smarted off to him once. I don't remember what I said—some wise-ass thing. He grabbed me by the neck and he goes, "Your little brother's quite a guy."

But his voice was saying "irritating little schmuck." And while he's talking nice, he's holding me real tight in these hands like a vise and he's moving my head back and forth.

When he left, I said, "Doug, I don't like that guy."

He was a good-looking stud, Ira, was. Another guy who died for no reason at all. They killed him during an operation in Culver City. He was having a slam-dunk operation, a nothing deal. Bled to death on the table.

Big scandal.

I didn't hate him anymore. I felt sorry for him.

Anyway, he was Ira, one of my brother's best buddies, and he turned out to be Jeff Chandler.

My brother always knew people and he did have a glimmer of hope for his future. Some of the films he was in were:

"The Red Ball Express" (with Ira).

"Purple Heart Diaries" (with a guy we knew as Bernie Schwartz at the time, whom the world later knew as Tony Curtis—another guy who was in and out of The Group.

"Frogmen" and "The Good Humor Man" with Jack Carson.

Heck, Doug was in "Butch Cassidy and the Sundance Kid."

He was just a punk in it. He got a day's work out of it because his buddies were doing some work on the film.

My brother kept writing at the same time. And him and his buddy, Jay something-or-other, decided, "We're going to go out on a limb."

They got enough scratch together to open up this Beverly Hills Playhouse over on Robertson. This was sort of a job, but it wasn't really a job because it was just kind of drifting.

As usual, it was good old Mom who came to the rescue again.

My mother got on the horn and started selling theater parties. She kept the Beverly Hills Playhouse going. She had these parties for all these groups coming through, and the place was always full.

Then, in the late '50s, my dad went out of business with the grocery. Same deal. Mom is the U.S. Cavalry again. In she comes, riding at the full gallop to save the day.

Sylvia got on the phone again. She picked up the phone book and said, "OK, we're gonna start another business. This time it's the meat business."

My mom started the meat business out of the back of our house. My dad would go down and get the meat.

They would cut it up on the washer and dryer.

I would wrap it on the kitchen table and deliver it in the afternoon.

Sylvia got the biggest people in Hollywood as customers. I was a movie star and I was delivering meat in the afternoon. It was 1958 and '59. I'm a regular on "Leave It to Beaver."

And I'm walking up to Edward G. Robinson's house with his meat.

I'm walking up to Jack Benny's house with his meat.

They all knew I was in the movies and on TV. But it was cool. It's just the way things were back then. Movie stars were more regular people. So it was only natural that I would be walking up their driveway with a load of meat and I'd be a guy they'd flip on the television that night and see on a hit TV series.

"Oh, look, there's Leonard and Sylvia's kid. Didn't he deliver nice meat today?"

That was their reaction, rather than: What in God's name is he doing soiling his delicate hands with common labor when he's a movie star?

It was only natural, you'd pitch in on the family business. Almost all the big stars just seemed more like normal, flesh-and-blood people.

I don't know how many times you'd go to a restaurant in the '50s and see a movie star and it was no big deal. "Oh look, there's Jack Lemmon." Go back to eating. Let them eat. No big commotion.

We'd go to a place called Wil Wright's on Saturday night for ice cream sodas and constantly see Humphrey Bogart or Jimmy Stewart. We never said a word to these guys.

Why can't we do this now? What has changed? I don't know. People are weird, I guess.

People weren't so much into idol-worshipping, it didn't seem to me, back then. We'd respect them. We'd leave them alone. I mean, keep in mind, I lived in West LA, where a lot of stars did live. They'd go to the market themselves, instead of sending the servants or whatever. A guy like Gary Cooper, maybe, had to hide a little. If you were Dick Clark, you hit the market yourself.

If you had a lot of confidence in yourself, you'd be a high visibility person.

To this day I don't know how many times I ran into Walter Matthau in West Los Angeles. A million times maybe. He doesn't hide from anybody. He leads his life the way he wants. He's a bright man, a really cool old guy. He used to live at the race track and I'd see him there when I went with my old man. Him and Jack Klugman. They were always at the races.

And speaking of off to the races, the meat business was doing pretty well with Mom and Dad busting their humps and me dropping deliveries all over town.

But Sylvia was far from satisfied. I told you she was a go-getter.

She was very creative. And when I was 5 or 6, I used to wonder why we didn't have a Christmas tree like you'd see on the lots all up and down Wilshire Boulevard.

I was a rotten little putz. "Wah! Why can't we have a Christmas tree?" I whined.

Well my mother always felt bad about that. All of a sudden she gets the bright idea. God's truth, Sylvia Bank, my mother, invented Chanukah decorations.

All Chanukah decorations.

At least any of them you ever saw out on the West Coast.

I mean, she didn't invent the dreidel—this toy top with the Hebrew letters on each of the four sides, which kids spin at Chanukah. That was invented thousands of years ago.

But Sylvia invented the folding dreidel, the folding star—all of the paper ornaments, all the paper streamers, the banners with the letters spelling out "Happy Chanukah," the electric menorah.

She invented all of this to keep me quiet.

Actually, some of it was to keep me happy because I was spoiled and I felt bad being a Jew in the middle of all this Christmas stuff. I sat there and watched her. I watched my mother with her scissors, take a great big white Christmas bell that she bought at Woolworth's and cut it into a folding Jewish star.

Sylvia started a company called Jewish Holiday Novelties, at our house. In those days there had been none of this stuff. My mother went to all the rabbis in Los Angeles and all the synagogues and all the gift shops, and they started selling.

Boy, they caught on big time.

We were living in the Fairfax area, which was the big Jewish district at the time. Still is, in fact. Within two years, our house and our garage was filled to the rafters with boxes of my mother's stuff.

Maybe it was watching my mother's motivation, the strong desire she had to accomplish and succeed at things, that got me to teach myself to read and do addition and subtraction along about the time I was 4 years old.

I learned to read and do math off the old Racing Form.

Maybe I was just bored. I was, in effect, an only child at the time. My brother had gone away to World War II, then come back, then moved out. He came over for dinner maybe twice a week and did his laundry.

Chapter Two

That was about it, because he was out with his pals and girl friends.

So what did I do with no television and time on my hands? I was kind of an introverted kid at the time. I wasn't really a loner. I had a few playmates in the neighborhood. But I was comfortable being by myself at that stage of my life, I guess.

Anyway, I would sit home and listen to the radio in the afternoon. Instead of listening to some other weird stuff, I'd listen to the race re-creations. From 4 to 5 o'clock, they'd run the races from Hollywood Park or Santa Anita or Del Mar.

I liked some of the names, like Citation and Coal Town. I got fascinated by this stuff. Then my dad said if I picked up the Los Angeles Examiner, I could see where they had all the horses rated. And he sort of helped me sound out the words. An "a", a "b", a "c."

I was born in '42 and this was '46 when we started with the words. And now I'm learning to read. But then came the numbers, because I was talking about prices. My dad wasn't a teacher, but he explained to me about a zero and a 10 and the way they worked.

Then I would put Tinkertoys together. I would put three together over here and three together over there, and I'd say, "Mom, if I have this and I put these Tinkertoys there and those Tinkertoys here and push them together, is it six Tinkertoys?"

And she'd go, "Yeah, honey."

And she'd walk away, not knowing that I was learning to add and subtract and multiply and divide. This was before school for me. I just sort of learned by accident. I figured it out for myself—with a little help. Because I had time on my hands.

Time?

Did I tell you I took the time, when I was in the second or third grade, to read the entire encyclopedia?

That's right.

I did.

I said there wasn't a whole heck of a lot to do in my neighborhood. Maybe there wasn't anything to do.

Because I read all 20 volumes of the "World Book Encyclopedia" when I was 7 years old.

Every word, A to Z.

It took me about three months.

I was kind of a knowledge junkie. I learned all these crazy things.

Here's the thing. I learned a bunch of garbage that didn't mean anything. I mean, I knew that the markets closed on Catalina Island at 6 o'clock. I knew that kangaroos sat on their tails.

I mean, how do you apply these things to regular life? But I dug it. I soaked up knowledge. I loved soaking up knowledge.

It was something my mom and dad had loved all their lives and they passed on to me.

They passed on a love of doing and accomplishing, even with all the hits and misses of life. You just have to keep on plugging.

That's what Mom and Dad did.

Eventually, the meat business got pretty solid. And Leonard-the-Sport was really proud. He bought my mom a 1939 Willys for 50 bucks. It was 10 years old, because this was 1949, but that was no small feat. And let me tell you, that son-of-a-gun ran.

It was this ugly blue color, and you know what? I'd give a lot of money for that car today. It was really cool.

In a way, the Willys was much like my old man. Kind of an ugly blue color, but the son-of-a-gun could really run.

I'd give any amount to see him today. He was just really the coolest.

My dad had one wish that I was glad that I was able to fulfill for him.

The Jewish tradition is, when someone dies, you dip 'em in the ground the same day so the healing begins. I mean, all you other guys are barbarians. You put 'em in a room and you drink with them for a week and once they start smellin bad, you plant 'em.

But us Jews, we gotta plant 'em right away.

I couldn't do that because my dad died at this dude ranch in Paso Robles, California.

It was a challenge.

He died on a Thursday night, late at night. And because he died away from home, they picked up his body at the hospital and they wouldn't release it. Until some medical guy, whatever they had in that territory, gave his OK.

In the Jewish tradition, you can't bury them on Saturday, the Sabbath.

So I couldn't plant Leonard until Sunday.

But it was worth the wait, I think.

If you were a famous Jew, you were buried in Hillside Memorial Park in Los Angeles. It's right near the airport, right off the San Diego Freeway, not five miles from LAX.

My dad always said, "Son, all I ask is that you just make sure I'm next to Jolie."

It took some doing, but if you were to go visit my dad, you will see that he currently resides on a certain hillside.

Leonard is not 20 feet from Jolson.

And so is Sylvia.

Both of them are there together, Leonard and Sylvia.

Like I said, I was so lucky to be together with them all the time I got to.

Chapter Two

I was lucky, the gifts they passed on to me, of inquisitiveness and persistence and an undying interest in people.

But one thing knowing them and reading my way through the entire encyclopedia had taught me.

I had experienced the most beautiful, full, rich, incredible life with them.

But I had experienced nothing.

I was missing something.

There was more out there for me to see and do and be.

Chapter Three
Beach Days and Knights

ool.

You hear me say it all the time, as if you haven't noticed.

But it's more than a saying with me, more than just a word.

It is a belief.

It is a core tenet of my existence.

The pillar on which my psyche stands.

It is both a journey and a destination. A motivation and an accomplishment.

It is a grail as palpable and reachable as any goblet in some faraway shrine.

To me, it became almost holy.

Cool is in my bones and in my fibers, in my heart and in my soul. It flicks at my eyes and licks at my lips. I see cool coming and going.

Cool should be on the periodic table as an essential element of life. Like both oxygen and carbon, I breathe cool in and I breathe cool out.

It has permeated my life since my early teens.

I guess cool always will.

Becoming a movie star, or becoming famous, was never a goal.

The first goal I ever had was, I wanted to be popular.

I decided I was going to be cool. And to be cool, I had to be nice, I had to be thoughtful, I had to be caring, I had to be remembered.

But it wasn't always so.

If there was such a thing as the antithesis of cool in school, that was me.

I was a dweeb long before there were dweebs.

Before anybody knew what a geek was, I knew.

I was a poster child for dork.

Take every lame-o you ever saw in teenage-angst movies, roll them into one, and you've got me in early high school.

Dial 1-800-IMANERD and you'd get Frank Bank on the other end of the line.

Part of the trouble, if I may say so, was that I was just too friggin' smart.

I know it's immodest to mention it, but here's the deal. I was the smartest kid at Hamilton High School. Out of 3,000 kids I had the highest IQ in school.

My IQ was 203.

Yes. It sounds absurdly high. I didn't even realize it was up there for a long time. But I can document it by the fact that I also was a screw-up.

What happened was, my junior year, my counselor calls me in. My grades had slipped from A's to C's. Obviously, up 'til then, schoolwork had been a slam-dunk for me. English, history, I breezed through all that. I knew the history of the world, Part I and II. I loved it. I really dug in. Politics. Geography. All that. The only thing I hated was science. I had to study some, but still skated through most of it.

But now my counselor calls me in, this guy named Leonard Rudolph, and he says to me, "What is the matter with you? You just took the IQ test and you dropped 25 points?"

And he showed me my IQ was 178.

I said, "Well, to be honest with you, I really wasn't thinking about taking the test that morning."

I didn't add: I was thinking of girls, which was all I thought about by now, morning, noon and night and all the hours in between.

"Would you like me to retake the test?" I asked.

He goes, "No. There's nothing wrong with what you scored, but I'm curious as to why you could have dropped that much."

The words "copping out" didn't exist as far as I knew at the time. But what I said was tantamount to, "I've just been copping out. I just wasn't thinking about tests."

So he tells me, "Well, I'm very upset because you've had the highest IQ in the school at 203. And how come the guy with the highest IQ is getting C's while everyone else is getting A's?"

I couldn't really tell him what was going on inside me.

But it was simple. In the eighth grade I was a real toad. I was socially backward. I was shy. I kept to myself. The guys I hung with were like the science club. We used to play chess, for God's sake.

In fact, if I may add an immodest footnote, I had beat the California chess champion when I was in the sixth grade. He was a coach at Shenandoah Grammar School. The guy was 40 years old and his name was John Keckhut. We'd turn a couple of trash cans over and set some carom boards across them, and play chess on top of these at school.

True story.

Beach Days and Knights

So I was still doing this kind of thing in high school.

I did all the things you expect a nerd to do.

And then it hit me.

Like the Elvis movie, I went Girl Crazy.

I discovered girls-girls-girls-girls-girls around age 12. My first real love was a girl named Joyce, who lived around the corner from me. Man, I was madly in love with Joyce.

I never had sex with Joyce or anything. You don't always nail the first girl you love, but Joyce just got me thinking about it.

Everything took a backseat to girls. I'm still doing the movies and television. But the movies and television took second place to my new-found ambition:

Getting laid.

And suddenly, I saw the way to getting what I wanted.

I would become the most popular guy in school.

I would become...cool.

My libido was pointing the way. But I also decided to train my mind on the whole matter of becoming cool.

That's when I decided to become a people person.

I realized as a kid I'd spent all this time listening to race results, reading the encyclopedia, doing all these mano a mano projects.

But gregariousness was a much better project and I honestly did love being with people. This was a natural part of me I'd inherited from Leonard and Sylvia, who never knew a stranger. I'd just never thrown the switch in that part of my brain or heart.

I loved being with people.

The cool thing was that I wasn't phony about it. Because I really did abhor phonies. I liked being genuine. And I genuinely liked everybody. I genuinely wanted to do good. I was a do-gooder.

Dudley Do-Right of the Mounties was cool. He was. That was another thing that goes back to my father. My father said to me, "I always want you to be the guy in the white hat, not the guy in the black hat. It's much better to be good than bad."

Everything was black and white to my dad. Black stood for evil, white stood for good. Well, I gotta tell you something. He was right. Leonard was really cool in his own funny kinda way.

And so my heroes were all good guys. I had so many heroes when I was a kid, it was terrible. I mean, more than the average guy.

Remember I am left-handed? I go to buy my first baseball glove and I'm all upset because my buddies are all righties and I can't borrow one of their mitts because I'm a lefty.

But my dad pointed out to me, "Hey, son, here's a lefty. His name was

Chapter Three

Babe Ruth."

And I went, "Really? Wow! Hey, cool. Babe Ruth is a lefty." I was so excited, I can't begin to tell you. I was thrilled.

Where do you think my love for Sandy Koufax comes from? It wasn't just the fact that he's Jewish and a lefty, was it? C'mon. Get real. Let's go for it. Sandy Koufax. The greatest pitcher in the history of baseball is a lefty?

Sandy was my man.

But it wasn't just sports guys.

Albert Einstein. Lefty all the way. I loved Einstein. Einstein was cool. He was great.

And I loved Jonas Salk, another lefty. I so admired guys who I thought were good guys and who were smart enough to figure things out and help other people.

I saw that if you weren't smart, you were going to get trampled on. You either had to be strong physically and fight—which I was fairly strong and was a fairly good fighter…I had my share of them. Or you could go one even better than fighting. You could outsmart 'em.

So smart guys were my heroes, too.

But my Big Three heroes, by far, were Ruth, Koufax and Einstein.

Pretty decent trio, isn't it?

And because I had that complex a lot of left-handers do about being lefty in life, my dad also told me, "Frank, lefties are special. They're probably a little smarter and they're probably a little more intuitive."

Whether that was true or not, my father thought it was cool, so I did, too.

So I wanted to follow my heroes and be kind and generous and do good to people.

This would help me be liked by them and popular with them, and I wanted that more than anything.

But especially I wanted that with girls.

I used to really get off when I'd have four or five girls around me. I liked that. I think I was interested in some of their causes. I've always been a feminist before feminism was popular. I know that sounds crazy for the son of the world's greatest male chauvinist pig—and a guy who's done some pigging in his own right. But I always thought chicks got a rotten deal in the world, in general.

So I played that chord and joined their chorus about uplifting and celebrating women.

Even more important than my baseline beliefs on the subject, of course, was the fact that I most definitely saw this as a good angle to lead me to the ultimate conquest.

I felt their pain.

I also was feeling for their bods.

But in order to get those bods, I decided I had to become the essence of cool.

I had this personal drive that I wanted to become king of the hill. And nobody could make me king of the hill unless I did it all by myself.

I approached it kind of like Bill Nye, the Science Guy. I made it a research project. I concentrated on gathering data and storing the understanding which would enable me to become knowledgable, witty and cool.

My bible in this spiritual awakening was the same as many a young man in the '50s.

What else?

Playboy.

OK. So it's predictable. Sure, it's a cliche.

But it was the main tool we teenage boys at the time had available to sharpen our girl-prospecting tools.

Remember when I said everything in my life has been timing? *Playboy* comes along in '53, '54. It was new. Cutting edge. At that moment it was bold, adventurous, pushing all the societal envelopes.

Shoot, I was at least one guy who honestly did read the articles. I looked at the picture, sure.

But I soaked up all the cool *Playboy* philosophy stuff.

What sort of a man reads *Playboy*?

A man wanting to learn how to get girls.

A man like Frank Bank.

I took to *Playboy* like catnip. Here I am, this young punk kid. I almost wanted to go out and get a smoking jacket and a pipe to be like Hef. I didn't go that far, though.

But I asked myself, self, what are chicks looking for? I didn't have the body of John Derek. I was a little chunky. But I had all my hair. I had bright sparkling eyes. I knew I was smarter than all these broads put together (in a completely understanding way about the noble struggle for feminine equality, of course).

So I decided what Cool was, was a version of being smart, witty, kind and fun. And really being hip about what was going on. I started reading newspapers, watching television. These were like self-improvement books before you had self-improvement books.

In other words, how are you cool at a party?

I knew at this point in time Johnny Mathis was getting popular. I loved Mathis. I went with that trend.

There were a few things my morals wouldn't allow me to do. Drugs being one of them.

Not in high school.

In fact, not in college.

Chapter Three

Well, there was that one time I dropped peyote with Carlos Castenada at UCLA, but that comes later in the "Idiots" chapter.

I didn't do alcohol in high school.

Sex, constantly, yes.

That was my drug.

But my science project was a success. I did, indeed, become cool. I had made the total transformation. I truly was a cool guy.

I pretty much would say that I became the most popular guy in the entire school.

Before I got there, I had to change my image.

So I went and got me a real buckle-butt chinos—those pants with little buckles halfway between the pockets and the belt-line. I got these double-button-down-collar shirts. I got them in pink and orange. Those were the two hot colors.

Black polished cotton pants. That was cool, too.

Then I started giving my own definition to cool.

I became a trend-setter. Honest-to-God. Me.

Right to this day, Fonzie had nothing on me when it came to establishing the cool agenda.

Things I would start and realize were cool, things I would do, six months later would become the fashion.

Like wearing my pants with tennis shoes and no socks.

Like a barracuda jacket with no shirt, zipped partway up, with the sleeves pushed up. A barracuda jacket is a beige jacket—everyone in the world wore a barracuda in the '60s. It's got a red-plaid lining, it's got two slash pockets and a flip-up collar. You wore the collar up, zipped up to just past halfway.

No shirt. No socks. Jeans. Tennis shoes.

Tennis shoes preferably with no ties. Preferably white loafer tennis shoes. Not too many people made them. Keds might have made them. But they were available. You had to have them.

Now, if you didn't have tennis shoes, you could have worn nice loafers with no socks.

But the no-sock look was invented by yours truly in '61 and '62 in West Los Angeles.

And then everybody did it.

Once in awhile people would say to me, "Where's your socks?"

"I feel comfortable. Get off my case," I'd say.

Pretty soon, a couple other guys showed up like that. And then...it just happened. Everyone started doing it. I'd see it at some other school later. It came over from our school. Somewhere outside of L.A. someone may have been doing it before, but in our group it was new.

In our group, it came from me.

The next thing I had to do in order to secure my position as the King of Cool was to get into the best "club" in school.

This was in the day of the social clubs in California high schools. This was snobbery. To the nth degree. You had dorky clubs. You had clubs that were smarter guys. You had the clubs that were the better athletes. You had Jewish clubs. Gentile clubs. You had the bums who were in clubs. Guys who had the fastest cars might have been in this club. The geeks were in the science club.

They all had distinct traits and personalities.

Most of them were based on being clean-cut. Remember, everything in our day and age had to be clean-cut. Tramps and bums were not normally part of society.

Our clubs were mostly named after British royalty. There were the Barons and the Regents, the Imperials and the Essex, the Counts and the Normans and the Argonauts.

Girls clubs were the Lorelles, the Sans Parelles, the Fidelts, the Adorians.

I was in the club.

I was a Knight.

I came into the Knights kinda like I did in "Leave It to Beaver." I wasn't there for the first meeting. But I was there for the fifth. The club was about a month, month-and-a-half old. We started the club in 1957. I think I was the sixth or seventh member.

We got pledges. We had our own medalions. Sweatshirts. Jackets.

Across the back of our jackets it said simply:

"KNIGHTS. West L.A."

Every guy in our school would have killed to have that on his back.

The Knights ruled.

Completely. Entirely. Abso-friggin'-lutely.

We wound up having hundreds of Knights.

Everyone in West Los Angeles wanted to be a Knight.

Every girl wanted to go out with a Knight.

Why?

Because we were cool.

What made the Knights cool was, we dressed right, we acted right, we did the right things, drove the right cars, we went to the right places, ate the right foods.

We cruised "DL's" hamburger place. That was our turf. On Wilshire and La Cienega in Beverly Hills.

That round drive-in...that was our domain.

DL's was actually "Delores.'" But when you saw the neon sign, the "D" and the "L" were bigger than any of the other letters. So we used to call it DL's.

Delores's was world-famous. They copied Mel's Drive-In, in

Chapter Three

"American Graffiti," after DL's. That was exactly what DL's looked like.

What you drove to DL's had to be cool. Not necessarily the fastest. Fast. But more importantly, the coolest.

You had to drive Chevys. Or Corvettes...'57 Chevys. Impalas. Four on the floor was OK...409's were cool...335 4-speeds. The hubcaps had to be Moons, Chrome Reverses. Had to have the tubular grille.

It had to be shaved and decked.

There used to be a big "V" and it said "Chevrolet" on the front of Chevys. And on the back there was also a "V" and it also said "Chevrolet."

You took off the "V's," filled in the holes, sanded and painted it. Shaved is the front. Decked is the back.

So it was painting. Nothing ostentatious. It had to be cool. Clean. Sharp.

I had a metallic turquoise '58 Corvette, one of my sharpest cars. My '57 Chevy was black. I later painted it that '58 Corvette metallic turquoise. I sold it for a ton of money, but I wished I'd kept it.

I had lots of cars. I had a ton of them. I used to get a car every six months. Like Kenny Osmond said, I changed 'em like underwear.

I had convertibles. Chevys. Corvettes. Always my cars were cool.

Saturdays, you drove your cool cars over to the Miracle Mile. The Miracle Mile started at Fairfax with the May Co. and went down toward LaBrea. You had men's shops like Phelps-Welger, and you had Broadway and Ohrbach's and all these places.

And you'd always meet girls out in front or inside the department stores.

Or we'd stop at Van de Kamp's for a cherry-lime Ricky. Van de Kamp's was this big bakery and coffee shop on Wilshire Boulevard. You'd get a cherry-lime Ricky for a nickel. A cherry-lime Ricky was a lemonade-limeade with some red juice and some cherries on top.

I don't know why they were called Rickies. They just were.

The other drink was a Green River. Green soda pop, more or less just coloration with cherries.

The cherry-lime Ricky was tart. The Green River was just sickenly sweet.

We'd walk down to the LaBrea Tarpits and hang out in front. There was a lawn there and we'd sprawl out on that.

Wherever you looked, you saw all these kids on the Miracle Mile hanging out all afternoon.

It was a major Southern California scene.

Everything you saw in "Grease," we did first.

You saw it every Saturday, on the Miracle Mile.

The girls wore poodle skirts. Sweaters. They had their bucks and saddle-oxfords. Ponytails. Girls would do the French twist.

Us guys, we greased. We were very, very big on pomade. I'd have to de-grease myself before I walked back on the "Beaver" set. We had to be pretty middle of the road, normal, when we walked onto the set.

But out on "The Mile," you did the pomade. Still, we were never greased to the max, because we didn't have that long of hair. Remember, flat-tops and butches were still fairly popular.

Sometimes, you'd bring the hair back on the sides with the flat-top. Bring it down in front to a point or flip it up.

Some guys wore ducktails. But ducktails were more for eses. That was the term we borrowed from the barrios for tough guys, rogues, punks.

Ese or ese vato mon.

That's what we called them.

We had our share of fights with them.

We used to have fun at these fights, mainly because we always won. We would kick butt and all the tough guys knew it.

We were Knights and we were tough, too, and we didn't back down.

Nobody screwed with us on Knights Beach.

That's right.

We had our own beach, named after us. Of us. For us. By us.

Knights Beach was the best stretch of beach in Southern California. It was right at the end of Wilshire Boulevard in Santa Monica. A couple blocks from the Santa Monica Pier. Right by the Jonathan Club.

That was our turf. Nobody messed with us on Knights Beach.

We invited our friends there, so you could come if you were not a Knight, but invited. If you weren't invited, you weren't welcome.

We protected what we had. It was part of the job. It went with the turf.

We'd walk up and go, "Hey, uh, I hate to tell you this, but this land is spoken for. But why don't you guys maybe head out over there somewhere else?"

We were very nice about it—we tried to be gentlemen.

Every once in awhile we ran into some jackass who wanted to stay.

"Screw you." You didn't say that to us.

Thirty or 40 kids might show up each night from the Knights. With the girls, it might be 50, 60 kids. If a Norman or an Imperial or an Argonaut tried to hit Knights Beach without being invited, he didn't last long. He was asked to leave.

Yet, he could come back the very next day with a Knight and all is forgiven and forgotten.

Crazy, but this was the law of the jungle. It's the way it worked.

The Imperials were an older club than we were and probably our chief rival. But we were much better. They thought they were cool, but we used to have what we called "pulling" guys from other clubs. We could have pulled any Imperial we wanted, and we knew it.

They all would have quit the Imperials like dogs to be a Knight.

Chapter Three

You know what I'm saying?

Club-jumping was fun for us, because we always won in that exchange.

A lot of this was to impress the girls, of course.

Hell, always to impress them.

That was pretty much everything...the whole idea.

We used to pull our cars into the parking lot by Knights Beach. The top was always down. Six or seven or eight people in the car.

We had this one guy, Bob Luskin. His car is in surgery down at the Chevrolet dealer, so he gets a loaner car. Of course, being L.A., even the loaner is a convertible.

It was this old beater, a '48 Buick convertible. This was in the days when everyone was role-playing and stuff like that. So he puts on this hat kind of like the Blues Brothers and he walks around the beach calling himself Capone.

He's going, "Hey, who wants to ride in Capone's coach?"

Anyway, Luskin winds up with only 24 people in his '48 Buick—by actual count.

I don't have to tell you what comes next. He piles the car up. Hits a streetlight. There's bodies flying everywhere. Nobody got killed. But everyone was walking around with, like sprained knees, cracked-up elbows.

I believe he didn't negotiate a turn. He wasn't going very fast. But we all remember the night Capone's coach ate it.

Mostly, though, you'd cruise into the lot at Knights Beach with only six or seven or eight people sitting on the back.

And the night at Knights Beach would begin.

First of all, we used to have static from the L.A. Police Department. Because you weren't supposed to build bonfires on the beach in L.A. County. You'd have to go to the other side of Malibu to Ventura County to build bonfires, or south to Marina del Rey.

So, of course, when we built our bonfires every night at Knights Beach, we dug holes in the sand and built them lower down and huddled around them. So we didn't get too much static, except if a helicopter came by.

But we used to have sleepovers and sleep-out parties there.

In those days, the biggest music system was a portable radio. Or we would take the cars and park them backwards with the top down on the parking lot and turn up the radios so we could hear them down at the water.

Because we had to listen to KFWB—that was the radio station. They had the disc jocks. Al Jarvis and Bill Balance, Joe Yoakum, Gene Weed, Sam Riddle, B. Mitchell Reed. Those were the guys you had to listen to. You had to quote them. You had to know them.

Balance would say, "I just got back from the Hollywood Library. Boy, books aren't the only things stacked there."

Ha, ha.

Hey, what do you want from me? It's supposed to be sophomoric humor. If they were Johnny Carson, they'd have been on TV. They wouldn't have been ditzoid DJ's.

But these real dumb innuendoes, you had to know 'em and spout 'em.

And if the sex jokes were lame, the sex wasn't.

We didn't drink at these parties. Oh, you'd have a couple guys hit a liquor store. They'd get Country Club Malt Liquor. Or Colt 45. I've never been a beer drinker, though. Most kids didn't at the time, either. We had one guy, Floyd, who put hard liquor in Cokes.

In the absence of a lot of drinking or drugs, we spent our time on something more worthwhile.

Making out.

That was much, much bigger.

The sex was very communal. At least in the sense that it was going on all around you.

Blankets. Sleeping bags. That type of stuff.

The actual sex that went on may not be as close as two or three feet away. But maybe 20 feet down the beach. You had a little bit of modesty in that situation.

But you knew that you were doing it and you knew they were doing it, too.

Sometimes, we'd stay all day and all night. There were hot dog stands. One of them was Roadside Rest. They sold dogs, sodas, Icees. Stuff like that. Or you could walk the couple blocks to Santa Monica Pier. There was access to all the good, cruddy junk food you wanted.

You never wanted to stray too far, though, because you never knew what was going to happen next at Knights Beach, and you didn't want to miss it.

Not that you could have missed this one incident which comes to mind.

You couldn't have missed it if you tried.

One night, one of us—Steve Wallace, I think—got the brilliant idea of pulling off a commando raid. It was going to be on the Los Angeles Coliseum.

Our military objective: Commandeer all the fireworks they were storing up for the big displays they'd shoot off there.

I guess "commando raid" and "commandeer" were euphemisms for "stealing." But back in those days it didn't translate that way to us.

"Caper" sounded better than "theft."

It was wrong, hell yeah.

But we were able to rationalize it as a teenage prank pretty easily.

We just thought we had to have those fireworks.

Reason? To shoot 'em off on Knights Beach. What else?

Chapter Three

Which we did.

Memorably.

Let Gen. Wallace debrief you on the results of the first annual Knights Beach Great Fireworks Shootoff.

"We didn't know what the hell we were doing," Wallace said. "We just sat the things down on the beach and started lighting 'em up. We didn't know what special handling they needed or anything.

"So we fire 'em off. The next thing you know, these rockets are zooming all over the beach. Half of 'em don't go up. They go sideways. Which means, they're shooting at us.

"We're running like mad. We're diving for cover.

"A whole bunch of these things are whizzing across the Pacific Coast Highway straight into the banks, into the ice plant and all that good stuff. Traffic has to stop. We actually stopped traffic on the PCH as all these rockets and buzz bombs and everything are ripping across the road.

"It looked like a war zone."

It was pretty spectacular, too.

I think it should have become an annual event. On TV. We should have negotiated the rights. Maybe sold tickets.

When we weren't making love or making war on the beach, the other big activity was dancing.

Lots of dancing.

We had great dances. Great dancers.

I had to laugh when Robert Shapiro, OJ's mouthpiece, popped off in People magazine that he was the best dancer at Hamilton High.

Horsefeathers.

Shapiro was in the class below me, and he would have given his left nut to be a Knight. He was a Count. We wouldn't let him in.

Shapiro was a slimeball. Still is.

And, in addition to being a slimeball, he was not the best dancer at our school. Not even close. He was not cool at all.

Not all Counts were slimes like Shapiro. Some of them were nice guys.

Joel Siegel was a Count. You know, the film critic who's on Good Morning America? Joel was a good guy. I would have liked Joel to have been in the Knights, but he was too fat.

I was the only fat guy allowed in the Knights. That's because I was the coolest fat guy in L.A. County.

But Joel was a good guy. I liked Joel. The Counts could be all right.

But Shapiro was a pud.

I, on the other hand, was what Shapiro wished he could be, in his dreams.

I was a very good dancer.

Not as good as Al Barbakow, who was the best dancer in school.

He was a Knight, of course.

What you saw on the beaches were the shakin' dances. Chubby Checker, of course, started the first one, the Twist.

Then we did the Monkey. The Jerk (hey, Shapiro mighta been good at this one). The Swim. The Fly. The Watusi.

Hey, man, we did whatever dances we made up, and whatever we wanted to. Because whatever we did, caught on.

We were the trendsetters for the United States.

And I know it was crazy, even to me, but I was the guy setting the trends the trendsetters set.

That's how it went down. Dumpy Lumpy, the squat kid you saw on the "Beaver," was the king of Surf City, USA.

The Frankie and Annette movies, those beach parties in the beach scenes? They all happened a long time before they ever showed up in the movies.

At Knights Beach with me and my buddies and our girlfriends.

Our crew.

The "Beach Blanket Bingo" movies copied us right down the line. We were there with our babes and our cars and our blankets and our radios.

Oh, wait. There's another thing. We had guys who sung.

We didn't always need the radios.

Because we had the people who later played on the radio.

We had some of the biggest groups that ever hit.

Phil Specter went to Fairfax when we were going to Hamilton. We'd party at the beach together. Ever hear of Phil Specter, the god of rock and roll music?

What about Russ Titleman, one of the biggest rock 'n' roll producers of all? He was a Knight, of course.

Annette Klinebard was going to Hamilton. She was the lead singer of the Teddy Bears: "To know, know, know him is to love, love, love him...and I do."

That was Annette's song. She sang at Knights Beach.

Richard Clasky had a No. 1 hit, "The Image of a Girl." He was from Hamilton.

Arnie Marcus was with the Hollywood Argyles that did "Alley Oop" and some other big hits.

All that good stuff.

It was down at Knights Beach first.

After the beach, if it wasn't an all-nighter or anything, you'd all meet later at DL's and hash out the happenings of the day.

And we'd wolf down big old double-decker cheeseburgers with "Z" sauce. More Suzi-Q's. The original curly fries.

That was the deal, congregating back at DL's. Like meeting at Arnold's on

"Happy Days."

They copied all that "Happy Days" stuff off what we did. This was our life.

We would go out on a date. I could take a cool girl out. I would maybe go to the movies with her. Or wherever. When the date was over, if she was your girlfriend, you would bring her back to DL's.

If she was just a date, you would take her home. If she was just a chick you were trying to make, you would take her home.

Of course, you would walk into DL's with a big smile on your face to let them know if you scored or didn't score.

Because everyone says, "Well, did you or didn't you?"

Just like Richie and Potsy and Ralph Malph on "Happy Days."

That's the way it happened.

Another common happening was the Stadium Theater where we'd work the old Popcorn Box Ploy. This is where you put your dick in the bottom of the popcorn box, let the girl reach down into the bottom of the box.

Surprise!

Say hi to Dick.

My friend, Floyd, got one of the best reactions I ever heard or saw. I don't remember the girl's name, but I remember her howlin' and screamin' and all the guys crackin' up.

The girls, by the way, were crackin' up, too.

If it didn't happen at the beach or the movies or at DL's, it was happening down on The Boulevard.

Hollywood Boulevard.

There has never been and never will be another scene like it anywhere in the world.

George Lucas tried to copy it in "Grafitti."

He failed.

Failed miserably, really.

Nice try, George.

No go.

The real Hollywood Boulevard was much, much wilder than what they showed in "American Grafitti."

Imagine what it would be like in a wall-to-wall traffic jam, with everyone's top down (the car's, hers, yours, more often than not). The music playing. Everyone hitting on everybody else from all angles for six hours a night.

You're on Hollywood Boulevard with neon that's almost like daylight.

Traffic would be about one mile an hour. It took about an hour and a half to go from Hollywood and Vine to LaBrea, a couple miles or so.

Guys are hanging out the window: "Screw you!"

"Yeah, up yours."

"Eat me?"

"You wish."

"Come 'n' get it."

People jumpin' in and out of cars. Swinging off into the side streets to get laid.

Again, back to DL's to talk about it. Share war stories. Keep score.

Hollywood Boulevard was one reason I changed cars so often. I wanted to keep my repertoire fresh.

I had a '62 Cadillac convertible, pale yellow with a yellow top.

I had a '61 Impala convertible.

I had a '61 Bonneville convertible. Metallic green. Tri-power under the hood.

A '62 Corvette.

A '61 Corvette that was red. Fuel-injected 4-speed.

But you couldn't just depend on cars and clothes and cuckoo buddies at the beach to impress girls.

I wanted the all-round approach.

I always wanted to use my mind—if not for grades, something far more important. To up the cool quotient. To impress my friends. Make them look up to me. So girls would want me more. So I could get laid more.

So I decided to make myself an expert on rock 'n' roll music. Well, actually, all kinds of music. I love music. My absolute favorite music was Broadway show music. I knew it all. I still do.

But rock 'n' roll was the way to go in high school. So I got real good at knowing it.

It used to kill me when people would say that "Sha-boom" was the first rock 'n' roll song. I'd say, "No. It wasn't. It wasn't even the second rock 'n' roll song."

People forget about the real roots of rock 'n' roll. The first hit song was called "Gee" by The Crows.

The second hit was "Work With Me Annie" by Hank Ballard and the Midnighters.

And "Work With Me Annie" also became "Dance With Me Henry," which Georgia Gibbs did. Georgia Gibbs did it on Mercury. The Midnighters did it on Atlantic.

These two songs were at the end of '53. Then "Sha-boom" comes out by The Chords on the Cat label.

Immediately, The Crewcuts cover it. A "cover" record is where someone records a song, and then along comes someone else and "covers" it with his own version. They would both contend on the radio for the most popular rendition. This happened all the time back then.

Both "Sha-booms" went No. 1, actually. Of course, the version that gets

Chapter Three

the most popularity is by The Crewcuts because they were more from the music establishment at the time.

Which sucked. The one that was really great was The Chords' version, which was the black rendition on Cat records.

Here's a guy who got famous, never did an original song in his life, until "Love Letters in the Sand" and a few others: Pat Boone.

Pat Boone started off covering records all over the place.

There was a guy named Randy Wood, who owned a record company in Mee-umphis—as Elvis would have pronounced it—Tennessee, called Dot records. And Pat Boone is this young kid who happens to be a direct descendant of Daniel Boone.

(Also, he happened to be a client of Frank Bank when Frank Bank opened his own financial-consultant business, but that's for another chapter.)

Anyhow, Pat was signed by Dot records—young kid, married this girl named Shirley, pumpin' kids out like Eddie Cantor. His first hit was called "Ain't That a Shame?" which was done by a guy named Antoine Domino on Imperial Records. Fellow we came to know by "Fats."

Within a week, a version of "Ain't That a Shame?" by Pat Boone comes out on Dot records.

Shortly thereafter, the El Dorados come out with a song, "At My Front Door"— "Crazy little mama comes, knockin', a-knockin' at my front door, door, door." Guess who comes out with a hit? They hadn't even let the ink dry on "Ain't That a Shame?" and here comes "At My Front Door."

So Dot records was made by covering records with all their original artists—they had the Fontaine Sisters, Pat Boone, Billy Vaughan, Jim Lowe. Well, Jim Lowe actually did an original record, a great hit called "The Green Door."

But anyhow, what I did, because I have pretty much of a photographic memory, I started using it on rock 'n' roll. I'd always had pretty good retention. If they showed me a script, I read it twice and I knew it. Reading the encyclopedia, things in school...anything that seemed worth remembering.

Now rock 'n' roll was worth it.

When a song became half-popular, I remembered the artist. I remembered the label. The chronology. What was on the other side of the record, how long the record was, who produced it, who the bandleader was, who the people in the band were.

I almost made a bundle off this essentially useless knowledge.

Almost, but not quite.

Remember my great timing?

Well, it almost always was perfect.

There were exceptions.

Such as this major one.

The "$64,000 Question" is on the air along about now. It's become the biggest show in the country.

In my quest for greatness, I said to myself, "Self, what could you do with $64,000?"

Then I tried to say to myself, "How could I get tripped up on a category when I knew every single record?"

I had every copy of *Cashbox* magazine in a stack in my room from 1953 on. I had every copy of *Billboard*. I knew how high the record got on the charts, when it hit the charts, how many weeks, how high the cover record was.

I was like so good, I was incredible.

You take songs like "Ivory Tower." Most people didn't know the original one was by Cathy Carr. To make a long story short, I didn't think there was any way I could lose.

So I went down and took all kinds of exams at CBS Television City. I'm just into teenage-hood, about ninth or 10th grade.

They would have taken me...the younger, the better. And they were going to.

So now I am scheduled to go on the show. But there was a waiting list of people in different categories. They wanted to switch categories around so it was interesting.

Five guys in a row come on doing English literature, it gets pretty boring.

So they went for odd angles. They loved it when Joyce Brothers was on and she'd do boxing. I mean it was all bogus in a way, because she didn't give a hoot about boxing. The whole deal was to have this cute little, sweet, petite, blonde psychologist come on and talk about boxing. She wanted her name around, so it was a good stroke by her. She got what she went after, but she wasn't really a boxing fan.

Boris Karloff was another good example of the off-beat contestant. Having "Frankenstein" come on for children's literature. I thought that was great and the whole country did.

So having me on—this was before "Beaver", so I wasn't Lumpy Rutherford yet—as a 13-14-year-old kid who was an expert on rock 'n' roll would have worked.

I was all set.

Then the Charles Van Doren scandal hit—the whole thing about Van Doren being set up on the show "21." They found out he'd been fed some answers and groomed as a star. The next thing you know, all those shows are poison. "The Question," "21," all of them go kaput.

It went from:

"Sorry, kid, we're puttin' you on hold."

To: "Well, we're gonna go on hiatus."

Chapter Three

To: "We're canceling the show."

Oh well, it didn't cost me anything.

Like hell.

There was no way I was going to be tripped up. I knew what records Elvis made before he went to RCA. What his first RCA record was, what his last Sun record was. How many copies did

"Blue Moon" sell?

All that junk...I was really great at it.

And they took it off the air.

The way I figure it, I got hosed out of 64 grand.

'Cause I woulda made it unless they drugged me or something. I didn't even need the "expert" they give you to help prepare you for the show.

I was my own expert.

And I got nothing for it.

Except lots of chicks.

Girls loved it when you could spout all that crap about records and artists and all that.

So what did I need with the "Question?"

I still had "The Quest."

To get laid as often as humanly, or inhumanly, possible, as the case may be.

Without the quiz show I could go back to concentrating on what really mattered.

Sex.

It's all I thought about, pretty much, anyway.

Hell, at that age was there anything else to think about?

Speaking of Lots of Beaver

have slept with over 1,000 women.

I don't exactly say that with pride.

I'm not exactly apologetic, either, although I'm sure there

are good reasons to be.

But the fact is, I engaged in a perpetual sexfest in my youth, and there's no expunging it from the past.

And if I stand back and take a clinical view, what I see it as, more than anything, is a kind of footnote to history.

It was the product of being in the business I was, in the city I was, at a particular time when the first furious fusillades of the sexual revolution in America were being fired in earnest.

That's what turned the sexual spigot on for me. Turned it wide open. I drank from it. I bathed in it. Heck, I did the backstroke and breaststroke in it.

When everybody went into the pool, I dived into the deep end, the shallow end and all the ends in between.

Which may seem preposterous when you think of the muddled, dumpy, awkward character most people saw in me when I played Lumpy Rutherford.

It also may also sound bogus, in a Wilt Chamberlain kind of way. Remember when Wilt the Stilt, the Hall of Fame pro basketball star, claimed to have bedded over 5,000 women? Malarkey, is what I'd say. I don't know if his stilt would have wilted, but it seems like a logistical problem anyway.

Figure the man-woman-hours available, and it seems beyond time management.

Five thousand? Can't be done.

One thousand? Can be done.

Believe me.

The bulk of my sexploits came in an apartment I rented at 8939 Cadillac

Avenue in L.A. Actually, it was left over from my first official marriage, to a woman named Marlene, hereinafter referred to as my Six-Day Wonder. Yes, that's right, I married this girl and six days later we ended the marriage.

We had it annulled. But I'll tell you more about that later.

What happened was, Marlene moved out. I kept the place on Cadillac and it became my first real bachelor pad. It turned into something of a drive-thru sex market. Every day women would show up at the front door. They weren't always there to see me. My buddies were in on the act, too. But starlets and harlots and girls from high school, college girls, girls we hustled cruising Hollywood Boulevard and the Sunset Strip several times a week—they just knew there would be action on Cadillac Street.

That's where the boys were.

That's where the girls were.

We each made sure we got together.

There were many nights and days when I had sex with four or five women.

Lots of toga parties.

Lots of towel parties.

I didn't even know the names of half my partners.

Was it socially responsible?

No way.

Safe sex?

Absolutely not.

This was before AIDS. This was even before Roe v. Wade.

I had one close buddy who had to get this one girl an abortion, and one of the reasons we could do it was because I knew the generalissimo of the Mexican army and his brother-in-law was the biggest abortionist in Tiajuana. So my buddy took her down there. The generalissimo's name was Victor Fuentes. He was a Beaver fan and he took care of it.

Of course, this was all selfishness on our part.

All I was looking for was a good time.

It was 1964. I was 22. What red-blooded American boy wouldn't have wanted this? What was the No. 1 thing on the mind of the average 22-year-old, single American male?

Girls.

Hey, I guarantee, every red-blooded, 22-year-old American girl, the only thing on their minds was boys. So I didn't do anything they wouldn't have done.

And, you know what? If they wanted to have sex with my roommate or my buddies after me, that was fine and dandy. A lot of them did.

So they had a wonderful sexual time.

Right about now, I can imagine some of you are skittish reading this. Or appalled.

What could we have been thinking? How could we have gotten away from the wholesome norm we'd all known as a country up through the 1950s?

How could we have left behind the puritanical ethic which had undergirded our culture?

That's just it.

The norm and the ethic and the culture were busy changing. The new wave became a riptide in the early '60s, then swelled to a tsunami throughout that decade and the next.

It engulfed the whole country eventually, but the first breakers in this new wave were definitely sighted in Southern California—as with many trends that swept society.

The epicenter of this sexual earthquake was right in my midst.

I rode it out—quite willingly—with the rest of my age group.

You can condemn us. And you may be right in doing so.

But it was a different time of life—both in our lives and the life of the country.

That's really the crux of the matter.

We didn't really stop to ponder all the nuances of this shift in morality. We were teenagers.

And we hardly were unique in what was to follow. The sexual revolution has lasted into the '90s with no clear sign of letting up.

We just happened to be Minutemen, as it were, in the revolution, firing some of the first shots heard 'round the world. We were at Bunker Hill and we had plenty of willing bunkermates.

When I say "we," it's safe to say that means the majority of kids who were my age in the '60s.

Some were conscientious objectors in the war on chastity.

Most were not.

Most kids joined up and fled to the frontline with reckless glee.

I'm not excusing us with all this social analysis.

I'm just telling you how it was.

Were the girls who joined in bad girls?

Nah.

I couldn't honestly say so. They were good kids from good families.

They were just looking to have a good time.

I mean, being a hormone-driven adolescent, I used to work hard to get laid in the 10th grade.

That was coming out of the '50s when nice girls just didn't do stuff like that. I used to take out a lot of cheap girls in the hopes that they would go to bed with me.

But by '62, it was the "substantial girls," as we called them, who wound up doing it more than the cheap girls.

That's just how the times changed. Everybody's morals were in a state of flux, and everybody saw that and picked up on it.

My first lieutenant in my own branch of the revolutionary army was my roommate, Billy Byron.

Billy moved in after Marlene split. I was there alone for a couple of months and then Billy needed a place to stay.

And I have to say, it worked out great because Billy the Kid, as we called him, was one truly amazing butt bandit.

Billy was one good-looking dude.

He made Richard Gere look like a monkey.

Every chick in the world loved Billy.

Billy had the same general type of look as Jan-Michael Vincent, only he was much better-looking than Jan-Michael Vincent. Blond hair, almost a Patrick Swayze look, but better-looking than Patrick Swayze, too. Great build. A personality so out-going.

"Hey-y-y-y, girls, hey-y-y, man, party's over here. Come on over for a towel party."

Wherever we went, Billy just reeled 'em in like Mark Trail snatching up boatloads of fish.

These chicks would wind up riding back to the apartment with us. And we gotta do it quick because these other chicks would come knocking on the door. It was like, take a number. They'd come over from West L.A. They'd come from Gazarri's on Sunset. The Whiskey-a-Go-Go. They'd drop by Billy and Frank's apartment.

When they got there, a towel party was often in progress.

A towel party went like this: You walk in and there's a towel sitting by the front door with a note attached saying, "Here's yours. Meet us in the other room."

You'd take your clothes off, put on a towel and go in the other room. The towel comes off and you put it down on the floor. We had a couple hundred bucks in the deposit for the apartment, so we didn't want to mess it up too bad, either the beds or the carpet. So the towel was just a house rule.

Billy and I started out in a one-bedroom apartment with him sleeping on the couch.

But traffic became so heavy we needed further accomodations. We switched to a three-bedroom unit.

It wasn't just total, wall-to-wall sex there.

We did a lot of cooking. Lots of gourmet meals.

We played lots of poker. There was always a card game in the dining-room-kitchen area while the other festivities went on in the bedrooms.

But sex set the undertone and overtones to each day.

We'd be playing cards, someone would want to change partners, come out and drag you out of a game. You'd excuse yourself, join your partner in the bedroom.

Come back out.

"Now where were we?

"Whose deal?

"Let's play cards."

You could say we took advantage of the girls who came and went at Cadillac.

I would say you were wrong.

We cooked meals. Billy and I were actually pretty decent gourmet cooks.

We'd have big feasts together. Sit and talk and eat and shoot the bull.

It's just that sex was always the dessert.

The girls weren't coerced. They weren't hoodwinked. Weren't sweet-talked or tricked into bed.

They were there fully aware of what they were doing.

They were there because they wanted to be.

Again, it was a time of life for them, just as it was for me and the rest of the country.

Girls just wanted to have fun.

And they did.

If I had to capsulize everything in one sentence, I'd say: We never left any of these girls not feeling like they haven't had a good time.

I guess it sounds arrogant, speaking of these hundreds of sex partners. But they weren't "conquests" to me. I always liked to think that I left all those girls a little bit happier for the experience.

That may sound immodest. Self-serving. Just plain selfish or insensitive or ignorant. And it definitely wouldn't fly in today's politically correct environment.

But that's how I felt. I'm not a malicious guy. I don't like malicious people. I think this world is such a great place and that if we don't take advantage of how good it can be, we can only blame ourselves.

I was simply dedicated to getting my share sexually. Mine and three or four other guys' shares.

Just like a Chicago election, I started voting early and often in throwing my support to the coming sexual revolution.

I broke my first cherry just before I was 13. I was 12 years and 10 months old. It was February of 1955.

Chapter Four

I was at a party, a junior-high school party house, and I was making out with this girl on the couch. She was in my class. She was 12 also, maybe 13. Her name was Diane. Diane was outstanding. Very lean. No breasts to speak of. I guess they were just forming. I don't know if they ever did get big. But she was awfully cute and slender and tight in all kinds of good places.

We got to petting heavily at this party, you know—on top of each other. She lifted her dress up and I opened my pants. I got, for a little kid, this great erection. And before you knew it, I got snagged on something.

She like wheeled on top of me and pushed and the next thing you know, we are doing it.

It was dark at this party and the whole scene was pretty scary, with a lot of people in the room. There were other people making out, but I don't think anyone else was doing it in the room at the time.

The only light you could see was the light on the phonograph. It was a 33 1/3. A Webcore, I think.

The music was Nat King Cole:

"Darling, j' vous aime beaucoup."

"Je ne c'est pas what to do."

"You've stolen my heart...night time too."

She kept calling me, "Frankie, Frankie."

I don't know what else she said. I was really trying to concentrate on what I was doing.

I wasn't too scared or anything when she called me and said, "I didn't get my period."

Suddenly, I'm thinking, here comes the bride. I mean, I was 12 years old, man. I didn't exactly sleep a heck of a lot. This was only six months after I decided I wanted to be cool, but I didn't want to be quite that cool, that I was gonna be a dad. OK?

Actually, I panicked.

I was real a-scared.

I was worried about going to "Juvie," as we used to call it. Juvenile Hall. I was telling myself, "Oh my God, I could go to Juvie." This was in the days of "Blackboard Jungle" and movies like that. I'm going, "My God, what did I do?"

I'm a stupid little kid. What did I know?

It was more than a week between the time she told me she didn't get her period and when we found out she wasn't pregnant. I felt bad because this was not a cheap girl and this was not a fast girl. I don't know how many of her girlfriends she told about this. I told no one.

I just told God. I said, "God, I'll never do it again if she's not pregnant."

And then after that, it was, "Sorry, God, I was just kidding about that."

The next time I had sex it was six months later, with a girl who was in the ninth grade.

I didn't get snagged like the first time. It didn't "just happen."

I did it to her this time, and I was really proud of it.

It was in her bedroom. My pants were offa me. I had a shirt on and I remember it was open, but my pants were off, my underpants were off, her pants were off, her underpants were off. I mighta had socks on.

This girl was Paulette.

Paulette was all-right looking. She had dusty blonde, curly hair. Real nice chest. Kind of medium-to-big butt, but she wasn't fat at all. She didn't shave her legs real good. I noticed a little stubble.

The thing with Paulette started out one night at the Stadium Theater.

Everyone made out at the Stadium in the balcony. There were times I could go to the Stadium with a couple of guys, and there were a couple of girls there and we would pair off.

So I was at the Stadium this one night and hooked up with Paulette.

Well, this one night, while we were making out in the balcony at the Stadium, I put my hand under her blouse and undid her bra and felt her breasts.

And I went, "Oh, my God, I went to first base by the end of the first movie."

It was a double feature.

I think "Giant" was showing.

Then I made a date to meet her at the Stadium the next Friday. The farther up in the balcony, the easier it was to do some serious necking. There wasn't anyone looking over your shoulder. We were in the very back row. I almost felt secure enough—and reckless enough—that I could pull her down and try and screw up there, you know? But I wasn't really about to try that because a lot of kids in my class were there. Not that it wouldn't have been cool if I did.

I'd have been a pretty big hero if I'd pulled it off.

She wore a three-hook bra, I remember that. A three-hooker was a tough one. But I always used the "one-hand pinch" to release them, and I felt pretty sure of myself with the pinch. You needed to have a good thumb to roll the bottom under while at the same time pinching.

I must have been doing all right in her eyes, anyway.

After the second movie, she told me that her parents weren't home. I remember waiting outside, watching her flash the porchlight, which meant that she'd put her brother to sleep.

I went inside, right into her bedroom, and we started making out.

The radio was turned to "Lucky Lager Dance Time." Lucky Lager was a beer and they were the sponsor to this radio show we used to listen to.

Chapter Four

I think it was on from 9 to 11 on weeknights, maybe on KMPC.

The music, the lights, the feeling was right. I remember taking her panties off because I wasn't real slick about it and they were all rolled up. I was disappointed that I hadn't been more suave with the move.

I mean, you don't want the girl thinking this is the first time you've ever done this. You want to just sort of nonchalantly, but sensually, draw them down to her ankles...and then deftly flick them off with the right look in your eye.

Skillfully, the way James Bond might have done. Leaving her stirred, but not shaken. Ready for the next step in the drama.

She, I might add, had no trouble with my underpants. They came right off.

I didn't last much longer than my first time. About five strokes or so.

But we made out for a long time afterwards.

I wasn't smart enough to know whether she had a climax.

She said she really loved it, and that was that.

Somehow, I don't think she really loved it.

She wouldn't go out with me again.

I asked her out a couple of times and she said, "No."

No reason.

She just said, "Don't bother calling me again."

It kinda hurt my feelings a little bit.

You know how women use us.

All they want is sex.

We're only good for one thing.

I don't know if I didn't satisfy her or she got an attack of conscience. This was a chick who was hot to trot. But I don't think she wanted word to get around about her.

One reason I think she did it with me was because I was an eighth-grader and she was in the ninth and maybe she thought I was safe.

I wouldn't run up and start rumors about her.

But the truth is, I did tell my friends about this one. I never told about Diane—well, I told a couple guys much later in life, but that was years after the fact.

But Paulette, I did talk about. You're really proud if you got laid in the eighth grade.

And Paulette was all I had to talk about for a long time. After my first two, it was a full year until I had sex again.

I was in the movies quite a bit by now. That did help get me girls, I imagine.

It didn't hurt, I'd have to say.

That was OK with me.

Whatever worked.

After my year dry spell, things started to accelerate. Big time. By now I am cruising Hollywood Boulevard. I am meeting 50 jillion chicks a night. We're going up and parking on Mulholland Drive—or Dick Lane, as we often called it.

There was this one dude, one of the biggest announcers on Los Angeles television at the time—he used to do wrestling, boxing; he used to sell cars and slap the fenders... "C'mon down!" That type of thing. His name was Dick Lane.

So the old joke around town was:

"What's another name for Mulholland Drive?"

"Dick Lane."

Any old part of Mulholland would do for making out. Anywhere you could park, look at the lights of the city and not have too many people around.

If we didn't go up to Dick Lane, we would cut off Hollywood Boulevard, go up Franklin Boulevard, up toward the "Hollywood" sign, up Beachwood or one of those other streets and park up there.

We would make love in residential neighborhoods overlooking the city. You never worried about rousting the neighbors. There were just lots of places we could go to do it in the car. We never went to motels. They cost money. The weather was always nice, we were always warm enough. As long as we had a towel or a sheet or a blanket or something, it was cool.

By now, I was beginning to feel, this was my city. I was getting famous. I was driving great-looking cars, in keeping with the reputation I had so carefully developed.

I wasn't looking too bad. I'm not saying I was Cary Grant or James Dean or anything. Heck, I wasn't Billy Byron. But I was about the best I was ever going to be.

Fairly well filled out from my football and baseball days at Hamilton High. Not fat yet, a little on the chunky side. But most people would have said "husky." There's a difference between fat and husky, and I was on the good side of the line.

I knew how to dress, as you know. I knew how to B.S. girls. I knew what was cool and, even more important, I had learned how to be cool.

I was ready to ride, daddy, ride, as they put it so well in the "Alley Oop" song.

It just all started falling into place.

I was in the 11th grade. I was 16.

I was perfecting my sexual repertoire.

Chapter Four

I learned the best cars to pick up in and the best cars to make out in. They weren't always the same.

The best pickup car ever invented was a Corvette. Any make. Any year. I owned several and loved every one of them. A '57 Chevy was good, or a '58 or '59 or '60 Chevy was good, too. They were all right up there. You had to customize or you weren't squat. You had chrome wheels, dual pipes, usually decked the hood, maybe with a tube grille, metallic paint job, definitely a great stereo system.

At the same time, the Corvette was by far the worst car to make love in. No. 1, you had to have the top down, which meant you needed someone with almost no inhibitions, or you had to hit it lucky with a really private parking spot. You had to get 'em up over the passenger side and arch their back over the rear of the Corvette, which sloped down. It was really difficult. Sometimes they banged their heads on the trunk and that was not cool.

I was better off taking them to the beach when I had a Corvette. I always carried blankets in the back of my trunk, stuff like that.

But the make-out limitations were the biggest reasons to get rid of the Corvette and get one of the '60 Impalas. I had a great '59 Olds 98 convertible. That was wonderful. Six-way power seats, real wide, real nice.

You could do it easily in the front seat because of the six-way power setup. You just get away from the steering wheel and go to the other side. Bingo. You were goin' at it.

However, obviously, the best sex-wagon ever created was the old Hudson Hornet, because the front seats used to fold all the way down. It was a great style car, too, in its own way. But the main thing was that it was a bed on wheels. So you had to try the Hudson Hornet, if for no other reason than just the experience alone.

As for the beach, we went wherever we wanted. But Knights Beach...our beach...the beach set aside for our club...was the best. It was dark. My club brothers were doing their thing, too. You felt comfortable. You felt right at home.

Still, a huge amount of our time was spent on Hollywood Boulevard, polishing our pickup strategies.

The Boulevard was an art form you honed over time.

Your paintbrushes were your clothes, your car, your conversation and your friends.

The easiest pick-up approach was striking up a conversation with a chick in a car with one of her girlfriends, dumping all the guys you were with, switching cars going the same direction and then going to make out.

Sometimes, you'd already know some of these girls' first names. Sometimes they'd get in and you'd introduce yourself: "Hi, Darlene, I'm Frank."

Some girls would go, "I know who you are." And I didn't like that. I would have rather had a little anonymity in this case. I wasn't there for a social gathering, per se. I was there for a bodily function.

By and large, I went for more dark-haired girls than blondes. I went for bigger breasts than small, and bigger girls in general because I was a bigger guy.

And I really liked outgoing, wild girls, rather than quiet, shy girls.

There was a period where it was cool to just come right out with it: "Hey, baby, wanna screw?" But it was a very short-lived period, I want to say around 1964 or '65. Then it got uncool.

But before it got uncool, irreverance was very, very big. Cops were pigs. Parents were idiots. Institutions sucked. And you could say anything to any girl and get away with it. Not only get away with it, it was encouraged.

The great thing about the Boulevard was that it was safe. You're not gonna get mugged and you're not gonna get killed. A girl would always know you would bring her back to the Boulevard after sex. You would either let them out in front of the Vogue Theater, the Egyptian, Graumann's Chinese...somewhere they could hook up with friends again.

The law of the jungle on the Boulevard was: You don't do another guy's girlfriend.

Or if you do, she has to be receptive and you can't get caught.

You know, you could say to her, "Hey, baby, you got great boobs." And if she took offense, you have troubles. Most of the time they wouldn't be offended. These comments were more or less expected.

If she did take offense, a lot of times you could say, "Hey, don't get all bent out of shape, because I'm just schemin'."

Scheming, they understood, is when you're plotting and implementing your strategy on a chick. You're coming up with a way to play her, almost as if she were a fish. OK? That's scheming. Struttin' your stuff. Layin' out your line. Showin' her what you got.

Some of them will laugh and think you're cute. Some of them will look at you and think you're a jerk.

You've just got to go for it, take your cuts and whatever happens, happens.

I mean, the way I looked at it, Babe Ruth struck out 1,330 times. But he also hit 714 home runs. There are a lot of girls who'd just tell you to buzz off.

I'd tell them:

"Well, maybe I'll have to."

Or, "I was just tryin'."

Real witty stuff, huh? Amazingly clever.

Well, unbelievably it worked, or a version of it worked. What can I tell you?

Chapter Four

Besides, I didn't insult easily. There was no reason for animosity in the pickup game. You'd just throw enough stuff against the wall and assume something's gotta stick.

If they didn't go, you wanted to convey one thing: Your loss, baby.

Another way we played the Boulevard was called Shuckin' and Jivin'. You're drivin' down the street and you see these two girls in a car. One of them is all uptight. But the one in the passenger seat's having a good old time. So ditch the first girl. You're shuckin' and jivin' on the second one. You're calmly polite to the other one so she doesn't drive off with your quarry. She's a sacrificial lamb for your buddies. If the chick on the passenger side gets out of the car, your buddy gets in the car with the stuck-up driver. He goes and buys that girl a cup of coffee.

He's your blood brother, and blood brothers did that for other brothers.

The girls knew the game as well as we did. They were being shucked. They were being jived. And, actually, they were jiving us back.

If your shuck-and-jive didn't work, you hoped your sounds would. Your tunes. Your car stereo.

The best stereo was a Muntz. That was the first car system for awhile. You had a speaker in each front door, the biggest you could cram in there. Maybe 12-inch, maybe 8- or 10-inch speakers. FM radio was pretty much unheard of then. So you had AM radio and you had 8-track tapes.

Pretty prehistoric, eh?

But again, it was what was happening at the time. And it worked.

By far the best make-out music was Johnny Mathis. If you're with guys, you don't want Johnny Mathis. Cruising music is entirely different. But if you're doing it with a girl, you've got Johnny Mathis—and only Johnny Mathis—on the stereo.

You could say, "Hey, look, wanna come into my car and listen to Johnny?"

You'd play, "When Sonny Gets Blue" or "Chances Are" or "Wonderful, Wonderful" or "12th of Never."

Any Johnny Mathis song, and you were halfway home. You ought to be able to make it the rest of the way and score.

Scoring.

It was the beginning and end of life through several of these years. It was your purpose for rising in the morning, and the only reason you ever went to bed was either to have sex or to rest up so you could go back to work on getting some more sex the next day.

Remember, I've said I always believed I was the luckiest man alive. And I feel like I was really lucky to come along at a time when sex was normal. It had changed from a taboo. It had switched from something only bad people or disturbed people did, or people who were somehow unbalanced or who weren't taught right. No longer were these the only people who engaged in sexual intercourse outside of marriage.

Now that may be bad to some people. But in a way, it probably was good we went through this transition. We may be less repressive. Women may get to enjoy sex as recreation, not just procreation, the same way men pretty much always have looked at it. Perhaps that's better for everyone involved. Maybe more of us are more comfortable with our sexuality and therefore mentally healthier as a whole.

All I know is I had one hell of a good time.

I had the best time you could possibly have.

But just up to a point.

I also had the worst time you could possibly have.

I can't say it was all fun.

I can't say it was all good.

Because it wasn't.

In fact, all you can say is that some of it was the opposite of good.

It was crap.

There is a price for over indulgence. One I never expected, not in 60 jillion years.

If you had told me this would happen, I would have looked at you like you just landed from outer space and would never understand our planet, and there was no way I could communicate how wrong you were.

But you, the space alien, would have been right.

I would have been wrong.

I got tired of sex.

After awhile, the thing on Cadillac Street, all the women, all the girls, all the faces that became the same, all the names you never knew—it all got to me in the end.

I remember coming home some nights and the towel-party note would be there and I thought, "Oh, no. There goes tonight. I was looking for some sleep. And we're 'entertaining.'"

Trooper in the sexual revolution that I was, I went and dived right in.

In the end, though, sex was not fun anymore. It was a chore. An obligation. It was something to live up to. It was a bog you sank down into.

Me. Frank Bank. I got tired of meaningless sex.

It drove me to my first wife. She wasn't ultra-hip. She wasn't flashy. She was a good person—still is. She wasn't real easy. She meant something to me as a person.

For the first time I saw the happiness that opened up to you from being with one person.

It only took me 1,000 or so women to get there.

Chapter Four

I'll always be glad I took the One Grand route.
I'll always be glad the route ended.

Chapter Five
The Idiot Magnet

am an idiot magnet.
They are drawn to me.
I am drawn to them.

I have spent my entire life away from the norm.

(Well, except for the most normal people in America, the Cleavers, but that was make-believe normal and doesn't count, even though, like I said, Hugh and Barbara were a very real-life Ward and June, so, in a way, they do count as normal. But they would be two of the very few I know.)

Clear?

Mostly, when you're talking about your normal, whitebread, 9-to-5 guys...I am not that.

I am the antithesis in every way, shape or form.

So are the people I have hung around with the majority of the time.

This is why I wound up bumping into guys like Jack Kerouac, the Father of the Beat Generation. This is how I dropped peyote with the famous author, Carlos Castenada. How I wound up rappin' with Angela Davis and Stokely Carmichael, the black activists.

This is how I wound up getting arrested with Cesar Chavez, the grape guy.

This is why I hung around Don "Big Daddy" Garlits and another Don of drag-racing, Don "The Snake" Prudhomme.

My thirst for crazies led me to that time me and my friend Jimmy peed in the radiator of my Cadillac and had the run-in with the Hell's Angels on the way to Yosemite.

And it led me to Marlene, Marlene, the Six-Day Queen, the woman I was married to for almost a week.

In recollecting these things, I kinda wish I could palm it all off on Leonard, the head cluck in the cuckoo's nest we sometimes called my home.

My Pop, most definitely, was completely nutty in every best sense of the word.

I loved the Old Man for his zany ways.

They inspired me. Uplifted and guided me.

But I don't really think I can dive into the gene pool on this one.

I am just naturally wacked-out in my own right and I seemed to seek other certifiably insane individuals from the lunatic fringes of society.

Sort of like wandering baboons finding each other, bonding and forming a pack together, scratching and picking fleas off each other's backs.

I liked the intensity and the unpredictability and the energy these crazy people projected.

I liked the action.

I liked the scene.

Any scene.

As long as it was what's happenin' or might even possibly happen, I wanted to be there.

Especially if girls were involved. Which they usually were.

Maybe it goes back to Kerouac.

Jack Kerouac was a guy we ran into in high school down at a place called Pandora's Box on the Sunset Strip. At the time we didn't know he was the father of all beatniks.

He was just a cool guy we'd see at this hot club where we liked to think we could nail a few women.

Pandora's Box was on a traffic island on Sunset and Crescent Heights. This was back in the days of The Troubador and Terrea Lea and the Garrett and Joanie Baez and all the folk singing.

Pandora's Box was a mainstay.

You would go in there and you would get your hot apple cider with a stick of cinnamon. Oh, man, it had all this stuff. It was cool. We would sit there and read poetry. It was dark and the fire was going and the bongos were going.

And if you happened to have a joint, well...I mean, that was my first experience of seeing people get loaded. I didn't do it at the time, although I did try marijuana a few times later.

I mean I'm not gonna be Bill Clinton here. Everybody smoked grass a few times in his life, me included. But I didn't really like drugs and basically avoided them.

This was about '58, '59, and Kerouac was in there in Pandora's and he was a very strange man. He definitely marched to a different drummer.

Quiet.

Very suspicious.

He sat in a corner of Pandora's Box and he had two drums near him. Bongos and a conga. And he had some coffee and some cigarettes.

He dressed like a bum.

The Idiot Magnet

Like a cutoff sweatshirt, torn Levis—he dressed like today's Valley fashion plate who would go spend hundreds of dollars for the look.

But in those days, you know, it was unacceptable, so that's why Kerouac did it.

His hair was fairly long, but not very full. He was somewhat balding. A grayish beard scraggle. No berets or baseball caps, but one time I saw him in almost like an Indiana Jones hat.

We talked about people and love, and he was one of the earlier flower children. His basic point of view, as I got it, was that we should all love everyone, but we're so distrustful of each other that we're blowin' up the world.

Which was fine.

I could dig it.

The only thing was, in the name of preaching trust, here was this guy sitting over in a corner, man, got a weird eye out for everybody.

Kerouac didn't want to be up front in Pandora's because he didn't want anyone bugging him. So a lot of people didn't even know who he was.

But Pandora's Box was this big, huge meat market and it was hard to stay hidden.

Everything was, "Heyyyy, man. Like, uh, you know the Kingston Trio, man. They're cool."

Berets, goatees and sunglasses were very, very big. Sandals.

Very much pre-Maynard G. Krebs.

Maynard G. Krebs—the beatnik sidekick of Dobie on "The Dobie Gillis Show"—was patterned after all these people at Pandora's Box. It's the first place where people started all this, "Hey, man" stuff.

And Gilligan was patterned after Maynard G. Krebs and all the people at Pandora's.

So, how, you are asking, did me and my preppy Knights crew fit into this scene? Here we were, walking in with our penny loafers and Levis, white socks, a white dress shirt with the sleeves rolled up twice and the collar open.

They must have thought we were very strange. They knew we were like high school guys. This wasn't a place that served alcohol. They were coffee houses. They were pre-Starbucks.

But these were the great meat racks of the '50s. And we didn't care whether we fit in or not. Or we tried to blend the best we could in spite of all the berets we were walking into.

Mainly, that's because, well, some of these flower children had nice bods.

It was a great place to go to score, man.

We would walk in, "Hey, man, what's happenin'? Let's go get lost in the stars."

Chapter Five

Anything to score.

That's actually how we met Kerouac.

One night this guy was sitting there reading poetry. I didn't think it was real good poetry, to tell the truth.

I mean, I loved the whole poetry thing in the coffee houses, but I'm saying, Kerouac...his poetry was just average at best.

So I made this comment, something to the effect, "Man, I've heard better than this crud." You know?

And this real scraggly looking chick that did not shave under her arms, raises one arm and I saw all this hair and I went, "Omigod."

And she's telling me, "Why don't you give a little respect?"

She was like, "Shut up. That's Kerouac."

That's how I realized who it was.

I'm...I wouldn't say forward...but I love talking to people. And the bigger the better. I walked up to Kerouac and I wanted to resolve all the problems at Walden Pond and be a little Thoreau-ish with the guy.

I'm never feeling 100 percent comfortable with him. And, I'm sure, I'm making next-to-zero impression on him, too. But the main thing was, there was always a good-lookin' broad near him. So it was a place for me to go to sidle up to something with very ample breasts.

We wanted to fake, at least, being interested in finding our Inner Flower Child, so to speak.

If it got us women, that's all we asked.

The dude would be reading his poetry and we would slip up next to some chick hanging around Kerouac and go, "Hey, man, Jack is doin' this, but why don't we go somewhere?"

Remember, all we had to do was drive up the other side of Sunset, the other side of Hollywood Boulevard, and park and talk about the world and our moons into their seventh houses, if you know what I mean.

But if they didn't want to make love, all right, we could just dump 'em off at Pandora's and we would go over to DL's, our club hangout. And we would change like chameleons. We would go from hippies back into soc's.

But hippie chicks were still some of the most fertile ground for scoring in the early '60s. And that led me into meeting Angela Davis and Stokely Carmichael, two of the major black activists of the '60s.

Angela was a very nice, quiet chick who truly believed in Communism. Out of all the black activists, she was the most real.

Stokely was only interested in white women. Stokely was an ass. He wasn't nice. He was nice when you first got to know him, but he just loved blondes.

You'd run into Angela and Stokely and the rest at UCLA and also on the weekends in Berkley, where they'd be holding protests and stuff.

See, that was another big thing for us. Back in those years, we would get in a van and we would drive up Highway 101 and we would hang out in the Haight. Haight-Ashbury.

We needed to take a van because Volkswagen vans were cool and then you could go more places. And, most importantly, it was a motel on wheels.

For this place, you left the yellow Caddie or the Vette or the Impala at home.

You were being hippies for the weekend.

You wanted some of that fine young hippie action.

The Haight was a strange place and still is.

There was this lamp post out front of this one place on the corner, where I met this fabulous looking girl and I mean, these were the days of no bra, and long hair. It was one block down from Ashbury on Haight. It was a real great hangout.

And I remember meeting this girl who absolutely turned me inside-out during sex. She was gorgeous. She was really nice. And, my God, she must have been a world champion gymnast.

Name?

You got me, pal.

The name was Gorgeous.

There were so many hundreds of willing chicks in the Haight at the time, you wound up doing it almost before formal introductions.

Free love was in. I took full advantage.

There was just so much up there. Omigod. Friday afternoon, we said, "Well, let's go up and screw all weekend."

And that's what we did. Morning, noon and night.

If they were receptive, that was cool.

If they weren't receptive, that was cool, too.

Go onto the next one.

Never force yourself. I was always a gentleman.

There were so many fish in the ocean, it didn't really matter.

You'd just drift in and out of these bars. A lot of them didn't have names. It's not like saying, "I'll meet you over at Joe's Bar or The Whiskey" or something. They just had the kinds of coffee they sold, like soaped onto the windows or something like that. That was the only signage.

But the Haight...the funny thing was, I did not get into drugs. I didn't want to, and I didn't have to, in order to score. I thought originally I would have to in order to get girls, but it turns out I could play it off and it wouldn't matter.

There were a lot of times I was with a chick and she'd take a hit of coke and she'd start to give me one and I'd go, "Nah, nah. I'm cool."

Everything was, "I'm fine."

Chapter Five

"I'm all caught up."

"I'm covered."

All these little things. You're dodging.

In other words, you didn't want the drugs.

You want the sex.

So that's how I ran into Angela at the Haight. I ran into Stokely. They would come up and do demonstrations. Angela, I want to say, was already a student at UCLA. But, actually, I'm not absolutely sure of her status.

I do know she was a nice girl. She had hair. She had a 'fro on her. Oh man, you shoulda seen her trying to get into a doorway with that massive hair.

She was strictly a Commie. She truly believed that everyone should share things together.

Angela was a good-looking girl. Man, she had great legs sticking out of these short little skirts. And she had an absolutely magnificent butt.

She was just hot. I salivated a little bit. But I never got close enough to Angela to try for her. I wasn't that much into the inner sanctum, at all. I knew them and they knew my name.

They knew I was Lumpy. And they tried to play me.

I didn't want to get involved with that.

You have to understand what it was like at UCLA, when I went there.

There were different areas around campus, these free-speech areas. You could be walking to class with a book and hear someone screaming out for the proletariat. Screaming out against the war. Against nuclear power. Against the government. Against wealth.

In my heart, I knew they were right, but I thought they were hitting their heads against a wall.

When it came to the black cause, Stokely was a manipulator. He was the head of SNCC, the supposed Student Non-Violent Coordinating Committee, and "Snick," as it was pronounced, was total B.S.

SNCC was about as non-violent as Fidel Castro. SNCC would have cut your friggin' arms off. OK? You couldn't believe Carmichael at all.

Like I say, all this guy was after was the white chicks. That's all he cared about. He was a real vermin.

But Angela believed in what she was doing.

She was very uptight. Always nervous. Fidgety. I can't say I remember anything Angela actually said that stuck with me. Much of it was the same rabble-rousing claptrap to try to get people who had an IQ of 3 to go, "Yeah. Yeah. Yeah."

That's how rabble-rousers are.

If you ran into somebody who really gave you verbal discourse, you avoided them.

You wanted the guy who sat there with a blank look on his face going, "Yeah, man. Right on. Let's do it."

They didn't want someone who could actually think.

They didn't want the guy who would say, "Hey, prove it to me."

They wanted me to be a representative of their causes. And I wasn't a cause guy. At the time I was very liberal. I believed the world had to be changed. I didn't think I was going to be doing the changing.

I was a pretty law-abiding guy. Remember, we were "Beaver" people. We were America and the flag and all that other good stuff. And all of a sudden, here I am, I didn't want to burn flags. I was raised to believe in, you know, God and family and all that.

Not to believe in anarchy.

These people were preaching anarchy. Anarchy wasn't my bag.

My bag was to have a little play-type anarchy with them and then go back to my disgusting existence and let them fight the war.

That doesn't sound very high or morally great, I suppose, but that's how it was.

I just wanted to be where the action was.

I had to be.

That was what made me tick.

And where could you get better action than a peace demonstration or a black-power rally in the '60s?

A lot of times, the activist leaders were aware I was there. When they knew, they were very nice to me. They always encouraged me to be close to them while they were talking. Of course, they wanted to see my fist in the air, going, "Yeah. Yeah. Yeah."

But my eyes were more on somebody's body and saying, "C'mon, let's get out of here and do our thing. And we'll come back. See how things wind up."

Something like that.

Aside from girl-hunting, I also liked the fact that you could meet some nice people at demonstrations. And some of these people, you would keep in contact with.

I just met so many people and my inventory of people that I knew grew to the thousands, not hundreds.

Anywhere I could go in Southern California or Northern California, I'd always run into somebody.

But there was only one occasion in which I actually got out and demonstrated and got my fine young Jewish tush arrested for it.

And that was with Cesar Chavez.

That was in East L.A.

Chapter Five

He was leading a deal called "MAPA." The Mexican American Political Association. And Cesar was out there trying to organize the brasseros. They were getting hosed so bad. The brasseros were the itinerant farmers. You know, they were all illegals. East L.A. was loaded with illegals and Cesar was trying to get people educated, he was trying to get people organized, he was trying to get people so they weren't getting messed over.

Cesar was a pretty good guy.

He was very, very loud. He was adamant. He was excitable. He was intelligent.

I've seen his eyes pierce through a lot of cops.

He really stuck up for his people.

Physically, he wasn't imposing. Not at all. He was dumpy. Cesar was nothing to look at. He wasn't tall. He wasn't short.

Cesar was a very nondescript guy. But he was a real good guy.

He had a big heart and big cojones.

Well, there was this lady we knew who was a Mexican. And this one night, she was talking about this demonstration on Whittier Boulevard.

Now, Whittier Boulevard was what Cheech used to sing about in the song, "Born in East L.A."—and, in fact, Cheech and Chong were at this very demonstration I was at. You bet they were.

But Whittier was where you cruised in East L.A. Kind of like the Hollywood Boulevard for the Mexicans.

That's where all the lowered Chevies were.

So now we're down on Whittier Boulevard and we come up on this demonstration. We're sittin' there and the next thing I know, there are all these coffins being paraded down the street.

And we're lookin' and goin', "Hey, that's pretty cool."

The coffins represented how they were tromping the Mexican Americans, and how their bodies were being buried in unmarked graves. And they weren't giving them any money. It was just a symbol.

Now all of a sudden, the cops are going, "Disperse. Disperse."

And everyone's going, "No way. We're not leaving, you pigs."

And I happened to be there, so, of course, suddenly I've got three cops coming up behind me, shoving me into the back of this van.

So we get our butts arrested.

Now, I haven't really been shouting, "Down with the pigs" and all this. I was doing my usual. I was schemin'. I was playing like I was all for the cause.

But I was there and I was part of it. I mean, actually, I did believe in what Chavez was doing.

If you didn't believe in Chavez's cause, you weren't human. Because the pickers and people like that were getting screwed over something fierce.

They really were.

Cesar was right on the money. He did a lot of good for a lot of people.

But, still, it wasn't like I was in any real role in the demonstration or anything. I was just down there to see a scene.

I was probably looking for some Mexican chick. I was usually in that mode.

But there was action.

It was the same thing. I loved the action wherever I went.

When things were happening, I wanted to be part of it.

So now these cops are coming to round everyone up at this demonstration and these three cops have me by the arms. I'm already almost in the van before they even start with me. Believe me, I did not exactly push them back.

I didn't say a word.

Why should I?

Because I knew I was already in there.

No way of talkin' my way out of this ticket.

But actually, we were more of a nuisance to most of the authorities than a real threat. Because, see, Cesar Chavez's guys really were non-violent. I mean, up in Delano and up in the farm country in the middle part of California they got pretty violent. But in East L.A.? The Mexicans were pretty laid back.

So the cops weren't clubbin' people. No Kent State scene. It was more like, "Get the hell outta here. Clean up this demonstration, and let's all go home and watch TV or something."

So now I'm taken down to Parker Center—the place they originally took O.J.— and they threaten us for about a half hour.

It was so disorganized. Finally some guy comes out looking like Michael Conrad from "Hill Street Blues" and goin', "Well, if all you people can act like human beings and stop with this civil unrest, you can go home. If not, we're gonna throw your butts in the slammer tonight."

So I'm sittin' there goin', "Oh, yeah. I'll go home."

I turned around and they let me go.

There were maybe 300-400 people arrested and they just wanted to get us out of their hair, if at all possible.

So that was my one time being arrested, although I wasn't formally charged with anything.

It wasn't long after that I ran into my next unforgettably crazy moment.

That would be dropping the peyote with Carlos Castenada.

This was at UCLA in the '60s. Drugs just weren't a really big thing for me then.

I dabbled some, like I said.

Chapter Five

TALKIN' 'BOUT MY GIRL...young love, first love, happened for me at Hamilton High School with Susan, my steady date for four years.

CHOW, BABY....me at four months, already figuring out that some of my most meaningful relationships will be with mealtimes.

CPL. FRANK T. BANK...eat your heart out, Beetle and Bilko...I own the Army now.

TAKE THAT TO THE BANKS....here's our happy family (from left) me, my mom, the fabulous Sylvia; my dopey brother, Doug; and my dad, Leonard-the-sport.

MICHELLE, MA BELLE...she was sweet, smart, funny and kind Michelle Dusick while we were growing up. Later she became Michelle Lee, the famous actress. We were friends through grade school, junior high and high school and we dated a few times. But we loved each other like brother-and-sister more than anything. I will always treasure our friendship.

LORDS AND MAS-TERS...here we are, some of the Knights, the best social club in Los Angeles, the one any kid would have given his right arm to belong to. As a one-time terminal nerd, who learned how to be the coolest of the cool, I, of course, belonged. That's me, back row, second from right, in case you have trouble picking out a more slender version of Lumpy.

ABSOLUTE RULERS...my social club at Hamilton High School, the Knights. As anyone in his or her right mind will tell you, we were the best, the creme da la creme of clubs in L.A. Our cars, clothes, music, girls, the drive-ins we favored, the beach parties and our cruisin' scene on Hollywood Boulevard and The Sunset Strip—all were copied by "American Graffiti," "Happy Days," and the Beach Blanket Bingo movies. That's me with the paddle, front row, far right. I was voted—me, "dumpy Lumpy, dumb as an ox"—as Most Valuable Member of the Knights my senior year.

FRANK BANK, ESQ., ACTOR...The way I looked in a catalogue of young actors, published by my agent, Lola Moore, and sent out to the trade. Lola was a superagent for tons of child and teenage actors in Los Angeles. Fortunately, I was one of them, because Lola helped me land plenty of roles.

LUMPY ON THE LOOSE...Lumpy, Wally and The Beav. I am causing trouble, as usual, for the Cleaver kids on "Leave It to Beaver." Some dispute over the bike. As always, Ward and June help the boys overcome my schemes and I am taught the error of my ways.

SUNDAE'S BEST... I am annointed with ice cream, becoming Lumpy a la mode, during a scene from one of the more famous "Leave It to Beaver" episodes... "The Soda Jerk."

PHONEY BALONIES...Eddie Haskell and I work out some phone scam—me with the old handkerchief-over-the-mouthpiece ploy—while once again trying to lead Wally and The Beav astray on an episode of "Leave It to Beaver."

CATCHERS IN THE WRY... "The Cleavers" baseball team gets ready to take the field at Baseball City in Florida, spring training site of the Kansas City Royals, just down Interstate 4 from Universal Studios. We had been filming "The New Leave It to Beaver" and someone cooked up a promotional game against a team of sports-casters. I don't think we exactly beat 'em, but we were funnier than they were.

ALL SHOOK UP...that's me pretending to be in deep mourning while I sprinkle the ashes of my wife Rebecca's ex-husband, Elliot, out of a Ziplock baggie, over Elvis' grave at Graceland. Notice nobody has come to arrest me while I pull off dumping this dude's mortal remains all over the King. I rank this as one of my highest acting achievements.

MORE BEAVER TALES....the cast of America's favorite family, and friends, as "The New Leave It to Beaver" airs in 1984.
Front row (from left) are Kipp Marcus, Troy Davidson and Eric Osmond.
Middle row (from left) are John Snee, Jerry Mathers, Tony Dow, Kaleena Kiff and Janice Kent. In back are Kenny Osmond and me. In the center is the queen of all mothers, herself, the thoroughly gorgeous and wonderful Barbara Billingsley.

THIS BUD'S FOR ME... Tony Dow, a dear friend on and off the set, and I relax at a social gathering during the "New Leave It to Beaver" years.

BOOK US, DANO... Jerry and I share an Hawaiian "aye" with a friendly island girl during a promotional shoot for a "New Leave It to Beaver" episode.

AIN'T NUTHIN' LIKE THE REAL THING, BABY... Rebecca, my true love, my best friend, my braintrust, my confidante, my lover, my sweetheart and my soulmate for life, on our honeymoon, 15 years ago.

But I would rather have gone to the Luau on Rodeo Drive and gotten a couple of whiskey sours, wearing slacks and a dress shirt, rather than go to some ratty place and stick something up my nose or whatever.

But these peyote buttons were real interesting and they were kind of a hallucinogenic. This was in my Playboy intellectual days. I was maybe 20.

I was about the same age for all these adventures I'm talking about.

From 19 to 22 I was a real hell-raiser.

But Carlos, I bumped into at the student union at UCLA.

Everybody hung out there.

And somehow I knew who he was and he knew who I was.

Remember, back in the early-'60s, by now I was a pretty high-level person.

People knew who Frank Bank was. They knew because of "Leave It to Beaver"—that was our zenith.

We went from '57 to '63, but from '60 to '63, we were like household names and I was going to UCLA.

I wasn't about to sneak up on somebody and say, "Hey, baby, let's jump in the sack." A lot 'em knew who I was. But a lot of 'em didn't.

I mean, I wasn't opposed to the fame thing working for me if it got me girls. OK by me. I mean, I was just such a casual guy, though. The word, "casual" was very big in my vocabulary.

So I didn't like forcing the name, Frank Bank, on anybody. If it helped me out, fine. If they thought I was a schmuck for the way I made money, so be it.

I heard remarks every now and then. Like, "Oh, that idiot thinks he's a hot movie star" or something like that. And I wanted to go, "I don't think that," but I didn't. I was a better listener than I was trying to fight back. I didn't have anything I had to worry about fighting for.

I knew I was cool.

I knew I was right.

I knew I was a good guy.

And I knew I was not stuck-up, conceited or any of those other weird things.

If there was some dork, I would never blow him off. I loved dorks. They just weren't with-it people. Because, see I started off in that area. Hey, I loved the movie, "The Revenge of the Nerds." I loved some of those nerds. Especially Booger, you know, the guy who was always sticking his finger in his nose? I loved him.

They were cool, man. They were funny. They had their revenge, too.

And I had my transformation.

I was really what I was. I wasn't a nerd trying to be cool. I really was cool. And I knew that. I belonged. I now knew that I belonged with the sweet people, the higher end of the proleteriat.

And Carlos Castenada was one of those people I met that day at the student union.

We used to call the place Disneyland. Because it was this brand new student union. And it had a couple of bowling alleys downstairs, where we used to bowl for 10 cents a game. And you could eat in there — burgers, grilled cheese sandwiches, chips. And it had the bookshop. That's where Bear Wear started getting popular. All these school T-shirts and sweatshirts—all of the casual dress that you see around the world today started at UCLA with Bear Wear.

I don't know if you know this or not, but UCLA clothing was the most popular clothing in the world. If you went to Asia or if you went to Europe, the No. 1 sweatshirt or T-shirt that you were going to see wasn't going to say, "USA." It was going to say "UCLA."

Sounds crazy, but it's the truth.

At our student union, people came from all over the world to buy clothing. They'd go in there and buy sweatshirts and T-shirts and all that stuff. We're talkin' 35 years ago, before you ever saw a Gucci T-shirt or before you ever saw a T-shirt that said "Eat at Joe's" or "Gates Barbecue" or anything like that. I do believe that we started that stuff before most colleges. I can't guarantee it, but it's a belief of mine and I think I'm right.

So now I'm in the Disneyland student union and there sits Carlos. He's just a heavy-duty Latin-American kind of guy. And he's kind of quiet.

And he goes, "You're the guy from 'Beaver.'"

And I went, "Yeah."

And he says, "I'm Carlos."

And I go, "Hi, Carlos."

And he went, "Uh, I wrote some books."

I went, "Are you the guy that wrote that 'Don Juan' stuff?"

And he goes, "Yeah, man."

He says, "I been there."

I remember him sayin', "I been there."

He meant to hell and back. Because, see, now we're into the drug-culture days. And those drug-culture days lasted a long time. A lot of people were talking about things. We used similes. We used the language.

It's like when I was young, we would say, "bitchin'." Meaning, something was really cool. Yet, when I was in my 30's "bitchin'" was a real stupid word and no one ever used that. Now I hear it's comin' back.

The verbiage of young America or the verbiage of a sect or a part of society was always different.

And "he had been there" was a big thing with drugs.

That was what Carlos was trying to say.

Chapter Five

Here was another guy, kinda like Chavez...nondescript. If I had to pick him out of a crowd today, I couldn't. I could get Cesar. But I couldn't get Carlos.

He was about five years older than I was. Other than that...he looked like your everyday Latino guy.

So how did we get from "You're on 'Beaver'" to popping peyote? It got to the point where he says, "Wanna do some buttons?" Something in that vein.

He says to me, "We're meeting somewhere."

We met over at someone's house one night. And it was on a school night.

It was in Beverly Hills. A major, heavy-duty Beverly Hills house. Pool. Tennis courts. Servants quarters. Theaters. You know. Crap like that.

Typical Beverly Hills house.

Whose? You never asked.

It was immodest to ask.

The house was in the Beverly Hills flats. Right near Sunset and Beverly Drive. Big estate, though.

I remember I was in the kitchen. Carlos was in there. And that was the first time I ever did any peyote. And it was really interesting because I got so damn dizzy. And I was just like...I'm not sure what I was like.

There were lots of good-lookin' chicks. And some very substantial-looking guys. And I'm saying, there were about 20 people there and only three or four of them were Latin. And the rest were all West L.A. types. They were just sitting there getting loaded.

For all I know maybe we were puppets set up for Carlos' next book or something. Remember, he wrote these "Don Juan" books really back a long time ago.

But he was a bright guy. I told you I got off on learning things. So I figured, OK, I'll try this...peyote. See if I can learn something.

I really didn't learn anything. Except I got loaded.

I was either with Wallace or Phil Kerbis, or one of those guys, one of my club brothers. And the next thing I knew I was in my bed. I was still living at home. I remember the experience of being lightheaded. I do not remember the experience of going anywhere.

After that I still saw Carlos around campus. I just didn't go to the parties. I think I did peyote twice, both scenes like that. That was all. It wasn't that big a deal because people were doing it every friggin' day.

I had more fun, when the word, "TGIF" was coined...Thank God It's Friday...where we would sit and drink and drink. And we would drink these two drinks.

One was called Skip and Run Naked. Because after you drank one, that's what you would do, skip and run naked. Skip and Run Naked was beer, vodka...you put the vodka in the shot glass and you drop it on top of the beer. There was a third ingredient, but I forget what it was.

If you were higher class, you would have what's called a French 76. In a French 76, you substituted champagne for the beer. Why was it a French 76? Beats the hell out of me. Probably "French" because it was champagne. I don't have a clue what the "76" meant.

But the most popular drink was Skip and Run Naked. You'd have a few of these and you would.

You'd go down to Julie's in Westwood. Or there were a few places down by USC. What was I doing down by the hated USC campus, when I was a UCLA Bruin, first, last and always?

The broads.

There were some good-lookin' chicks at USC.

We went wherever the action was.

One of our favorite hangouts was the Luau I mentioned before. The Luau was one of the fanciest, hippest restaurants on Rodeo Drive.

It was the place I drank 56 whiskey sours on a bet.

After I drank the 56 whiskey sours, I walked outside and the bet was that I had to walk the double-yellow line between the manhole covers. Now, on the corner was an old Atlantic-Richfield gas station. And I had to walk halfway down the block to the next manhole cover, and I wouldn't miss a beat.

I won the bet.

It was 2 in the morning. There was a little bit of traffic. Not much. They kinda steered clear.

And the Beverly Hills cops were there and they didn't bug us. Because we were "cool." We were "substantial."

I was wearing an alpaca sweater—white tennis shoes, no socks, Levis.

We belonged.

See, here's the deal.

If you belonged to the Beverly Hills neighborhood, the cops were cool. But if you looked like you were from the barrio, or you were from South Central, if you were there to cause trouble, those cops were brutal.

They were among the most violent officers you ever saw...they were not nice guys.

But they were really nice guys if they saw you were driving, say, a new Impala convertible, you had this nice-looking girl and you were really clean-cut. If you were clean-cut, they were your friends. If you were there to loot a house, they'd cut your freakin' heart out.

But, you ask, how I did 56 whiskey sours? I couldn't really do that many, could I?

Oh yes, I could.

In about three hours.

They were regular-sized whiskey sours, four ounces, I believe, and you'd drink 'em half a dozen at a time.

The waiter was a guy named Alfred. Our favorite thing with Alfred, every time we saw Alfred, we would say to him, "Sip-sip?"

I think that is Polynesian. Or it's Filipino. It's something down in the South Pacific. But when you say "Sip-sip?" to someone, that means, "Do you eat it?"

The whole phrase was, "Sip-sip boogie?"

"Sip-sip" means "do you eat" and "boogie" means "it."

Ask a Filipino about that.

But when you said that to Alfred, he would just laugh and you'd go, "Bring me another half-a-dozen, Alfred."

I did get up and whiz a couple times. I did do that.

I don't know why the bet was 56. I don't remember what was supposed to be magic about that number. But 56 was the number that came up.

Whereas I didn't drink a whole hell of a lot in high school, obviously I was making up for it in college. The bars were just too much fun.

The greatest women in the United States went to the Luau. I'm tellin' ya right now, the dreams of your life walked in the door of that place.

And we would walk out with them.

They would come in wearing short-shorts. They would come in wearing very tight jeans. That's just about the time bras were starting to get burned. You would see halters. You would see the "California Look," you know.

Bright colors. Silk blouses, so you could see the nipples underneath the silk.

Big blonde hair. Bouffants and all that were really popular. Bubble-flips, they called them. It was like the one Nancy Sinatra used to wear when she sang, "These Boots Were Made for Walkin.'" Kinda like a matchhead.

It was the "That Girl" look.

Mary Tyler Moore.

When we weren't prowling Rodeo Drive, we were driving through another major Los Angeles scene, looking for action and finding crazy people.

We got into drag racing.

And we met "Big Daddy" Garlits. We met Don "The Snake" Prudhomme. Tommy Ivo was a young Hollywood movie star when he started racing. He was the king of the dragsters there for a couple of years with his Buick.

Me and Wallace and Dickie Schwartz would go out to the drags all the time and I had my Corvettes. We used to hang out in a place...nowadays you wouldn't go down there because it's too dangerous. It's in the heart of deep do-do...Crenshaw and Slauson. It was in "Boyz 'n' the Hood." That corner, that's where the kid got shot in the movie.

Slauson is also where Johnny Carson used to talk about on "Tea Time Movies" in the old bit on his show: "You take the Slauson Cutoff and cut off your Slauson."

But at Crenshaw and Slauson back then, there was a place called Harry Mann Chevrolet.

It was the largest Corvette dealer in the United States. Your Corvette was not a Corvette unless it came from Harry Mann Chevrolet.

If you went to Beverly Hills and bought your Corvette, you were a complete and total wuss.

You had to go to Harry Mann because first of all you were going to get an injection. A fuel injection was a big deal. He had this mechanic down there named Jimmy Viedenoff. Jimmy could make fuel injection sing. He was the best mechanic in the United States.

There would always be one or two Knights down at Harry Mann Chevrolet getting their Chevys tuned or their Corvettes tuned. Then we'd go race them at these drag strips around L.A.

There was the Lions Drag Strip which was down in Long Beach, just off the newly named San Diego Freeway. It was below Gardena. Then there was San Fernando which was out in the San Fernando Valley. And we had Pomona, where the L.A. County Fair is. And then Fontana was a big drag strip.

This was where drag racing got popular.

I raced with them. You bet I did.

I raced in my Vette and I had a '60 Impala, 360, 4-speed, a honkin' Chevy that really was cool. My '57 Chevy was good. My fastest car was my Corvette, though.

I won a lot of trophies with that sucker.

This Corvette was painted regal turquoise, which was like a metallic turquoise. It had black leather interior. It was a '58 and it was fuel-injected.

We did some minor modifications. Like we "polished the ports." We "tuliped" the valves. That means the valves can move faster. It's called "legal cheating." You're doing everything you can to make your car the fastest in your classification.

Every drag strip had a different classification like dragster or a funny car. Matter of fact, funny cars were invented, I believe, in Lions. The girl dragster that became real famous, Cha Cha Muldowney, started in Lions, I think.

But Garlits is from Florida. Garlits would come out West. Our guys out here that were the fast ones were Don "The Snake" Prudhomme, and Ivo was pretty fast, too. The Snake was probably the most high profile, although we also had a guy named Tom "The Mongoose" McEwen who was very fast.

I was there one night when The Mongoose ate The Snake.

My buddies and I were chump-change guys. We drove what were called "stockers." You had stockers and you had dragsters and you had funny cars. Stockers was "A Class," "B Class," "C Class." Then when you got up into high-stockers, that was Corvettes and Cobras and stuff like that. There was A-Gas, B-Gas, C-Gas. And then you had the old Model-T's. They'd put engines in that were 25 times bigger than the cars. Those also were gas-classes.

I used to race in A-gas and B-gas and Supersport.

The A and B stood for the size of the engines and the Supersport was for the Corvettes. And T-Birds...ha-ha-ha. I don't think a T-Bird ever won a trophy at a dragstrip. It was always either a Chevy or a Corvette or once in awhile a Cobra. And then, for awhile, the Dodges and Hemis and some of the Chrysler Corporation products.

They were screamin'.

But Corvettes ruled. That's why there were so many songs about them. Ask the Beach Boys. Ask Jan and Dean. Everything was Corvettes. The Ripcords and all those guys. They sang about them.

I won some trophies. Not all of the time. But I would be competitive.

There were different degrees of idiots and cool. There were some icky guys that hung out at the drag strip. There were some greasers. And then there were cool guys that hung out at the drag strip.

You could always tell who was cool. Let's say a guy goes out and buys the right car...obviously a '57 Chevy was a right car. But it was only a right car if you bought it the right way and in the right color. If you bought an automatic four-door with a center-post that was copper-colored, you might as well have had your pencil pocket-protector on. Your hornrimmed glasses and your braces. You're an absolute geek.

But if you bought a two-door hardtop, all black, or if you bought one that was red with a black interior or if you bought a convertible that was white, red, black, turquoise...something like that...cool.

If you went out and bought a convertible that was beige...c'mon, man. You're a friggin' toad. You don't buy a friggin' beige convertible. Or mint green.

I shouldn't have to explain this to anyone. You wasted your money there, man. These guys are losers.

But the best of the best, guys like Big Daddy and The Snake, were out there at the strip...they were professionals.

We were just there for the scene.

This was a very rare scene.

It was not for chicks. It was for having a good time with the boys.

Our avocations, aside from girls, were hot cars and hot poker games.

It was what Southern California was famous for. Still to this day, if you want to see more Vipers, more Ferraris, more of every hot car in the world, come on out to L.A. I'll take you over to Ventura Boulevard or Sunset or to the beach or anywhere, and you're going to see the kind of car you want to see.

I talked to Big Daddy on a few occasions. Total shit-kicker. He's a Southern bo-ah. He had that heavy-duty accent. I was a local boy. So we were totally different.

Let's put it this way, I was always rooting for Don Prudhomme to beat his hind end. Prudhomme was a local boy. From Pasadena, I think.

He beat Big Daddy a lot. And Big Daddy lost to some other local guys, too. Big Daddy was a foreign guy, coming in to try and kick our butts and take our trophies.

We wanted to keep our trophies.

Territorial. Damn straight we were.

Big Daddy was good, though. He was tough. And he loved to win. And you know what, he did win a lot. He was great.

There is no question he's the big daddy of drag racing. His longevity is incredible. He's got to be the greatest who ever lived.

But we had some good ones. Mickey Thompson was a good one from Long Beach.

We'd always go down to the speed shops. We had speed shops all over L.A. You'd go get an Iskendarian Cam. The nickname is "Isky" cam after a guy named Ed Iskendarian. He invented the roller cam. And the roller cam was a faster way to get that engine moving. He was big-time stuff. General Motors had a guy named Duntov and everyone had Duntov cams. My car came from the factory with a Duntov cam, and it came with General Motors fuel injection.

B&M Automotive was cool. They made B & M transmissions. They were like auto-sticks. If you had a B & M transmission it was faster than a 4-speed. It shifted so fast—it would cut time off your "ET." Your ET was your elapsed time.

See, these guys would say, "Oh, I went out to the drags and I turned a hundred."

That meant you went 100 miles an hour in the quarter-mile. That didn't mean squat.

Because you could go 100 miles an hour and have a 15.5-second ET. But if you went 100 miles an hour at a 13.4 ET, you beat the guy by 16 car lengths.

Every car length was 10/100ths of a second, I think.

I did 13.20 one time. Which was fast.

I mean, nowadays it's laughable. You know, some of these big dragsters do six seconds. You can't even open your mouth and they're down the quarter-mile.

Chapter Five

But back in those days, 13.20 was pretty damn good. I had no complaints.

I was making plenty of money from "Beaver" by now so I could afford the cars. This was about '62.

But I sorta outgrew it. It wasn't cool enough for me in '63 to '65.

I was busier and involved in classier events. I was hanging out in Beverly Hills, not Long Beach or Pomona.

But that didn't mean I was outgrowing my love—and crying need—for crazy people.

Far from it.

Along about this time came one of my all-time favorite days with Jimmy Winston and the Hell's Angels.

You have to first of all understand who and what Jimmy Winston was.

Jimmy Winston was a big, big kid. Barrel chest, I want to say 46 minimum, more like 48. About 6-2, 6-3, a 29-inch waist. Blond hair, blue eyes, a really good-lookin' guy. Jimmy was strong as an ox.

Of all my friends, my father loved Jimmy the best.

Because Jimmy was an eater.

He'd come over to our house and eat three or four steaks. And my dad couldn't wait to get the food on the barbecue to feed Jimmy. He'd see Jimmy walkin' through the door, he'd say, "Here comes Hollow Legs."

Jimmy once ate 19 pizzas to win a contest on TV. That's right, 19. Another time he ate an entire 23-pound turkey.

Channel 13 would hold these contests. Why? Why did you jam people in a phone booth? Why did you eat goldfish? People in the Midwest used to have pie-eating contests.

We had pizza and turkey-eating contests.

If you won, your prize was: You were cool.

Or else a pig.

You won the admiration of other devout guttersnipes, I guess.

We loved it.

Anyway, Jimmy was always winning these eating things. And I called him "Smiley' because Jimmy had this big old smile. He won the Smile of the Year contest when he was a young kid.

Sounds perfectly Southern California, doesn't it?

The L.A. school district used to have this contest, Smile of the Year, and Jimmy won it. You know, for having good teeth and all?

People used to accuse Jimmy of being a mooch. Which he was. But I loved Jimmy.

So anyhow, Jimmy calls me up one day and says, "My uncle is inviting us to Pine Flats Lake."

I said, "Where the hell is that?"

He says, "Up near Yosemite."

The Idiot Magnet

I said, "What's the story?"

He said, "He's gonna teach us how to water ski."

Says, "He's got this great big boat. Got this blown-Chrysler engine."

So here is his Uncle Dick up there with the Chrysler engine and the lake and Pine Flats is the destination.

OK. I said, "I tell you what, Smiley. You're supplying the boat and the cabin, so I'll drive."

We're going up to the Redwoods, the High Sierras. That's the area.

Now, back in these days, I don't even think the San Diego Freeway was finished that took you out of town, heading up to Highway 99.

But Highway 99, we used to call the Grapevine. And the reason it was the Grapevine, is you went up this huge mountain and came down into the valley by Bakersfield and that's where you got to Delano and all the farm country.

We went up 7,000 feet.

Anyhow. I had my Cadillac convertible, my '62 pale yellow, yellow leather and yellow top. Just beautiful. Me and Jimmy in there. It's Labor Day, 1963.

So Smiley and I go down to the Shell station on Robertson and Airdrome and fill up with gas. We pull into the station and there's this lox that takes car of my car. I tell the guy, "Make sure you check the water and the oil. We're takin' a trip."

He goes, "OK."

Oh, what is a "lox?"

A schmuck, a dullard, a dimwit.

Anyway, I'm sittin' there and, you know, gas is about a quarter a gallon or something like that. So it was about six bucks worth of gas to fill the tank.

I go to pay the guy and I say, "Is everything OK?"

He says, "Oh, yeah, everything's fine."

So we start driving out of town. It was Labor Day Weekend. It was hotter'n a son-of-a-gun. There was a heat wave goin' on.

But me and Smiley, we got the top down and we're lookin' good which, of course, is the main thing.

We're listenen' to some "Pipeline" by the Chantays and some "Wipeout" by the Surfaris. You know, some good surfin' music.

"G.T.O." by Ronny & the Daytonas. "California Sun" by the Rivieras.

Car songs. Girl songs. Sun songs.

Cool stuff like that.

Good tunes to climb the Grapevine by.

I guess what we should have been playing was some Commander Cody and the Lost Airmen. Because the Grapvine was the Commander's inspiration for his song, "Hot Rod Lincoln." You know the one — "My daddy said,

Chapter Five

son, you're gonna drive me to drinkin' if you don't stop drivin' that hot-rod Lincoln."

Just a little factoid I like about the Grapevine.

Anyhow, now we're goin' up all these hills when, all of a sudden, I notice my heat guage.

It's like over to the side, almost all the way across.

We're not even up the mountain.

I'm goin', "What the hell is goin' on here?"

Now, we're in bumper-to-bumper traffic. Friday afternoon. Everyone is trying to get out of town.

And now I'm startin' to see a little steam comin' out of the old Cadillac hood and I'm goin', "Uh oh."

I'm prayin', "Just let us make the hill and we're OK." Because when we get to the top, you coast all the way down and there's a bunch of gas stations down there.

So, we're about one mile from the top of the hill and the car craps out.

It sounds like we're rollin' balls around an empty oil drum or something, and the engine stops.

We're still goin' enough that I pull out of the lane and get it over to the side of the highway. Jimmy and I push it just to get it straight and out of traffic.

And then we open the hood.

Damn.

That stupid moron did not put the water cap back on my radiator.

All the water'd boiled out.

I said, "When I see that guy..."

I was doin' the Moe Howard, "Why, I oughtta..."

I mean, we were beside ourselves.

But here was our problem.

Bumper-to-bumper traffic, like 4:30 or 5 o'clock on a Friday afternoon. And our car's just sittin' there doin' the boogie.

And there's no way.

We're hosed.

We can't find water anywhere. And we're sittin' there, like, signalling to people: Anybody have any water?

There are two lanes of bumper-to-bumper goin' by us. Nobody would stop for anything.

Jerk-offs.

So finally, I said to Jimmy, "I think I gotta go take a leak. If anyone's tank is filled up, it's mine."

So I stroll over farther along the side and Jimmy says to me:

"Uh, don't waste it."

I go, "What do you mean?"

And Jimmy just looks down at me.

The realization suddenly comes to me.

Jimmy, you're a walkin', talkin' genius.

A regular Ein-freakin'-stein.

Hey, man. We got some radiator juice right here.

Mother Nature's very own Prestone.

I got some Frank Bank in the Tank.

So I stood up on the front bumper. Dragged the boy out. Got him lined up in the right direction.

Allowed for windage. Elevation. Trajectory.

Ready on the left.

Ready on the right.

Ready on the firing line.

Aim.

Pow.

Hey, man. I didn't waste a drop. Davey Freakin' Crockett couldn't have hit the bull's eye better than I did.

Talk about your Deadeye Dicks.

I'm totally unloading as people are drivin' by.

They're gawkin'.

Lookin'.

Cranin'.

Pointin'.

Laughin'.

A few hoots from the guys in the audience.

A few appreciative whistles from the ladies.

I heard a few, "That's disgusting" remarks.

But I also heard a few, "Hey, baby, save some of that for me."

And now it was Jimmy's turn.

I said, "Smiley, you gotta take a whiz, too?"

And he goes, "Well, maybe I can brew somethin' up."

Then he gets up there, jerks the old Johnson, and he does his bit.

We put the cap back on the radiator.

We crank the engine.

It starts.

One guy was staring at Jimmy and stopped and said, "Hey, give us a gallon."

I was thinking of bottling it and marketing it.

Drain-the-Lizard Radiator Lube.

So now we're done.

Chapter Five

We take off and we don't even try to get back into the lanes with the traffic. We drive on the lip all the way to the summit, about a mile.

As soon as we got to the top, I put the car in neutral, leave my foot on the brake and start coasting downhill.

People are looking at us passing them. They're steamed.

But hey, you think a few scowls are gonna stop us now?

We were laughin' so hard, we rode the shoulder all the way to the bottom of the Grapevine.

We stop at this little gas station. We fill the radiator with water.

Everything was cool.

OK. So now we go on a little bit further and we're up on the other side of Bakersfield on the way to Modesto, which is where they shot "American Graffiti."

When you heard Wolfman Jack growlin' on the radio, "It's gon' be fo' hunded de-grees in de valleh today," that's the valley they were talking about.

The San Joaquin Valley.

Now after all this it's about 7 o'clock and we're really hungry. So we find this roadhouse restaurant.

Don't know the name of it.

It was a big old roadhouse between Bakersfield and Modesto on Highway 99.

We pull in and there's this old couple, right out of American Gothic, across the aisle from us. Jimmy and I sit down and we both order the standard California dinner—big half-pound hamburger, French Fries and a Coke.

They had just started to serve us our dinner and we hear this humongous racket out front. It sounded like all hell breaking loose.

Which it literally was.

The next thing, the doors fly open and in comes all these smelly, grimy guys with the Hell's Angels. They were having a Labor Day outing.

I'm telling you, there were over 100 bikes out front of this restaurant.

They were the smelliest, roachiest-looking guys. Long scraggly hair. Unkempt beards. Ugly old tatoos. Levi jackets with "San Berdoo" on the back.

Meaning San Bernardino.

These girls looked like yesterday's latkes. That's Yiddish for yesterday's pancakes.

Boy, were they terrible.

Jeans. Leather. Lipstick from ear-to-ear. And they smelled and they were dirty. And they had their fat rumps hanging out of these chaps.

They had the chains out of their back pockets and the cycle boots.

And they had their stupid little sailor hats on.

The Idiot Magnet

That's the pile of puke that walked through the door.

All of a sudden, 100 of them walk in and they start sittin' down anywhere and everywhere.

Two of them come over to Mr. and Mrs. American Gothic and wedge into their booth.

Next thing I know, these two big dudes come in, followed by four more right behind 'em.

Four of 'em sit behind us and the other two say, "Move over, boys."

They slide in with us.

Did we object?

No, we did not.

You think we're stupid or something?

We didn't do diddly.

We had looks on our faces like, "Yessir, Mr. Hell's Angels."

I mean, we didn't say a word.

Jimmy is a big boy and I'm not exactly a flyweight, but neither one of our mommas raised no fools, either.

We moved over, right?

Afraid? Yeah, my heart was bouncin' pretty good there.

Because, see it was just me and Smiley.

If it was two-on-two, we wouldn't have had any compunction against any two of those guys. I mean, believe me, I would have stood up with any of them.

But this was 50-to-1.

It was 100-to-2.

Our bodies would not have been found.

Understand, this was before today's new-and-improved Hell's Angels, sanitized for your protection, with a Surgeon General's warning on the label.

This is before Toys for Tots and other goodwill, public-relations stuff by the Angels.

This was when they were for real. This is when they put the actual Hell in the Angels.

They were known for messing people up. They could care less. They did what they wanted and nobody stopped 'em.

Just about the time they say to us, "Move over," the lady comes and slides the burger plate in front of Jimmy and a burger plate in front of me.

So Jimmy was sittin' there with this look on his face, which is the same thing I'm thinkin'. We have a split second to do something and as he's reaching down to pick up his hamburger, this one guy sticks his big old greasy, smelly mitt over on Jimmy's French Fries and says, "Pass the ketchup."

And he starts pouring ketchup all over the place.

Chapter Five

Jimmy takes one bite out of his hamburger and I go, "You know, Smiley, I think we're parked in a bad place."

He goes, "Yeah, I think you're right."

"I'll go with you to help you move it."

We turned to the guys and said, "Hey, would you watch our food for us?"

And they said, "Surrrrre" with these big grins on their faces.

As we got up, we walked real quickly. We were only three booths from the door. We looked back and they'd already scarfed the meals. Jimmy's whole burger went into this big beef's mouth.

But we didn't care.

We saw a little daylight to run to.

They thought they had a couple of geeks to play with.

They'd have squashed us like bugs on their windshields.

We'd have been roadkill.

We bailed into the Cadillac and peeled out of the parking lot.

We go half an hour or so up the road and duck into this market and grab something to eat and tear out again.

I was trying to be as cool as I possibly could be. Just get us out of the scene alive. It was something you'd see in a movie.

The Angels were famous for going up to Yosemite and Sequoia on holidays. We were going to Pine Flats Lake, which wasn't too far from there. Labor Day and Memorial Day were their two biggest days, but we weren't even thinking about that until they showed up at the roadhouse.

They were 100 percent USDA, Grade A scarier'n all-get-out.

You know if a major moose who had the size and appetite of Jimmy was willingly giving up his food without a whimper, you've run into something genuinely frightening.

If Smiley gives up food, life and limb are involved to a serious degree.

I don't blame Jimmy for one second. He was one brave hombre normally, but he wanted to cut and run, and so did I. I was scared out of my boots, too. And we should have been.

But I didn't have to go all the way to the national parks ordinarily to get my dose of crazy. I usually found it all too close to home. With my closest friends.

That calls to mind the time I faced another form of Hell—that being Hell Night when I was first pledging the Knights.

You know, this is where you have to clean stuff and go around quacking like a duck or clucking like a chicken or drink some kind of disgusting gunk or stand naked somewhere or do some kind of weird, demanding physical activity.

All that good stuff they're basically trying to outlaw nowadays in fraternities. Back then it was still fairly common.

Didn't strike me as something I wanted to participate in.

But I wanted in the Knights real bad.

An opportunity presented itself for me to sidestep the bullcrap of Hell Night and get what I wanted...membership.

This one guy gets up in front of the group and he's got a mayonnaise jar. A small mayonnaise jar. And it's filled with jalapeno peppers.

This was 1957 and jalapenos weren't real popular in West L.A. People thought of them as gut bombs.

So they're laughing, all these guys, and there are two guys pledging at this moment, me and another guy named Marty Hochberg.

So the head guy says, "Well, tell you what. We're going to give you guys a choice. Taking Hell Night or eating this entire jar of peppers. With no water. And you have to stand here for 10 minutes after you eat the jar of peppers."

Marty didn't even think twice. He says, "I'll take the Hell Night."

Me, I'm standing there like I'm really mulling the whole thing over.

Marty goes, "You crazy? Are you actually thinking of eating the jalapenos?"

Well, remember that I was an actor.

I'm sitting there and all of a sudden I say to the guy with the jar, "Boy, you guys are somethin'. How about I eat a quarter of the jar?"

"No," he says. "You gotta eat the whole jar."

"How about half a jar," I say. "And I'll take 50 swats."

"Nope. The whole jar or nothin'."

"But what if I only get halfway through and I faint or get sick?"

They said, "If you get sick, we'll beat the crap outta you. And if you faint, you're on your own. And you gotta take Hell Night."

I said, "Boy, that doesn't sound very fair to me."

They said, "Make up your mind."

"Well," I said, uncertainly, kind of stammering. "L-l-let me try it."

I pick up the first pepper.

I take a bite.

"Omigod!" I cry. I'm rollin' my eyes and stuff, kinda clutching at my throat and carrying on.

These guys are falling all over themselves, laughing their butts off. They're on the floor. Whacking themselves on the back.

They're lookin' at me, like: This is even better than we hoped.

I reach in. I take a second pepper.

And I go, "Maybe I'm gettin' used to this. Well, I'm gonna try not to faint."

I take the whole second pepper, stick it in my mouth. I chew it.

I say, "You know what, guys? I might be gettin' used to it by now."

Their laughing fades to a little chuckling now.

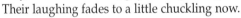

Chapter Five

I proceed to pick up the jar and hold it out in front of me. I pause for dramatic effect. Then I suck out all the juice.

They had some carrots and onions in there.

I ate those.

I look in. There's, oh, maybe 15 more peppers in there.

I tip 'em over into two hands. I start shoveling 'em in, one after another.

I'm popping 'em like gumdrops. I've got my cheeks full like a chipmunk.

They stood there with blank looks on their faces.

The room is dead silent.

Finally, I'm chewing all these peppers at once and the place goes nuts.

I swallow the last pepper.

They say, "You gotta stand there for 10 minutes. If you pass out, you gotta take Hell Night."

I went, "Wel-l-l-l, I'll try not to pass out."

But they knew it was ovah...it was all ovah, as Howard Cosell would have put it.

Clock winds down.

Bank wins. Bank wins.

They all gave me a huge round of applause.

I say, "Hey, look, for a hundred bucks, I'll eat another 50 of 'em."

They went muttering away.

My private triumphant moment was complete.

See, what they didn't know...what I had to hide with my superior acting talents...well, by now you know...

I love jalapenos.

Have ever since I was a little kid.

What my brothers-to-be didn't know was that my mom and dad used to take me down to Tiajuana. Never the bullfights. Usually to the jai alai. Before the matches, we'd go down and eat tacos at Tiajauna Tilly's, this great, great Mexican restaurant.

My dad used to buy these big one-gallon jugs of jalapenos whenever we went down there, which was pretty often.

And what my fellow Knights-to-be didn't know was that on the Bank table, every night of the year, there was a big jar of jalapeno peppers.

I'd always eat at least one or two with dinner.

Cleans your sinuses out wonderfully. Really good.

I couldn't get enough jalapenos.

Hey, Br'er Rabbit never fooled Br'er Fox with the briar patch any better than I duped my bros in the Knights.

Not only did I duck the Hell Night bullet with the help of my jar of gut-bombs, I had become a living legend in my club.

Nobody ever performed the jalapeno feat again. One guy tried. He barfed his guts out after about three peppers. He was miserable.

But I, in the meantime, was able to parlay my renowned cast-iron stomach into further handsome dividends.

Our base of operations for these capers was a hamburger joint named Alex's.

Alex's was on Pico Boulevard, about one block from Rancho Golf Course.

My buddy, Steve Wallace, as he often was, was the instigator in this scene. He'd wait till Alex's had a few patrons file in for lunch and then he'd start talking about me in the third person.

"I heard some guy say he could drink a whole bottle of tobasco sauce," Wallace would say in a loud voice so everyone could hear. "But my dad's a doctor. He said, hell, if anyone tried to drink a bottle of hot sauce, their insides would cave in."

Whatever it took to get some patron interested.

Next thing you know, some poor schlub would be betting Wallace that I couldn't drink a bottle of tobasco sauce.

We're not talking one of the tiny bottles they often have on diner tables with your scrambled eggs or something. I mean the next bottle up from that. A pretty-good sized one.

Well, of course, we did have people pay to watch me down the tobasco sauce—and, of course, I could do it, no problem.

We'd win $10, $15, $20 a pop on the bet.

Which was pretty good money for kids in those days.

I won my buddies a lot of free lunches at Alex's.

Once again, it is I...Superbelly...defeating the forces of evil. Or at least some moron trucker who didn't believe I could do it.

Restaurants always seemed to inspire us.

One staple of every Knights' school year was to whip up a huge batch of oatmeal and then take pledges down to some of the nice eateries in Westwood.

What the pledges had to do was, cram their mouths full of oatmeal until it was running down their chins. Then they had to go up and look in the window until they'd gotten the attention of some people eating, point at their food and make faces like something was wrong with it, groan and hold their stomachs—then spew the oatmeal all over the windows.

Oatmeal: The Perfect Vomit Substitute to Blow Chow With.

Somehow I don't think Quaker Oats thought of the slogan.

But it worked for some morons like us.

The oatmeal routine was, I believe, one of the more inspired rites of pledge passage.

Chapter Five

I mean, we had some of the usual stuff—guys had to go up and stand naked on this one billboard on Wilshire Boulevard.

OK, so it's a cliche. But we still thought it was pretty funny.

Besides, it's kinda like Moe bopping Curley with a ballpeen hammer and Curley doing the "Nyuk-nyuk-nyuk."

You gotta do it if you're the Stooges.

Us stooges—we had to do the naked-billboard thing to pledges

It was expected.

When I say stooges, I mean it endearingly.

We were lunatics, me and my Knights brothers. Mostly harmless although I guess not always.

But the thing about it, life was never dull.

Like Roseanne Rosannadanna used to put it, it was always somethin'.

Take the time Fingers Freeman walked out of J.W. Sloan with the grand piano.

Which he hadn't exactly paid for.

"Fingers" was actually Jimmy Freeman, and Fingers' old man was a millionaire.

I guess that's why Fingers didn't have anything else to do but dream up stunts. The more audacious, the better.

In this case, it was the bright idea of strolling into Sloan's, the hottest furniture store in L.A. at the time, dressed in coveralls, claiming to be "here to pick up the piano."

That, apparently, was all the credentials required for the good folks at Sloan's to help Fingers and Wallace, I believe, as his accomplice, to wheel the piano out of the store.

The store employees all but rolled out a red carpet for Fingers and Wallace to boost that baby. Opened doors for them. Helped hoist it into a truck.

It was a scene right out of Clouseau where Peter Sellers, playing a beat cop striding the sidewalk, holds the door for fleeing bankrobbers to pile into their getaway car.

In a way you have to lament the passing of such an innocent time when a store just naturally assumed some yokels dressed like moving guys were, in fact, there to legitimately cart the piano off.

In a way, I guess you have to blame jerks like us for pulling such shenanigans, destroying the trust we used to have in these situations.

You could say "shenanigans" was a convenient euphemism for "larceny" and probably be right.

But to us, it wasn't stealing.

It was hijinx.

The Idiot Magnet

Wrongheaded as that may be, the story had a happy ending in a way.

While the baby grand never was returned to Sloan's, Fingers delivered it to an old-folks home.

Some senior citizens are still tickling them ivories to their pace-makered hearts content today, thanks to Fingers and Wallace.

And they say crime doesn't pay.

The story also has a sad ending—although with a zany twist.

Fingers was an outstanding athlete—he could drive a golf ball 300 yards back in the days when everyone didn't have some space-age material in the shaft and clubheads bigger than a manhole cover, launching every ball like a Saturn rocket.

But Fingers one day got too energetic and broke his neck diving into the surf at our beloved Knights Beach.

It was an incredibly terrible incident.

Fingers was left paralyzed.

He later passed away in Mexico City while attending the 1968 Olympics.

And then Fingers achieved an eternal place in Knights lore.

He missed his own funeral.

That's right.

His loved ones had set such-and-such a day for the ceremony and all the details were set.

Only one problem.

Somehow Jimmy missed the plane ride home from Mexico.

Beats the hell out of me how it happened.

We never knew.

Somehow, someone boogered up loading his coffin on the flight.

Meanwhile, back home, no one knew that exactly until the ceremonies were about to begin.

We were all assembled there, ready to raise some serious lamentations.

Which a lot of people did.

But Wallace and I wound up sitting down in the front row and we heard the whispers that Jimmy was a no-show.

I believe that Wallace and I were about the only ones in the congregation who knew at the time:

They'd wheeled a box out there for the funeral.

The box was empty.

We went through all these gyrations for about an hour.

We all paid our last respects to Fingers.

Wherever he was.

Somehow, we could see Fingers somewhere with a satisfied smile on his face.

Not even the Knights could have plotted a better gag.

Chapter Five

When I think of it, a whole lot of our goofier pranks as Knights were aimed more at ourselves than at innocent bystanders.

We had what we called the "B.F."—Buddy Fuck.

Sorry. There is no politer way to put it.

The best buddy-fucker of all time had to be Wallace.

And Las Vegas was the setting for two of his best B.F's.

In the first one, we're drivin' back from Vegas one night.

Wallace is at the wheel, goin' about a thousand miles an hour or so.

I'm sleepin' in the back and Dickie Schwartz is riding shotgun.

He shouldn't have been.

It turns out some of Nevada's finest notice our car and take exception to us going a thousand or so.

Wallace sees the red lights in his rear-view mirror when they are a speck on the horizon.

He has just enough time.

He pulls over to the shoulder.

Nudges Dickie.

Yawns.

"I'm...kinda...tired," Wallace goes, nonchalantly, stretching his arms up over his head, rubbing his neck.

"You drive for awhile, Dickie," he says.

I wake up in time to see Dickie slide over into the driver's seat and Wallace take Dickie's place.

Dickie Schwartz, still coming back from dreamland, is too groggy to see the troopers barreling down on him just as he pulls out onto the highway.

He drives about 29 feet.

The fuzz pull him over.

They hand Dickie the ticket.

Wallace sits there lookin' at the officers like:

These hot-rodders.

Whatta ya gonna do?

Wallace's second great Vegas B.F. came after I'd been holing up, as it were, all weekend with a girl named Mickey.

We're sleepin' up in our room when Wallace and someone else—I don't remember who—slipped in and stole Mickey away (with her complicity, I might add).

The boys spent a couple hours with Mickey and then drove off with her.

In my car.

I mean, hey, I didn't mind the Mickey part.

I'd had my fun.

I was always willing to share.

And Mickey obviously was going with the program.

But my car.

That really hurt.

I had to make it back to L.A. on my own.

But then I guess there's supposed to be a "gotcha," at least a little one. Otherwise it wouldn't be an official B.F.

Thanks guys.

Speaking of thank-yous, I can't get out of this chapter without a note of appreciation to a couple of women in my past for providing some of my crazier moments.

The first one is Sarah.

I'm in this apartment on Cadillac. I'm single. I'm seeing all these fine-looking young girls.

So I went after 'em.

Needless to say, they responded.

Arrogant, yes. True, also yes.

The best I met in the building was the girl in Apartment 311.

That was right upstairs from 211, which was my apartment number.

Now, the way these buildings were laid out, 311 was cleverly over 211 and that was over 111.

So the girl in 311 had a balcony and I had a balcony in 211.

Which, fortunately, would come into play later.

It turns out the girl in 311 was Miss Mississippi of 1962. She was probably one of the most beautiful women I have ever seen in my life.

She was about three steps better than Farah Fawcett. With a better body. Blonde hair, delicate thin face, blue eyes—just incredible-lookin'.

Her name was Sarah.

I find this out when I run into Sarah one day on the elevator. She looks at me and I look at her. I never thought anything else of it.

A couple of days later, there was a knock on my door.

There she was in a trenchcoat. She had a cup in her hand.

OK, so it sounds like some fiction out of spy thriller or a Playboy fantasy, but I can't help that.

There Sarah was standing in my doorway, and she says, "Ah beg yo-ah pahdon, suh, but could ah borra a cuppa sugah?"

And I said, "Well, shet ma mouf. You surely can."

She had that Southern accent and I just melted like butter.

So I walk into the kitchen. I take the cup out of her hand. I turn my back to her.

And—this is the God-honest truth—I reach up into the cabinet to get the sugar, I turn around to hand her the cup and there she is.

In her birthday suit.

Totally buck-naked with her trenchcoat open.

Chapter Five

She's got this big grin on her face.

It was no bigger than the one I got on mine.

I don't think I ever emptied that cup of sugar.

We just headed right for the bedroom and that was it.

Now, here's the deal.

The reason she has that apartment...this was a pretty nice apartment building...there was a guy named Billy Gray. He was an old guy who owned a big nightclub in Los Angeles. It was named Billy Gray's Bandbox.

It was a famous nightclub. Mickey Katz used to be there. Billy was Joel Gray, the actor's, dad.

And Sarah was Billy's mistress.

And he used to call her at, like, 1 o'clock in the morning to make sure she was home.

Enter the balcony.

What we did was, I got Sarah a 25-foot phone cord and dropped it over her balcony into my bedroom. So when the phone rang, Sarah would pick up the phone, and she'd go, "Hi, dahlin'. How ah ya?"

So we used to have that phone in my bedroom down below, pumpin' away. She tried to make it sound like she was sleeping and, meanwhile, we'd be goin' at it while he was on the phone.

She'd go, "Oh, dahlin', ahm jus havin' a terrible nightmare. Ah gotta go turn ovah and I'll talk to ya tomorra."

Bam. Hang up. Bang. We're back at it.

This went on for a few months and then Billy "The Kid" Byron moved in with me. And I liked to share things. So I shared Sarah with Billy a couple of times.

But Billy was smaller. Billy was very thin and Billy was about 5-7, 5-8. I was about 6-foot tall and about 180 pounds. Plus I had a hairy chest; Billy didn't have a hair on his bod.

So, actually, Sarah liked me, which was an upset, since Billy The Kid was one of the great ladies men of the western world, as I've mentioned before.

Not often did someone prefer me over The Kid.

But that was neither here nor there, anyway, because I liked the world in those days.

Which got me into some pretty deep trouble, I might add, with the second girl I was gonna tell you about.

That would be Marlene.

I had been dating this one girl—her name was Susan—off and on for about five years. So Susan and I break up and it was pretty much mutual, but, you know, you're still kinda torn up about that.

So the very first Saturday night after we were broken up, I was up on Sunset Strip.

First we went to the Whiskey. Then we went to Gazzari's.

Gazzari's was like, at the time, a very "in" dance club.

So I'm leaving and I'm in my Knights uniform...white tennis shoes with no socks, good-lookin' jeans, no shirt and a barracuda jacket zipped up about three-quarters of the way with the sleeves pushed up. And a gold chain around my neck.

I'm feelin' cool, even if I haven't scored so far that night.

Now I'm in my yellow Cadillac convertible, and it's about 3 o'clock in the morning. I'm over on La Cienega and Third Street, in front of this flower shop.

I look over in the left-hand lane and I see a girl that, oh...was about a 13 on a scale of 10.

She was just flat-out beautiful.

But, even better than that, she was smiling at me.

Needless to say, I smiled back at her.

And before the light had a chance to turn green, I just yelled out, "Hey, let's go get some coffee somewhere."

She cranks the smile up to about Mach 3 and says, "Sure, why not?"

So the coffee happens to be at my apartment and the next thing you know, we're makin' it for about three or four hours.

And then she stayed over and slept.

And the next day she stayed over.

And then the next day she stayed over.

And we were havin' a really great time.

And then, about...I don't know...about a day or two later, she says, "Why don't we get married?"

I was crazy. And I went, "Hey, why not?"

You know, real cavalier.

So before you know it—she's from this real nice family in West L.A.—I'm over at her parents' house and they start planning this big ol' wedding.

I don't mean a little wedding.

I mean a big -ol' wedding.

Which we held—let's see, I broke up with Susan on Thanksgiving...this was like the first week of December that Marlene and I met...we held the wedding on December 29th. At this temple over on Pico.

So it was that quick.

But, see, Marlene was a real beautiful broad. She was a gorgeous girl. I was 21. This was 1963. "Beaver" had just finished. And, like I said, she was just absolutely beautiful and she was a great lover and all that good stuff.

So I said, "Yes," crazy fool that I was. She was great in bed and I didn't want to lose her. I mean, what did I know? I'm 21 years old—you're not smart enough to figure those things out.

Chapter Five

I didn't dislike her.

She was nice.

And I knew that we had a good time.

So we got married.

And my old man was just the cutest guy at this wedding. I'm standin' there, I'm smilin'. Because Leonard is sitting down on the first row with all my buddies. And he's saying to all my friends, "Screw him. I'm the best-lookin' guy here."

I'll never forget that.

That was so funny.

I got a kick out of that.

I'm laughin' and all my friends are having a big old time. We had a great time at my wedding.

Then Marlene hopped in my car and we drove to Las Vegas for two nights.

Then we went up to Lake Tahoe for two nights.

Then we went to San Francisco for two nights.

And then back home.

The night that I get home, I'm sittin' there and I'm talkin' to Wallace on the phone. He says, "OK, you're back. Now whatta ya do?"

And I went, "Yeah. What do I do?"

All of a sudden it hit me and I went, "Am I crazy?"

The answer, without missing a beat: "Yeah. You're crazy. You're absolutely a lunatic."

So I walk into the other room and I say, "Marlene, we have to talk."

And I said, "You know what? We had a good time.

"But," I said, "I want out."

She said, "We just started."

So she goes ballistic on me.

I don't remember all the verbiage. It was 34 — years ago.

But the gist of it was, "I'm madly in love with you. How could you do this to me? Ta-da, ta-da, ta-da."

And she called me every name under the sun.

But, hey, I was every name under the sun, I guess.

That was fair.

But I also figured that getting out was the right thing to do.

Better then, than waiting another five years or 10 years.

I mean, maybe it would have worked out...I don't know. But I was still too young and I was just having too good a time chasin' everything in—or out of—a skirt.

So anyhow, my biggest mistake in this whole deal was when I left the keys to the Cadillac on the dining room table.

The Idiot Magnet

In the middle of the fight—we were in the bedroom fighting—she runs out of the bedroom, she grabs the keys to the Cadillac, she bails.

Now I'm sittin' there in the apartment and I'm sorta scratchin' my chin and I'm sayin', "What the hell's goin' on here?"

So I call Wallace. I say, "Hey, Wallace, I just told Marlene I want a divorce."

And he started laughing like Steve does.

He goes, "What, are you crazy?"

And I went, "No. For the first time I'm sane."

And he says, "Well, yeah, we all thought that, too."

Because, you know, my friends were always my best critics. That's what friends are for.

Sure.

I think Wallace said something poignant like, "Well, you're not going to be able to bang her anymore."

And I said, "I know. But I'm really worried about the car."

He goes, "You're kiddin'."

I said, "Yeah, she's got the Cadillac."

So Wallace comes over. And then I get a call from UCLA NeuroPsychiatric Center.

The cops had caught Marlene going 90 miles-an-hour down Sunset Strip, headin' toward the beach.

And they brought her in through UCLA Neuro Psychiatric in a strait-jacket.

She was hysterical.

And it wasn't too cold of me, was it, when I said, "Is the car OK?"

Because that's what I did say.

Cold? It was real cold.

Maybe I'd apologize to her all these years later if I saw her, because that was very vicious.

But when you're 21, I guess you're capable of doing things like that.

I would never do it now.

I would never do something one-one hundredth that mean or uncaring to someone now.

But the only thing I thought of in those days was me.

That's the true name of that story.

I don't have the slightest idea what happened to Marlene. I don't think I ever saw her again. We wound up getting an annulment. I think the annulment was something to the effect: we didn't love each other.

So that was grounds for annulment instead of divorce. But I don't know what happened to her. I really don't. Oftimes I wondered.

Chapter Five

As for her folks and the money they spent on a big wedding, yeah, that was really bad.

And I felt bad about that.

But I didn't ask for the big wedding. That was my rationale.

And I wasn't planning on doing what I did. I just came to my senses. The way I figure it, shit happens. And that was also before people said that shit happens—but, if no one else was aware of it at the time, Marlene and I definitely knew that shit happened.

(Although maybe Marlene more than me.)

That's the story of my Six-Day War with marriage.

It lasted about as long as it took Israel to take over the Sinai Peninsula and the Gaza Strip from the Arabs.

But it taught me one history lesson.

Sometimes the biggest idiot I met was me.

Chapter Six
Beetle Bilko Minderbender, PFC

love John Wayne.

We used to see him in the commisary at Universal, gliding through in that walkin'-tall, sidewinding gait of his, that leatherneck look in his eye, the battleships of Guadalcanal stuck in the jut of his jaw, the shores of Iwo Jima seemingly washed across his face.

He was an honest-to-God, GI Joe action-hero figure come to life.

He looked like he could kick every goose-stepping butt that got in his way.

He looked like he could fight World War III all by himself, with one hand tied behind his back, and have time left over in the afternoon for World War IV.

He was nice and kind to everyone on the lot—stars and extras alike—and just as larger-than-life impressive in the flesh as he appeared on the screen.

I was glad he was on our side if we had to take on the Commies or the Castros or whatever bad guys anyone threw at us.

You'd think The Duke would be my military hero.

Nope.

Not even close.

Sgt. Bilko was.

That's right, Sgt. Ernest T. Bilko.

I speak, of course, of the Sgt. Bilko of 1950s television fame. The wheelin'-dealin', conniving, flim-flamming master of artful dodging was Beetle Bailey with juice. Not only did he want to spend every day of military life ducking, rather than fulfilling, assigned tasks. He had just enough power to wriggle off the hook. If he could just devise the proper scam, concoct the correct mixture of hoodwink and hokum, he could not only get out of whatever it was he was supposed to do. He could look good getting out of it. Put one over on the Dudley Do-Right dufuses in charge of everything without the poor schnooks realizing they'd been put on. No...better than that, with them congratulating you for the con you just ran on them.

Pure, undiluted, 24-carat gold-bricking. That was the Bilko Code.

That was many a red-blooded American boy's dream of life the way it ought to be in This Man's Army.

At least it was the right color of red for this American boy.

Why choose The Ducker over The Duke?

Maybe it was just my personality, some let's-make-a-deal, beat-the-system genetic defect deep down inside me.

Maybe it was a sign of the times.

It was the early-'60s and the national philosophical axis had turned for kids growing up now. We were about flouting authority. Trashing institutions. Thumbing our noses at traditional values.

Irreverence was our daily bread.

It was pre-Kennedy Assassination. It was pre-drug era. It was still Happy Days. It was I-don't-give-a-rat's ass, who-cares. There was nothing nasty about it, really. Not yet, anyway. It was really cool. Wonderful.

In that spirit, I am proud to say that I spent my time in the service in what I deem the cushiest job in the history of the United States Army.

I am also extremely proud that I won my wussy job—and the only stripes I ever wore (however briefly)—in a crap game.

Let Bilko beat that, baby.

Let me take you back to the beginning.

It was 1960. I'd just graduated from Hamilton High, and my buddy, Al Levine, and I decided we were going to go into the Army Reserves.

We didn't want anything hanging over our heads about ever getting drafted. The draft was really big back then. We signed up immediately after high school, instead of starting college. I told Al, "Let's start college in the fall, instead of starting in February."

February? Uh-huh. We had graduations every six months back in those days in L.A. We had "A-12" and "B-12" in the 12th grade—two graduations a year. Mine and Al's happened to be in January. So we figured we would take this time and opportunity to get our little military bit out of the way. I wanted to start college after Labor Day, anyway.

Now, the next item was to carefully select the outfit we would go into. In tribute to Sgt. Bilko, our main objective was to have as good a time as possible and do as little as possible.

We found the perfect unit.

We joined the 311th Logistical Command in West Los Angeles, over on Barrington and Wilshire.

The first sweet thing that hit you dead in the face about the "311th Log," as it was called, was that we would be reporting for duty at Ford Ord, which just happened to be on the Monterrey Peninsula.

Sun-drenched days. Gorgeous beaches. Beautiful homes. Quaint village atmosphere. Babes.

That struck us as a proper vantage point from which to defend the country.

Secondly, the 311th Log was a quartermaster company. We found out in case there ever was an act of war that President Eisenhower would issue orders activating our unit to go over to the Beverly Hilton Hotel and type out quartermaster commands for the Pacific Theater of war.

That would have been our job should there be an outbreak of hostilities.

Typing.

We liked the idea of that.

Somehow, it just seemed better than going, say, to Korea and getting our keisters shot off, you know?

It had an even better ring since the California National Guard almost got wiped out in the Korean War.

Monterrey. The Hilton.

We liked the sound of that much better.

Upon joining up, we received our Military Occupational Speciality—what is called your MOS. It was 711-10. In common English, it's called clerk-typist. We were ready to go peck our pinkies to the bone for Old Glory.

We are off to Basic Training at Fort Ord.

Al and I reported to the welcome center where they proceeded to shave our heads, take our clothes and give us the usual ill-fitting outfit. They gave me brown boots, knowing I had to wear black boots. Then they handed me a can of black shoe polish. Some guys got black boots. I got brown boots and they said, "Color 'em."

Because I was dumb.

It was just my first day and I hadn't begun to achieve full Bilko-hood yet. They'd shaved our heads, taken our identity, dehumanized us — same as Elvis or anybody else. We were just numbers in a line in this particular place.

But right away, life seemed OK in the army.

I remember the guy that welcomed us was Sgt. Love.

"Ahhhm Sgt. Love and Ah run the indoctrination center here, and you-all are in the Yoo-nited States Awmy," he said in some Southern drawl out of Central Casting.

I looked at Al; Al looked at me. We cracked up.

I got my buddy there and, you know, I'm not scared. That night we heard guys crying in the barracks and we couldn't quite figure out why. There wasn't any war going on in February of 1960. Here we were on the Monterrey Peninsula at Ford Ord, OK?

What are you whining about?

So they separate us into all these different basic-training companies, and

Chapter Six

we start the daily grind. We're doing OK. I mean, I'm as out of shape as I can get at the time, but still all right. Nowadays, I may look like I couldn't win a footrace with Nell Carter, but back in those days I still looked like the jock I was. I had played high school football before signing up. At the start of basic, I was one of the guys in the back of the pack and they're going, "Hurry up, you guys back there," when we started marching.

But I started falling in line with the physical part of basic and by the end of it I was pretty trim.

I did get pneumonia three weeks into basic and had to spend a week in the hospital. I got what was called "re-cycled." Set back a week before I could finish basic.

All in all, though, the Army was quickly turning into a pretty milquetoast deal.

And by now, Al and I had begun to work our Bilko scams. Our first accomplishment was to alienate everyone in our entire company. There were about 300 guys in the company and every single one of them was pissed at us.

Not that I can blame them.

Every Friday night our whole company had what we called G.I. Parties. That's where the guys would get out the buffers and the waxers and all the cleansers and clean the latrines and clean the windows and get the floors shining like glass.

The sad thing for Al and me was that this whole thing occurred right after chow on Friday. It just so happens that the Jewish Sabbath also started on Friday right after chow. At formation after Friday dinner, the company commander, a captain, yells, "All Jewish personnel, please fall out."

There's me. And there's Al.

We fall out.

"Everyone else," the captain shouts, "get in and start those G.I. parties."

Regrettably, Al and I were unable to join our comrades-in-arms.

Instead, we were forced to go over to Friday night services, where we cleaned house in our own manner by chugging wine all night.

Turned out, the ranking clergy at Fort Ord was the Jewish rabbi, who was a full-bird colonel. And every Friday when we'd go over to the rabbi, he'd divest himself of pretty much the same speech: "All right, guys, don't take any crap. I know you're in basic. I know they're gonna give you crap. Just remember, you don't give them any crap on Sunday morning—you don't let 'em give you any crap on Friday night."

We took him at his word.

On Friday nights at the temple, they served challah, which is egg bread and glasses of Mogen-David wine. It's really only one cup they're supposed to give you. They say, "Blessed our lord, King of the universe, thank you for giving us the fruit of the vine," and they give you the wine.

Being in basic training, Al and I figured we needed even more blessing than normal. We'd sit around and drink three, four, five glasses of wine. The rabbi was benignly tolerant toward two of his people. Don't let 'em give you any crap. That was our cue to loll around and get half-schnockered. Then, about the time we figured the GI party was over, we'd stroll on back to the barracks.

The floors are standing tall. The bunks are all lined up. The mirrors are all gleaming. The toilet lids are standing at attention, just like Andy Griffith had them in "No Time for Sergeants." They are sparkling white.

And here come Bank and Levine back from services.

They wanted to kill us.

"Hope you guys had a good time," they'd taunt us.

"Hey, we smell alcohol on your breaths."

"Well," we told them, "we tried to hold it down to three glasses of wine each."

They were livid.

Our attitude: Hey, screw you.

That remained pretty much our prevailing attitude whenever we had a chance to dodge serious duty.

Did I tell you I drew barracks guard? On the surface, this may sound bad, but it actually was a wonderful stroke.

Everybody, when they get to basic training, they have to go out on what they call bivouac. What bivouac is, is being a Boy Scout for a week. You get a tent, a back-pack and a little shovel, and C-rations. Everybody goes out and lives in their little tents and eats their C-rations, and takes their shovel and they dig a hole. And they take a dump in the hole and they bury it and they get one ration of toilet paper for the week and that is bivouac. Pretty fascinating stuff, huh?

Everybody has to engage in this wonderful business of bivouac. With one exception. Somebody has to stay behind and guard the barracks. Just in case the Communists want to come in and take over our barracks at Fort Ord on the Monterrey Peninsula, someone has got to stop them from doing that.

It worked out—I honestly don't remember how; just the old Bank luck kicking in again, I think—they went through this big rigamarole and all I heard was, "Private Bank, fall out."

"Yessir."

"Private Bank, you will be barracks guard this week. You will watch this barracks and we expect it to be standing tall when we get back."

"Hmmmm. Yessir."

So I spent the entire week jacking around.

I was reading comic books.

Chapter Six

I was smoking cigarettes.

Yeah, I guess the worst thing about basic training, I did learn to smoke for the first time.

I mean, there's always that thing where they stop you when you're marching on some detail and go, "Smoke 'em if you got 'em." I never smoked 'em. Never had 'em. But somehow, you just seemed like you were missing out if you don't got 'em and don't smoke 'em in the military.

Otherwise, you're just standing there with your finger up your nose.

One day, some guy goes, "Hey, Bank, wanna butt?"

I go, "I got a butt."

Old joke.

He gives me a Pall Mall. I'm choking away on this thing. But the next day I had another one. Within a week, I went to the PX and bought a pack of cigarettes. By the time I left the Army I was smoking two packs a day.

Bivouac week, it might have been three or four.

God knows, it was tough keeping the Commies out of our barracks. A guy can jack around just so much. I needed something else to do while the guys were out there digging holes and dumping in them.

Me and my Pall Malls somehow made it through the week.

Finally, however, the fun of basic training ended. It was time to break up our beloved company. All these fine young Mormon men from Utah are signed up to become Airborne. They are all shipped to Fort Benning, Georgia. Then all these other fine young men signed up to be tank guys, and they sent them to Fort Knox, Kentucky. The rest of the clodbusters wound up to be spearchuckers. They were "111s" and "112s". That's the advanced infantry training. Nothing comes any worse than that.

Then there were two guys in the entire company of 300-and-some-odd who stayed right where they were at Fort Ord.

"Bank and Levine, fall out for BAAC school," the captain hollered.

BAAC stood for Basic Army Administration Course. It was at the top of the hill at Fort Ord. We had to move over two whole barracks for our next assignment in the United States Army.

No sooner did we get there, than we started giving Sgt. Bilko a run for his money in earnest. In fact, not even the Old Bilkmeister, himself, may have topped what happened next in my distinguished military career.

In the Army, it is important to note, you get paid once a month. Key factoid in my next little drama. I don't remember, really, whether it was the last day of the month or the first day of the month. But I was what was called an E-1. That's pond scum. That's the bottom of the scale. That is buck private. That is no-nothin', man.

I got 77 bucks a month.

Likewise, Mr. Levine got 77 bucks a month.

What ever would we do with it all?

We were about to find out.

Our very first night in BAAC school also happened to be payday. That night, these two young, enterprising Jewish boys, Bank and Levine, pooled their $77 and between them had $152. Doing the math are you? OK. The reason we had $152 was that we went to the PX and we got some of that 3.2 beer and two grilled cheese sandwiches each. So we each blew off a buck there.

Then we took the $152 and we decided to introduce ourselves to our new soldier-mates in the latrine with these two little white things with the black spots on them.

We cracked out the dice and we started a crap game.

Now, on that payday, there were half a dozen guys in our company called RAs. RA stood for Regular Army. Those are the morons that are either drafted for two years or the total nimrods that enlist for three years. Al and I were both what were called RFAs. RFAs are Reserve Forces Acts, otherwise known as "Six-Month Wonders."

We were extremely proud of that handle.

Extremely proud, because it did have a certain connotation of intelligence. Meaning we did not fall off the turnip truck, nor did we walk along scraping our knuckles on the ground as the other guys did that were RAs.

So here we are on payday. It's about four hours into the night — because the crap game started around 5-ish — and Al and I were up, I want to say, about 1,200 bucks.

See, some of these guys got what was called "re-up money." If you signed your name on the bottom line and you re-up, or re-enlist, for three years, you get like three months pay. If you re-up for six years, you get six months pay. We had, like I said, maybe six or eight guys in our little company that made that major patriotic move for their country.

They also liked to shoot dice and we cleaned their clocks.

About four hours after they had received their re-up money, a serious quantity of it had rearranged itself into the pockets of Mssrs. Bank and Levine.

Now, along about this time, about 9-ish, this man who was to become our new superior officer walks into our bunkhouse.

His name was Capt. Jenkins.

Capt. Jenkins comes into the latrine and says, "What's going on in here?"

And one of the guys says, "Just havin' a little crap game, sir."

"You know you boys aren't supposed to be gamblin'," the captain says.

"But," he says, "since it's goin' on..."

He reaches into his back pocket and drops 20 bucks down.

I immediately fade him.

I hand the brass the dice. And Capt. Jenkins proceeds to throw an ace-deuce.

Craps.

Capt. Jenkins then reaches into his pocket and says, "Well, I'll just try one more.'

About 25 minutes later, we have relieved Capt. Jenkins' wallet of his entire paycheck. Approximately $420.

During that period, we were hotter'n hell ourselves. Our bankroll had grown to over $2,000. All right?

Well, along about 11 o'clock, Capt. Jenkins asks for Bank and Levine to please fall out and meet him outside.

"Boys, you know I can't let you keep that money," Capt. Jenkins says to us.

"Captain, you know we won it fair and square," we retort.

He says, "Look, I'm a married man. I live here on the post and my wife is expecting me to bring home my paycheck."

"Captain," I said. "It wouldn't really be fair. You know you were holding the dice, and you lost the money to us."

"I'm aware of that," he says.

Then he looks directly at us and says, "Boys, here's what I propose to you. You will no longer be privates. You will be E-4. Corporals. You will also get a three-day pass every weekend for the entire amount of time you are at BAAC school."

The way the Army worked for us Six-Month Wonders was: two months of basic training, two months of your MOS training and then two months OJT (On-the-Job Training).

The captain added, "The final stroke...you give me the money back and I will make sure you each get a very choice assignment for your last two months."

To this, I mentioned the subject of my '57 Chevy, which I had brought to Fort Ord. They used to make the raw rookie recruits park their cars in this huge old lot like a cattle pen that was all gravel-pitted.

"Captain," I said, "I have this '57 Chevrolet that I really love, and is there a really good parking place somewhere near the barracks?"

Capt. Jenkins must have had some Bilko in him. He really admired the crust I had in asking that question, seeing as how I was standing there with his money in my hands. My car, indeed, would have a new home if we struck a deal, he promised.

"Well, Bank...?" he asked.

I handed him back $210 and Al handed him back $210.

"You boys go on up to the PX and buy some corporal stripes," he said.

And we did. But then we could afford them a little more than we could have just a few seconds before that.

Remember, an E-1 gets paid $77 a month? E-4 pay was about $180—more than double. I gave the guy back $210 and I got four more months to go in the Army. I wound up making money just off the promotion. Not to mention the three-day holidays and the pick at the end of BAAC school. Plus my car no longer had to eat dirt in the ratty parking lot.

Yes, military life was beginning to strike me as really cool.

Somehow, I felt, Milo Minderbender, the scheming quartermaster of Joseph Heller's classic, "Catch-22" would have been proud.

But that, actually, was just the beginning of my Minderbending days in uniform. By now some higher-ups had begun to recognize me as Frank Bank of Lumpy and "Beaver" fame. I also got passes to make movies for Beaver whenever Hollywood needed me.

Capt. Jenkins also had the pleasure of signing those temporary passes so that I could go perform my patriotic duty for Hollywood.

But even better than any getaways to make movies was the gig I wound up with back at Fort Ord. To pay off his craps debt, Capt. Jenkins had promised Al and I would get our choice of plush assignments. Well, I defy anyone to come up with a job to top the one I got. Capt. Jenkins more than kept his word.

That is how I wound up in the 17th Aviation Company—again stationed at Fort Ord.

Here is what comprised the 17th Aviation Company:

One Maj. Worthington Mahone, pilot.

One Sergeant-Major Milton J. Spritzer.

A typewriter.

An airplane.

A pool table.

One Corporal Frank T. Bank.

Tha-tha-tha-that's all folks.

Here is what the 17th Aviation did to heroically keep America the land of the free and the home of the brave.

Sixty miles down the coast from Fort Ord is Camp Roberts. Camp Roberts is usually a place for Army Reserves and National Guard units to do their two-week summer encampments.

Each morning at 4 o'clock, a small airplane at Fort Ord is loaded up with cartons of milk, butter and half-and-half. After it is loaded up by whatever donkeys are ordered to do so, Maj. Worthington Mahone boards this airplane, gets it up into the bright blue Pacific sky, makes the 10-minute trip over to Camp Roberts. Fresh donkeys take the milk and half-and-half and butter off the plane and over to the mess hall for the summer-camp guys. They wave bye-bye to Maj. Mahone, who flies back, lands the plane, goes home and goes to bed.

At the same time, the inventory of what Maj. Mahone has just delivered to Camp Roberts is handed to Sgt.-Maj. Spritzer, so he may log how much milk, butter and half-and-half has just been delivered, how much gasoline has been used and how much flying time has been used to accomplish this harrowing mission.

Because this is such a heavy task, Sgt. Spritzer lays it off on his Assistant Company Clerk, Corporal Bank, Esquire. (Did I say I had the cushiest job in the history of the U.S. Army? Now that I think of it, maybe one Sgt.-Maj. Spritzer may have topped it with the awesome duty of handing the piece of paper from Maj. Mahone to Cpl. Bank. But I still had to be a close second.)

I sit down at a typewriter, where I have been painstakingly trained.

I type: "Sixty miles, 22 cases of milk, 20 cases half-and-half, 16 pounds butter. Blah-blah gas."

I throw the report into the "out" box.

I whack my hands together.

Another job well done by your Armed Forces in action.

I spend the rest of the day sharpening up my pool game.

Or going down to the PX and hanging around there, which was, I want to say, almost a block away. Almost. Four barracks away. Outrageous that I had to walk. I should have really gotten a driver from the motor pool. I could have requisitioned one.

You'd think I would have become amazing at the game of pool, but I actually only got fairly good at it, despite all the time I put into it.

You'd also think I would have treated the post rabbi better than I did. But I didn't. One time after finishing my grueling milk-butter, etc., task and heading for the PX, I ran into the good rabbi.

The rabbi looks at me and goes, "Bank, you're a corporal."

"Yes, Rabbi," I said.

"Where are you now?" he said.

"I'm at the 17th Aviation Company."

"Bank, I'm a little disappointed in you," he said.

"What's this?" I asked, already well aware of the answer.

"I haven't seen you at Friday night services since you were in basic training," the rabbi said.

"Rabbi," I said. "I'm gonna make a note of that. I'm going to talk to Cpl. Levine about the same situation. I promise that we will make a very strong attempt to rectify it."

I walked away real sheepishly.

The rabbi was a really good guy.

What am I gonna tell him—I've had a three-day pass the last three months and on Friday nights I'm out in L.A. having a good old time?

Hey, man, I'm not up for there for that services stuff.

I'm down in L.A. My God, Thursday night at 5:01, I'm outta there like a rocket. Four hours to get back to L.A. I'm home by 9 o'clock to watch Alfred Hitchcock on Channel 4.

Not that I have exactly been slaving away all day on Friday anyway. It turns out, I am only required to perform my amazing milk-butter-etc. military feat four days a week. Because, I don't know if you were paying attention, but if you happened to catch the name of Sgt.-Maj. Milton J. Spritzer, you might be aware that "Spritzer" could be a German name. But it is very definitely a Jewish name.

Now, we have a situation where Sgt. Spritzer and his new young administrative assistant, Corporal Bank, who has performed his duties in such exemplary fashion, are both of the Jewish persuasion.

And because of the ethnic makeup of the Monterrey Peninsula back in 1960, there were no delicatessans on the peninsula. Sgt. Spritzer had a very specific yearning, because he came from the New York-New Jersey area, for kosher hot dogs and kosher salami, which were both extremely hard to come by in those days. Unless you happen to be passing Cantor's Deli on Fairfax in LA. We drove down, went in and spent a buck-and-a-half on the hot dogs and $2 on the salamis. Of which that wonderful Corporal Bank reached into his own pocket each and every week and took that three-and-a-half bucks out and got the sergeant-major his hot dogs and salamis. And every other weekend, I would also get him a really neat seeded rye bread, sliced, so he could make sandwiches.

Therefore, my job, instead of taking me 20 seconds, five days a week, took me 20 seconds, four days a week.

I was proud to serve.

On Aug. 5, 1960, Frank and his buddy, Al, jumped into his '57 Chevy and cruised down the winding Pacific Coast Highway to the dazzling sounds of Duane Eddy and the Cannonballs twanging, "Walk, Don't Run", out of Fort Ord and out of active duty in the United States Army.

But our Bilko-ing doesn't end there. It only gets better.

Al and I now have to start going to reserve meetings. I'm having a pretty good time at UCLA. These reserve meetings are sort of cutting in on my style. They're definitely cramping my Monday-night sex because we had to be at meetings from 7-to-10 and I could always schedule at least one girl in there. And then I don't want to be up too late that one Saturday night because one Sunday a month, we're supposed to show up at the reserve meeting out on Wilshire and Barrington, right near Brentwood, not too far from O.J.

Anyhow, in come Bank and Levine to the old 311th Log Command. Remember, this is the unit that will rush over to the Beverly Hilton and type out orders for the Pacific if marshal law is ever declared or some crisis like that. Well, this unit is so large we happened to have a two-star general and a one-star general. It's one of the biggest reserve units on the West Coast.

Gung-ho as they can be.

In this reserve unit was a certain dickhead sergeant, Gordon Duvall. Gordon Duvall used to be a linebacker for the USC football team, so you know going in he's a double-dickhead already, as far as a UCLA Bruin like myself is concerned. Dickhead Duvall has achieved some notoriety during the Frank Gifford days at USC. I think he was a total flop in the pros, but he tried.

In the meantime, he still got his jollies by being a sergeant and getting to yell at people. Probably wound up being a disgruntled postal employee the rest of his life. But during this period he was a sergeant.

Now, a couple of months into our reserve military life, Mssrs. Bank and Levine happened to notice that on one certain Sunday our two-star general was retiring. Mssrs. Bank and Levine really felt like that day should not be observed by going to the meeting. Rather, it would be appropriate to honor the old coot by going down to the end of the Santa Monica pier and doing a little fishing.

But before we headed down there, true Americans that we were, we put on our little uniforms and we went to our meeting on Wilshire and Barrington. They fed us lunch. After lunch, we're gonna have the general's retirement parade. Halfway into lunch, Mr. Bank and Mr. Levine decided that it was again time to have a little crap game in the latrine.

Sort of our own observance of a sacred event, the day we took Capt. Jenkins for all he was worth and earned our stripes.

We get this crap game going and again we are on a roll. This time, however, the door flies open, it's Dickhead Duvall. Old Sgt. Duvall comes in and we get arrested. That's right. That's it. The jig is up. We're busted.

Well, they really did it to me. They ruined my life. I guess that's why I turned out the way I did today.

They took my stripes.

I was friggin' heartbroken.

It really just flabbergasted me.

The crap game gaveth stripes and the crap game tooketh away.

But I somehow had to live with the shame.

Somehow, I found the strength to carry on.

Anyhow, I loved being in the 311th Log. If nothing else it provided one of the best lines I ever heard, anyplace, anytime, TV, the movies, nightclubs, you name it.

It came courtesy of a chap named Kip Kattan.

He was an actor. That's redundant, of course. Where can you swing a dead cat in Los Angeles and not hit an actor? Anyway, I'd seen him around Hollywood.

He was a nice guy. He was also almost as big a jerk-off as Al and I.

He had the same wonderful attitude toward the United States Army as we did—to become dedicated Beetle Baileys.

Well, one day the aforementioned Sgt. Dickhead Duvall was roasting everyone in formation. Everybody in our company was standing at parade-rest with our rifles at our sides like we're supposed to.

Everybody, with the exception of Pvt. Kattan.

Pvt. Kattan was standing at parade-rest looking forward when the ever-alert Dickhead Duvall walks up. He stands with his face in Pvt. Kattan's face and we all look around. We look down. Pvt. Kattan is standing there in the same position as the rest of us with the minor variance that he is pretending to hold a rifle, when, actually, he has no rifle.

Maybe it was method acting or something.

Anyhow, Sgt. Dickhead, who likes to get off by yelling at people sticks his mouth further into Pvt. Kattan's face and screams:

"Soldier, where is your gun?"

To which Pvt. Kattan immediately retorts, without skipping a beat:

"I left it on my horse, sir."

Well, about 300 guys hit the deck, laughing and rolling.

I mean, it was probably the funniest remark I'd ever heard in public.

We were laughing so long and so loud. The man caused total pandemonium.

It really was the greatest remark I ever heard in the United States Army. In civilian life, it's in the Top 10.

Think about it. "I left it on my horse, sir."

Nobody knew what the hell he actually did with the rifle. Probably left it in the toilet.

I later saw Kattan in a lot of commercials. He did a lot of comedy work.

The man proudly earned his comedic stripes that day.

Not that I had time for all this constant hilarity.

My attention was getting diverted by more serious military maneuvers.

By this time, there was this nice young man in the White House. His name was John F. Kennedy. John F. Kennedy, good Democrat that he was, decided it was time to cut back on all military expenditures. God love that man.

He didn't want to trim all these active-duty guys. So what's he gonna do—whip-crack-away, whip-crack-away, Chippewa, Chippewa, shut down, I believe, it was about 15 to 20 percent of all these U.S. Army Reserve units around the country.

It was going to save millions of dollars.

Chapter Six

Even more crucially, it was going to save Mr. Bank and Mr. Levine millions of boring hours at reserve meetings.

If we played our cards right.

By now, if you know anything about me, I tend to play my cards right.

Instantly, we knew that the 311th Log unit at Wilshire and Barrington would never go away. Can't break that up. It was one of the biggest units in Los Angeles.

But one great thing about being in the 311th Log. It only stood to reason that we would get a copy of the list of the units that were probably going to be deactivated long before it ever went public.

Now, if I remember right, the proposed group of shutdowns in the Southern California area arrived at our Barrington address and our first sergeant—I forget his name—had that list.

And if I remember right, Al and I had a $100 bill.

What we did was, we got ahold of this list and we proceeded to ascertain what were absolutely the most useless outfits you could find on this list. We came up with about a dozen candidates.

But about three of these units really stood out.

Whereas we had 300-400 reservists at our place, some of these units on the list had 20, 30 guys. I mean, nobody was gonna know that they were gone.

So we came up with this one unit. We were sure this had to be right at the top of the deactivation list.

It was the 25th Tank Command in Maywood, Calif.

Commanding officer was a captain.

This was a dogmeat unit.

So we go walking into our company commander's office of the 311th Log Command and I said, "Sir, we are going to transfer from UCLA to Compton Junior College. And it would be a hardship for us to come to meetings here in West Los Angeles. Is there anyplace out there in Compton we could attend meetings? Also, is there any possibility that there could be a unit that was a mechanized unit? We really had an interest in going to tank school and becoming full-time reservists."

Well, they had to research it. They said they'd get back to us.

We got a phone call a couple days later saying, as luck would have it, damned if there wasn't this unit in Maywood that specialized in tanks. There was plenty of room because it was a small unit. They'd be glad to give us specialized attention.

We ran, we didn't walk, over to Barrington to get our orders cut so we could rush to our very first meeting the following week in Maywood. Once you decide to be tank guys, you just can't wait to jump in those tanks.

Naturally, none of the geniuses we were dealing with asked us why we would be wanting to transfer from UCLA to Compton Junior College. I guess it was pretty obvious. Who'd want to spend all his time on a gorgeous campus in a beautiful little city crammed with unbelievable women like Westwood when you could go to school in an urban hellhole like Compton?

Obviously, there was more ethnic charisma out there than in Westwood. We had an intense desire to live in Watts.

I remember when we went in to request our transfer, I almost lost Al.

I hadn't told him how we were going to ask to be switched to this Compton unit—in fact, I didn't even know exactly what I'd say when we went in there.

So when I began this impassioned plea about wanting to quit a dump like UCLA so we could follow our dream of going to a really good school like Compton Junior College—and this Einsten company commander is actually buying it—well, Al damn near went south on me.

I see out of the corner of my eye he's getting red, then purple in the face.

I can see water forming in his eyes.

He's starting to shake.

Now he's standing there and he's beginning to make little animal noises.

We just made it out into the hall before Al starts howling. He's laughing so hard he has to hold onto the wall.

I can't believe the CO doesn't come out in the hall to find out whether we've flipped out or what.

I guess he figured we were just overcome with joy getting to further our academic pursuits at Compton.

Well, anyway, we're allowed to transfer.

We go to our first meeting at the 25th Tank Command and, of course, it was a total crock.

Guys are talking Greek. They're all into tanks, big time, and we don't know what the hell we're listening to. We grunted our way through the first week-night meeting.

But then, like two weeks later, there was a phone call right before the Sunday meeting. Make sure we all were there. Don't miss this meeting. This was a very important meeting. Mandatory attendance.

What happened at the meeting was that the commanding officer got up in front of all his troops and he gave the us bad news.

The United States Army was deactivating this unit.

Aww. Shuckie-durn.

We joined the rest of the men in lamentation. How could they do this to us?

The good old 25th Tank Command.

After all our years of faithful service as Greek-talking tank geeks, this is the thanks we get.

Chapter Six

A shutdown.

Goldurn it.

In our grief, we barely were able to absorb the rest of the news. Our commanding officer would make sure that if any of us wanted to get into another unit, he would do it. If not, he would just automatically put our name down in a control group. An inactive control group.

It was with a heavy heart and hangdog look that we approached our commanding officer and mentioned that we were, unfortunately, ill-trained for the other tank units where the other guys were going. Us just having arrived and all. Barely knowing which way you turn the turret and key stuff like that.

"Well, to be real honest with you boys, we feel you would be much better off in the control group. If the Army needs you, they could call you up," the officer in charge said.

"Well," we said, damn the luck. "We feel pretty bad about it. But can we please get a copy of this order. Like now?"

We were in a control group 60 days later. Then we petitioned to Washington for an honorary discharge from the United States Army. We'd already served our active-duty portion, we pointed out. And there was no reason why we should stay in the control group and waste all the taxpayers' money and all the paperwork.

We knew they were cutting back. As patriots, it was the least we could do to step aside.

Three weeks later, I received an honorary discharge from the United States Army.

Four months later, Vietnam broke out.

I got out at the end of '62. It was right before the Cuban Missile Crisis.

Once again, the Bank timing is better than Greenwich Mean.

Once again, I am the luckiest man alive.

But I can honestly say I miss the military days. My experience in the United States Army was second to none. I loved every minute of it.

And no one—not Beetle or Bilko or Milo Minderbender—I am proud, to say, can claim he was less of a soldier than I.

I'm sure The Duke would agree.

e were finishing a pilot for a new sitcom, "Life With Archie."

I was supposed to play the lead, Archie Andrews.

You know, the guy from the "Archie" comics.

This was after "Leave It to Beaver" had just finished its first run.

This was 1963.

"Archie" seemed like it might be a pretty cool thing to do.

I was 21.

I'd play the title role, instead of second banana.

I'd be a real star.

Keep the career on a nice, steady climb.

After six years and dozens and dozens of parts in show business, this was a chance to become more of a headliner.

Barbara Parkins from "Peyton Place" was going to be Veronica.

Would you play kissy-face with Barbara?

I know I would.

Cheryl Holdridge, the cute, sweet girl who used to play Mary Ellen Rogers on "Beaver," the one who was married to playboy race car driver Lance Reventlow, was going to be Betty.

I could see laying some serious Archiekins on her.

Jimmy Hawkins was supposed to be Jughead.

Paul Ford, the guy who played Col. Hall on "Bilko," was going to be Mr. Weatherbee.

Great cast.

Great people to work with.

All systems seemed go.

Then we shot the pilot. We were over at some screening room. We were talking about it.

The sponsor was going to be the American Tobacco Company.

And I heard a representative of the American Tobacco Company talking to a representative of the American Broadcasting Company.

They're talking about me on the screen.

And the tobacco guys says this:

"You know, that's not Archie Andrews.

"That's Lumpy Rutherford."

I did not say another word.

To anyone.

I turned on my heels. I walked out the door.

Next morning, I called my agent.

I said, "I'm going back to finish college now.

"I'm going to get on with my life.

"Good luck to you."

That's how I walked away from show business.

I could see that I was always going to be typecast.

I could see I was never going to truly be considered a leading man.

I could see that show business was going to be a never-ending process of trying to convince someone you were good-looking enough, or big enough, or small enough, or average enough or freakish enough or ordinary enough.

It was never about your basic ability as a professionial actor.

I could see that I was going to continue on a treadmill whose speed was always set on: "No. 2." Or "No. 3." Or "No. 4."

It was not going to be about my reaching No. 1.

I could see you were going to be able to pick up my resume years down the road and on page one would be "played Lumpy" and on page 2 would be "was Lumpy" and on page 213 would still be "the Lumpy guy."

As much as I loved the experience and thrill and honor of being a part of one of the greatest pieces of American entertainment ever— "Beaver"—I couldn't see playing Lumpy...and only Lumpy...the rest of my days.

I decided to go back to one of my first loves in life, something at which I felt I could be my true self and excel, something at which I could be No. 1.

The world of finance.

I decided I was going to seek fame and fortune as a wizard of economics. And I did.

I rose to the top of one of the most successful financial groups in Southern California, opened my own brokerage firm and became truly successful.

I did not become wealthy from the reel world of showbiz, but the real world of business.

Yep, me. Dumpy Lumpy, Dumb as an Ox.

I made it on my gray matter. My smarts. My brainpower. And my other qualities as a person.

I made it as Frank Bank, just-another-guy, not Frank Bank, the broken-down ex-actor.

I started from scratch and made a bundle.

I'm very proud of that.

As proud as anything I ever did in the entertainment industry.

But it wasn't without its fits and starts. And no one's beginnings could have been more humble than my own.

But I knew I would make it. I knew I would be successful.

Finance was right up my alley.

It was mathematics. It was people. It was personality. It was guts. It was about learning. It was about diligence and persistence and helping others while you were helping yourself.

Even when I was fairly young, the whole idea of finance fascinated me.

I'd be on the set, between takes, when I was 15, 16, 17 years old. A lot of actors were busy reading the Hollywood Reporter or Variety.

I was reading The Wall Street Journal.

I liked reading about the stock market. Keeping track of the market fascinated me.

I'd read the Journal because I thought it was cool to be able to know about, say, Univac. How Univac was going to change our lives.

I thought that was ultra-cool stuff to know.

So I went and enrolled that fall in UCLA

Back in that time, the most popular thing in college—at least until the hippie culture started to discredit them—was law or medicine.

All my friends—they had to be doctors or lawyers.

I almost fell into that trap. But as I saw my sophomore year at UCLA unfold, I realized I didn't want to be one of them. I mean, I loved the Knights. I wanted to become one of them and I did. I'll never forget them. A lot them became attorneys and doctors and are outstanding people.

But as far as the people I was seeing in my classes at UCLA, who were headed for law school or medical school, I didn't want to go out with these guys socially.

I thought they were a bunch of self-centered jerks.

Why would I want to become one of them?

So I set about to get my degree in business.

I never made it.

Fate had other things in store for me.

Fate and one Leonard Bank.

It turns out that Dad, God bless him, had been working too hard in the meat business.

He suffered a heart attack my junior year.

I don't know how much you know about guilt, or Jewish guilt for that matter.

Chapter Seven

But Jewish guilt is exponential guilt—guilt to the two millionth power. It is guilt through the ozone layer and the stratosphere, straight into outer space.

Jewish guilt is where the Mars probe is out there looking at red rocks and red dust.

You can clearly see Jewish guilt orbiting the universe from the Hubble telescope.

And so there was no question what was going to happen once Leonard-the-Sport had his heart attack.

My mom called me up and said six words:

"Your dad had a heart attack."

She didn't need to say anything else.

There was no other discussion or discourse required. No family summit about what would happen next or what my plans might be.

We all knew Dad suffering a heart attack meant one thing for his youngest son.

Frank Bank. Meet the meat business.

It was kind of sad, strictly from a selfish point of view. I was having the time of my life in college. I was on the Dean's list. I mean, actually...college was pretty easy.

I had 89 1/2 units at UCLA. I had put in three years.

That was all I was to get.

I left my beloved life as a Baby Bruin and was delivering baby-backs before you knew it.

And it went well, if I do say so myself.

I enjoyed the meat business, to tell the truth.

We were boppin' along, building it up pretty good, my brother, Doug, and Sylvia and I, while my dad was recovering.

Throughout the rest of the '60s, from '64 on, I was in the family business. And the meat business actually could have been really fantastic.

We could have made more money than you could shake a steak at.

Except for one thing.

My idiot brother botched it all up.

I had a big fracas with my brother over the direction we were taking.

I could have had all the hotdogs and hamburgers at the L.A. Coliseum for an account.

I could have had the Weight Watchers frozen dinners for an account.

But my brother and my dad wouldn't go out and modernize our business and borrow money to expand it.

They said, "We don't want to do that. We don't want to screw up a good thing."

That's how my brother and I got to tearing up this restaurant.

Remember, my brother was a dreamer.

Well, we had leased a truck and one day, like a fool, Doug went out like three months before the lease was up and bought four brand-new tires for this truck

So now it's coming time to take the truck back. I go over to a gas station, I find four old used tires and pay the station 20 bucks to put the cruddy tires on so we can keep these four really good tires.

My brother blows his stack.

He says, "Why did you undermine me?"

I said, "I'm not an idiot."

I said, "I'm not givin' those tires away."

They were like 400 bucks.

But he felt I was usurping his authority.

Of course, I was.

But of course, he was drinking, too, and wasn't thinking straight.

So we were in this little coffee shop where we used to have breakfast every morning. It was right next to our meat place.

It was The Bluebird Cafe on Santa Monica Boulevard.

Now we're sittin' there eatin' breakfast, and we're both wearing our cooler coats. He grabs me by the shoulder.

He says, "You son-of-a-bitch, you took those tires off the truck."

And I said, "Of course I took those tires off the truck."

And I can see him winding up to hit me.

So I sorta grabbed him by the neck and wrestled him down to the ground.

And he started swinging on me.

And I started swinging on him.

Next thing you know, it's something right out of a John Wayne movie and we tore apart about four or five tables. There were chairs all over the place.

And he didn't exactly make it into work that following Monday.

His back was just killin' him.

But both of us were pretty beaten up.

We basically beat the crap out of each other.

So that was a hairy fight. We had to pay poor Herman and Betty, the couple that owned the restaurant, to fix it up. It cost a few hundred bucks.

Just about the price of the new tires? Yeah, I guess it seems pretty stupid when you think of it that way. I could have just let the tire thing go and we'd have been money ahead.

Or about even, when you consider Herman's repair bill.

But it was a fight over more than a few hundred bucks.

It was about a basic business philosophy. More importantly it was about fundamental approaches to life.

My dad was teed off at me.

Chapter Seven

He said, "Why are you doing that to your brother?"

I said, "That bum did it to me."

Why didn't my dad take my part in the fight?

Well, he usually did take my side more than my brother's side. He really did. But once in awhile, in the interest of fairness and justice, he'd take Doug's part. He'd try to be balanced.

Which was hard to do, considering my brother was a totally screwed-up human being in my estimation.

Herman was not real happy with us that day, either. But after it was over, he and Betty were fine.

Matter of fact, Herman came over to me a couple days later and he says, "Geez, Frank, when you got him in that hammer-lock, I thought you were gonna break his arm."

And I went, "Did I have him in a hammerlock?"

I didn't even know.

I said, "I was just tryin' to think as fast as I could."

He says, "You guys were really good."

This was after we paid for the damage.

I mean, there was no doubt we were gonna pay for it. We apologized to everybody. God, there was one couple in there, we sorta scared both of them.

But, to be honest, I wanted to hurt Doug.

I really wanted his butt.

I wanted to seriously rearrange his landscape.

He deserved it.

Inside me was a lifetime of frustration over Doug being a dysfunctional butthead, never taking responsibility for anything, then palming it off on someone else.

This was more or less the straw that broke the camel's hump.

It was time for me to hit the road.

We had passed up two huge opportunities to make the meat business really take off and realize its full potential.

I guess it was just too daunting for everyone else to contemplate.

We'd have had to push out and build a place next door. Put in a bunch of hamburger-patty machines and expand our cooler.

Probably had to borrow maybe 50 grand.

Back in those days, my dad thought that 50 grand was 50 million.

And to get the Weight Watchers would have probably cost us $200,000 to borrow.

Because we'd have had to put in all these machines to make Weight Watchers dinners.

Would have cost a lot of money, without a doubt.

But we could have made millions and millions and millions.

Bux-Up Bank

I saw Weight Watchers comin' all the way.

It was a no-brainer.

I knew Weight Watchers would take off.

My dad thought it was a flash in the pan.

He thought that as soon as we built all this stuff, they were gonna walk away from it and give the account to somebody else.

He was wrong.

We would have kept Weight Watchers as long as we wanted. How? Simple.

I would have 'em sign a contract. It wasn't really rocket science stuff. But, basic as that sounds, my dad wasn't from that kind of thinking.

Besides, I knew the lady that founded Weight Watchers very well. Her name was Jean Naiditch.

She was a meat customer of ours in Brentwood. We had a lot of very famous customers and Jean was one of them. We delivered meat to her house every week.

Weight Watchers hadn't been going more than a couple of years when she approached us about preparing their meals.

Nice lady. Real nice lady.

I believed in her concept.

She believed in us.

But when my dad wouldn't let us take on this contract, that was it for me in the meat business. That and the fighting with my brother.

I just felt like it was time to take off on my own.

So I did.

I had been a finance major. I'd heard some friends, including Dennis Angel, a fellow Knight, were making a great living selling municipal bonds.

They worked for a company called MuniciCorp.

I went in and talked to them one day and I said, "Well, this is where I should be."

And they said, "You got a deal."

They hired me.

I didn't really know what a municipal bond was. So I went and found out, I studied and I took a chance.

I was married to my first wife at this time (after the annulment from Marlene, of course). We had a baby girl, Julie.

My parents helped me a little bit the first six months. Not much. But a little bit. As much as they could have. Which obviously, was very nice of them.

I said I started from scratch.

What's the level below scratch?

I started off with no salalry, no draw, no nothing.

It cost me 30 bucks a month to work there because I had to pay to park my car in Century City.

Chapter Seven

The office was at 1888 Century Park East.

I was 30 and starting over.

I already had a big house in Tarzana to support.

It took me six months before I started making a living. In the first year, I did OK. The second year I did great. The third year I was a monster.

The first year I made about 50 grand. The second about a hundred. The third about 250, or 300 thousand.

By now I'm a vice-president. Then I became a branch manager. I opened up an office in Rancho Mirage, suburb of Palm Springs, California. And then I became a member of the board of directors.

In the Rancho Mirage branch I had about a dozen people under me. But in 1984 I became the general sales manager, responsible for 250 brokers.

I was back in Century City for this stretch, running sales for the whole company.

I was on the board and the executive committee of the company.

How much am I making now?

A lot.

And I had other things going, too. Real estate investing. Investing in stocks. Investing in bonds. Investing in partnerships.

I was in a bunch of limited partnerships on multi-family housing properties. I had some in Oklahoma. Some in California.

I had some of the craziest investments you ever saw in your life. I bought these oil wells once and we hit oil in Texas, up in the Panhandle.

The day we hit the oil, I went over to King's Western Wear on Van Nuys Boulevard and bought this big, huge old honkin' 10-gallon Stetson. Like J.R. Ewing?

OK. So it was a cliche. But I just felt like it anyway. Hell-fire, man, I was gonna be an oil baron.

And the very next day I get a phone call from the guy at the drilling site. And he says, "We got a lotta water comin' into the well."

He says, "It's gonna cost us more money to bring up the oil than it will to cap it off."

I think he left me swinging for two days before I found out what was happening.

So he capped it off. My J.R. Ewing persona went right into the trash basket.

But it was a good write-off.

What can I say?

The oil well did not exactly pan out. And the J.R. hat drew a little dust. But you gotta try.

And overall I was doing quite well at the financial game.

And that is because of one major reason.

I loved it.

Bux-Up Bank

I loved making people money.

Nothing made me feel better than to call a client and say, "Hey, these bonds that we bought for this price are now worth 'this,' and your income is more."

I really made my reputation in 1974 when I put all of my clients in New York City bonds right at the bottom of the market.

My clients made a fortune.

It worked because I had faith in the American way of doing business.

I knew that they couldn't take New York City and let it default and go broke. There were too many people there.

There was no doubt in my mind. When President Ford said, "I will not bail out New York City," he was lyin' through his teeth.

There was the famous headline in the New York Daily News:

FORD TO CITY:

DROP DEAD!

I knew right then and there when he said that, he had to bail 'em out.

You know why he had to? Because if you take 16 million people and let 'em apply for unemployment all at the same time, it'll cost them more money by that than it would to bail out New York City.

Everyone was making fun of New York and scorning it.

And I was selling bonds like crazy.

Johnny Carson was on "The Tonight Show" talking about how "Bombastic" Bushkin, as he called him—his business manager—was buying him New York City bonds.

And I wanted to scream through the tube, "Bombastic Bushkin did the right thing!"

Carson would be talking about his guy making a stupid deal for him.

And I'd be watchin' TV goin' nuts: "Shut up, man, you're shootin' me in the freakin' foot."

My clients were nervous about the whole thing with New York City. They were buying because they had faith that I knew what I was doing.

And, as it turned out, I did.

Johnny Carson was making jokes. New York City was great joke fodder, as always.

But my clients and I had the last laugh.

And you know what? It turns out this is normally the case in these situations.

My New York experience gave rise to one of my fundamental business precepts.

You've heard of the Laffer Curve, which has to do with tax rates, government revenues and production?

We'll call this other thing the Laughter Curve.

The Frank Bank Laughter Curve.

I have since learned as I got older that whoever the comedians are using

Chapter Seven

for the butt of their jokes is usually the greatest investment in the world.

Another example would be Orange County. When it went belly-up in the early '90s and everybody and his brother was riding the place unmercifully for being bankrupt...what a great opportunity.

My insights proved true on Orange County, too. In fact my fame and my knowledge as a business advisor and a stock advisor grew.

I mean, I had a radio show on the local CNN radio affiliate for three years in Kansas City—called "Frank Bank on Finance"—and it was a joke how badly my predictions beat everyone else's. It was unbelievable. I was giving out stocks that tripled and quadrupled and hardly ever had a loser.

And now that you've got me here to advise you, here is a prediction you can take to the Bank. The Frank Bank Bank, if you will.

The stock market will go to 16,000 to 18,000 in the next 10 years.

We will have five billion new customers from around the world.

These figures may seem preposterous.

But they are what is going to happen.

At minimum.

My reasoning is simple.

I believe in America.

Five billion new customers? They will be all the former Communists, all the former Third World countries. They all want to become like America.

And we've got the products to sell and the technology to do it.

My business theories worked well enough from '73 to '89 that my family and I were living in style.

We had almost a full acre in Tarzana, a house over 5,000 square feet. Electric gates. Stables in the backyard that I tore out to put in a park.

It was a beautiful house.

Robert Wagner used to live across the street. Lee J. Cobb lived around the corner, but then he died.

But eventually, much like showbiz, I saw that I couldn't go any higher in MuniciCorp. I was the general sales manager. I was offered stock options to become a partner, and I didn't exercise the options.

Instead, I quit.

We had certain philosophical differences.

Equally important, I wanted to open my own firm.

So I opened F.T. Bank & Associates in Rancho Mirage.

"F.T.?"

Uh-huh.

I just decided to add an initial to my name.

My full name is actually Frank Bank. The name on my driver's license, the name on my diplomas, the name I use for the National Association of Security Dealers...everything...the name on my marriage certificate is Frank T. Bank.

See, I was one of those equal-rights kids. And I remember when I was 5 years old that I made a rather traumatic trip to Minnesota for my grandfather Tom's funeral.

I knew that Frank Bank, the man I was named after, had died about the time I was born.

But I said, "Wait a minute. I'm named after my dad's father, but what's wrong with my mother's father? He got a raw deal."

So I said, "I'm gonna be named after both my grandfathers."

So I legally added "Tom," after the guy who accidentally shot Frank James—remember that gunfight back in Northfield, Minnesota?

Well, that made me Frank Tom Bank.

But more than anything, I use the initial "T."

One day I remember starting arbitrarily to sign my school papers, "Frank T. Bank." And my mom asked what this was about.

I told her.

When my dad came home from work that night, my mother says, "Len, d'you know that Frankie took a middle name?"

And my dad was really excited, you know?

Like, "Who gives a damn?"

Who's pitching tonight for the Hollywood Stars, he's wanting to know. That's the important thing.

And he goes, "Oh yeah?"

And my mom goes, "Yeah, Frankie took my Papa's name for his middle name."

My father just sort of smiled and laughed.

I said, "Yeah, Dad. I'm Frank Tom Bank."

And Dad goes, "Good boy."

I remember that. He was happy for me, too.

So anyway, it had some extra meaning for me somehow when I opened my own securities firm, that's why I decided to make it—F.T. Bank & Associates.

Making the business flourish was no problem, actually.

I had developed a distinguished list of clients by then. I took them all with me.

Famous clients?

Over the years, I've had clients such as Kirk Douglas, Jane Fonda, Aaron Spelling, Juliet Prowse, David Brenner, Norm Crosby, Red Buttons.

Mr. Irving Paul Lazar, impresario extraordinaire. You may know him as "Swify" Lazar.

He was a client.

Bud Yorkin, the guy that did "Sanford and Son" and "All in the Family" and pretty near everything with Norman Lear—Bud was a client.

Chapter Seven

Pat Boone.

The girl from "Rhoda," Valerie Harper was a client.

Dom DeLuise is a client.

Lloyd Bridges is a client.

These were my personal accounts.

A lot of very famous industrialists were clients, as well.

For one, the May family from the May Co. department stores.

I had a very special spot in my heart for Anita May. For many years, I treated her as a sister. She was my prodigy, if you will, and I taught her everything I could about my business. My ex-wife was her kids' godmother.

We were very, very close.

The industrial giants were my biggest clients. I loved dealing with very big people.

Because I can talk to them.

And they know they can trust me.

Doctors and lawyers usually drive me crazy (maybe it goes back to the classroom of my UCLA days). I don't know why, really.

The doctors and lawyers—I'm not saying they're bad, but I've always preferred doing business with industrialists. They have more business savvy.

Here's why:

Because of their proclivity to understand the risk that they are taking in their investments.

I think that's a pretty good sentence, don't you?

I think the word "proclivity" is a particularly strong part of that sentence.

Makes me sound rather erudite, no?

Anyhow, what happened was, F.T. Bank & Associates was a huge success.

Larry Gordon was a client. He was a huge, huge producer.

Oh, geez, Ray Stark, I almost forgot about that one. Ray Stark, "Goodbye Girl," he's got—what?—about six, eight Oscars?

He was a client.

Of course, I had virtually all the Beaverites.

Jerry and Kenny and Barbara are all very active clients to this day.

But virtually all of my clients have been very successful because of me. I have been good for them.

And I love it. There is nothing more thrilling than, after you've recommended something, to call up and say, "Well, you made about 40 grand today. Were you too busy to understand that?"

Or something like that and they love it.

They sit there and they go, "Really?"

And you go, "Yep."

And it makes you feel wonderful.

You don't ever, ever want to sell a client on something where they're going to lose money so you can make a commission. Because it's just as easy to make a commission on good merchandise as bad merchandise.

Sometimes you do try and find bonds maybe that are in trouble that'll give a client a higher yield. You love that. That makes you feel very, very good.

Oh, Jaclyn Smith was a client for a long time. One of the "Angels."

I keep bringing these people up as they pop into my mind.

As I'm talking about how wonderful the business is to me, the question might arise:

Do I like making people money for the ego stroke of being able to say I was right...or simply for the joy that accrued to the other people?

I think it comes back to the responsibility that my parents ingrained in me. How you have to try to be a good guy. You have to try and help people.

You have no idea the feeling, when somebody comes up to you and says, "Here. Here's my life savings. Try and invest it as good as you can."

That's an incredible responsibility.

It doesn't matter how much a client has to invest. It's the same principle whether he or she has $5,000 or $5 million.

You don't ever want to mess it up.

You want to try and do your best.

God knows, I'm not 100 percent. I mean, Babe Ruth struck out 1,330 times.

But he also had a lot of mighty clouts. I have, too.

When a guy walks into your office and says, "Listen. I'm 65 years old. I've worked hard all my life. Here's how much money I have. Let's start doing some investing"...well, it's the greatest feeling in the world when you can tell that guy, "Look, we made 25 percent this year. We made 35 percent this year."

It's like a sacred, solemn oath.

You owe the general public the fact that you've got to do the best that you possibly can. If you don't do the best, you can't even live with yourself.

Because that's not fair.

You've gotta be fair.

I can't tell you how many times I've given trades away because maybe something didn't work out exactly right. So I didn't have the heart to charge people commissions just because the law says that I can.

I've got to do things that are right.

Otherwise I might not make it up to the Big Game in the Sky.

That's one game we all want to make it to.

You don't want to make that your 1,331st strikeout. You want to hit a home run on that one.

And, see, by doing the best, that's when you get referrals. That's the

Chapter Seven

whole thing about my business.

The saddest part of my business is all the friends that I've lost because they've died. It's heartbreaking.

There was this man who I loved. His name was Melvin Berman.

I thought of him as my second father. He taught me so much. So much about life.

Melvin was a very, very wealthy man. Very wealthy.

He made a lot of money in the dairy business. And then he made a lot of money in real estate syndication—shopping centers and things like that. He was the chairman emeritus of the Rouse Corportation. He was the chairman of the board of Federal National Realty.

Here's a good example of who Melvin was—you've heard of the South Street Seaport in New York?

One day, Melvin walks into my office. I didn't even know who he was. This was in the desert office in Rancho Mirage. And he'd bought, like a million dollars worth of bonds from me.

Well, while I was at it, I had just gotten a syndication on the South Street Seaport in New York.

And I said, "By the way, Mr. Berman, this looks like it might be a very, very good buy."

And I said, "How would you like to own the South Street Seaport?"

And he says, "Not very much."

And I said, "What are you talking about? This is a terrific project."

He says, "Well, if I thought it was that good, I wouldn't have sold it in the first place."

I said, "What?"

He says, "Yeah, I sold it to those guys."

In other words, to J & B Carlysle, who's a big real estate syndicator.

But I guess that wasn't all that impressive to Melvin since Melvin used to own the entire thing all by himself.

But see, the thing I admired most about this man, he was generous and he was brilliant. But he could drive people crazy.

Details. He was always worrying about details, and it drove people nuts.

But you know what? He was always right. The other people were always wrong. And it's scary how that worked out. There were people that could not talk to Melvin because he would say things that sounded like they were so far off base that it was ridiculous.

But, son-of-a-gun, the guy was right every single time.

Melvin taught me so much about people. He taught me that I have to be generous. He taught me how to share my love and my wealth with everybody else.

Because that's one of the reasons we're here.

He taught me how to be wise. He had a wonderful family. And his family really, really adored him.

When I first met Melvin in 1984, I had been a big success in the business. When I met Melvin I was absolutely one of the experts on tax-free bonds, not only in California, but maybe in the whole country.

I thought I knew everything. I thought I was a hot item.

But he taught me, and he didn't know what a tax-free bond was. It was just due to life and how things were constructed and what was going on. Melvin used to come into my office almost every day. And we used to sit there and talk. And salesmen used to come in and try to sell us stuff, and he had a ball.

And it was like a father and a son. It really was.

When he first walked into my office, he said his account was at Merrill Lynch. He was frustrated, he said. He said he'd heard about me.

He says, "Maybe you can help me."

I said, "I'll do my best."

At first, it was a greed thing because he was a very big client. But the greed didn't last long. It didn't last maybe more than a month.

All of a sudden I started falling for this guy.

When he died, it just crushed me.

See, one of the worst things that can happen to you in my business is— these people get under your skin. You get crazy about them.

I mean last year I lost David Loew from the Loews Corporation. I'd known him for 25 years. He passed away.

I had so many big clients who've passed away. Really, really good guys. And they mean a lot to you.

But no one ever meant as much to me as Melvin. Melvin was at the top of the list.

One of the things Melvin taught me more than anything else—is if something negative happens with an investment, don't wait to get out. Do it quickly. The first loss is your best loss. If something doesn't look right, get out of it right away. Don't sit and try to make something right that couldn't ever be right. There's always other fish in the ocean.

He also taught me: Deal with people who get right back to you immediately. If they don't call you back right away, you don't need to deal with them. All little things like that.

Any success I've had in business life comes from a few things.

One, I think my expertise in reading people comes from playing poker. Sounds silly, I guess, but I know it's true, and I'll explain more about that later.

Two, is a knowledge base that comes from reading the encyclopedia—I guess it was good to be a geek at one time in my life.

Chapter Seven

Three, being able to look at a good stock from a bad stock, which helps me to be honest with my clients.

Just like Melvin and my Dad preached to me.

I used to always laugh and say, "Well, my role models were Albert Einstein and Sandy Koufax."

Because those are my two biggest heroes.

But when you look at it they actually took a backseat to my dad and Melvin.

Melvin, like my dad, was a real good Jew.

And that means something to another Jew.

I mean, it's like when you're a Catholic and you meet someone who's a really good, devout Catholic, you look up to them.

Melvin was like that, a man of his beliefs.

So were a lot of my clients, which is why I loved them. I got to know some of my celebrity clients fairly well, too. Some better than others.

You know what? Kirk Douglas was one of them. He is a lot like Melvin. He doesn't hide anything. Kirk is a wonderful guy. I love Kirk.

He is what we Jews call "haimish."

It means he's a regular person.

He's thrilled about what happened in his life. Proud of who he is, but humble.

Kirk is a great guy.

I knew Kirk well enough because I was with Kirk on many, many occasions. We spent time down in the desert together, time in Beverly Hills together with his family and his wife, Ann.

His son, Peter, and I were very, very close friends. We used to go out together all the time. As a joke for his birthday, I bought him a beret, a riding crop and a whip, because I used to call him "C.B." for Cecil B. DeMille.

Peter went on to do some movies. Peter's a good guy.

Kirk's other son, Michael, was older and I think he'd already done "Cuckoo's Nest." I didn't really get to know him.

When Kirk and I first got together, it was around 1976. And that came through my relationship with Anita May.

You know, when I first met the Douglases, I could have walked in and giggled and laughed and said, "Omigod, it's Kirk Douglas." Because he's a Hollywood legend. But I couldn't do that, because, you know why? I was looking at a really nice man. And you can't do that to a really nice man.

The value and the wonderful things that he had given me my whole life of going and seeing his movies, I could repay, not by gushing, but by trying to do the best job I could for him.

And I understood what it was like to be in my celebrity clients' profession, which often helped.

I was one of them, in a way. Certainly nothing like the stature of a Kirk

Douglas, but having been generally in the same industry, I had a sense of "been there."

They knew I would treat 'em right. They knew they meant something to me.

All my clients meant so much to me.

Lloyd Bridges was a wonderful family man.

Bud Yorkin is a genius.

Same thing with Aaron Spelling.

They were clients and I admired them both a lot, just on the basis of intellect.

But there's also a warmness.

A lot of my clients are very warm people.

I will have to say, though, that I never quite understood Jane Fonda. And it had nothing to do with her politics.

I just couldn't quite understand some of the business moves she made. For instance, she would never buy bonds from places where there was a nuclear facility nearby.

But it wasn't the city's fault that there was a nuclear facility nearby. They were really good cities, and it didn't make sense to me.

I mean, my God, there are serial murderers living in Los Angeles, but I would buy Los Angeles bonds. Things like that.

On the other side of the coin, I'd have to say Jane carried her principles very highly. I think that's a good thing. I think she might have carried it to an extreme at the time, though.

But that's not a negative to say about Jane.

I only met her maybe a half a dozen times. She's a very serious person.

But she's a nice lady. She was always a lady. Always.

And I think she's a dynamite person. I like people who stand up for what they believe, whether I agree with them or not. And there's no doubt she believed them.

That old Hanoi Jane stuff? Baloney.

People thought that she wasn't a good American?

That was a crock.

She was as good an American as any guy who's waving a flag. Believe me, she is.

She just didn't agree with what was going on with the war. You couldn't really help it. I mean, who the hell really wants to drop a bomb on all these people?

Other than a bunch of bloodthirsty ghouls.

I'm not one of those guys.

I guess I'm a different kind of an animal.

I'm a Republican, and fiscally I'm very conservative.

Socially, I'm kind of a liberal.

Chapter Seven

I've got a lot of warmth and I've got a lot of feeling toward my fellow human beings.

I guess in doing all this name-dropping, it sounds like I'm just a suck-up to celebrities and that's all I care about.

Juice. Starpower. Box office muscle.

"I know (Fill in the Blank) and blah-blah-blah and yadda-yadda" and all this stuff about what good people they are is brown-nosing B.S.

Not true.

If you've gotten to know me at all by now, you know I pull no punches about what I think of people.

And your name or face aren't what dazzle me. It's what's inside that counts.

I had a lot of other clients who weren't major stars, but they're really good people. Boy, their money counts every bit as much as anyone else's.

I had one of the Jackson Five. I didn't have Michael. I had Sigmund. You don't even know who he is, but he's one of the Jacksons.

Sigmund Jackson had a lot of this rock 'n' roll money.

Besides, I never really set out to create a Celebrity Clientele Collection, and mount them like a bunch of butterflies on my wall.

The clientele just happened. Red Buttons chanced to be the first one. I ran into his agent in Century City one day. Things worked out pretty decently for Red, and things just sorta snowballed.

I didn't go out and say, "I only want to deal with famous people."

But it made me happy to know that a Jack Benny would be buying his bonds from Frank Bank.

Don Rickles.

Steve Allen.

They both did.

Oh, did Don Rickles ever "hockey-puck" me—lay one of his famous insults on me?

Uh-uh. Rickles was a nice man on the phone. Very. Nothing like he is in the industry. Real nice guy.

Ever since the first celebrity clients came my way, I think the thing I've tried to impart upon them is that I know that they are targets.

And they would never be a target with me.

I would have their best interests at heart.

Just as I would whether you were an actor or a mechanic.

I know that I have tried the very best that I can for them.

And that is why I believe I made a name for myself in business that rivaled any I ever had in the entertainment world.

Not bad for a lummox you only knew as Lumpy, eh?

Chapter Eight

The Name is Bank... Frank Bank

t was New Year's Eve, 1964.

Las Vegas.

I was dressed to kill.

I was cool.

I was so cool, I could have frozen hell over.

But I was in heaven, actually.

I had on this beautiful suit. A black mohair suit with a silk dress shirt.

Beautiful silk pocket handkerchief.

Matching tie.

Gorgeous manicure.

I was looking good.

I was feeling good.

I had money in my pocket and we were playing chemin de fer, also known as baccarat.

The James Bond game.

The same game Ian Fleming always had Bond playing in Monaco or the Bahamas while he was makin' a fool of Ernst Stavro Blofeld or some other maniac trying to take over the world.

I thought I owned the world that night in Vegas.

I decided to go partners with these two other guys I was up there with, Richard Trugman and some other guy from L.A. I don't remember.

All three of us were at the Dunes Hotel.

And there was this Asian woman who was always at the tables. Every night she came out with her hair dyed to match her dress—green or orange or whatever.

She was a highroller.

She was a red-hot rollin' mama who was too hot to handle and too cold to hold.

She used to bet like $2,000 a hand. In those days they played the game with cash. There were no chips. It was all cash on the table.

They had stacks and stacks of cash.

I remember this night so well because it was the first New Year's Eve I didn't spend with my parents.

How's that for a guy who thought he was the hottest item ever to hit Hamilton High?

But it was true.

I may have been a bounder and I was always out runnin' around, but I always spent New Year's Eve with Leonard and Sylvia.

I had made it a tradition. I never went out with the guys or dated on New Year's Eve.

I enjoyed being with my parents.

But I was 22 now.

I was entering a new time of life.

This was my first big night out on New Year's ever.

And I was doin' it right at the chemin de fer table in Lost Wages being Sean Freaking Connery.

I think the three of us guys put up $200 apiece.

That was our grubstake.

The first guy takes the money, sits down and does OK.

Then it's my turn to sit in.

I turn to my two partners.

I adjust my tie.

I go, "Bond. James Bond. International exports."

I am looking ultra-cool.

I am looking so clean, man.

Ah, it was so great.

I am looking straight at the Asian woman, an absolute Thoroughbred of a beauty, who tonight has chosen purple hair and a purple dress with a banded collar for her racing colors.

Right behind her is the prize filly in the place, her daughter. Her daughter comes up in a bright yellow silk dress with bright yellow hair, and her daughter is flat-out gorgeous.

You know what?

She had boobs.

We're talking Asian chick with boobs.

This is an unusual thing.

Mama-san is looking really good and daughter-san is looking extra good. And I am starting to stare at this girl.

Just about then, though, they pass me the shoe containing the cards.

I put out $40 or something.

I win the hand.

I could write that same sentence 16 times in a row.

Because that is what happened to me next at the chemin de fer table.

I held the shoe for 16 straight passes.

Of the 16, I had two natural 9's and three natural 8's. One hand I beat an 8 with a natural 9.

The Asian woman with the purple hair and purple dress and her entirely edible daughter in yellow-on-yellow are betting right with me.

They are hanging on my every move.

I am the center of their universe.

I want to say they were now betting $5,000 a hand on me.

And I made her and her daughter about $100,000.

I made for our group about five grand.

I was so proud.

I felt so cool.

I was James Goddam Bond.

In fact, let Commander Bond beat that—16 straight passes.

I'd like to see Q dream up some fountain pen or laser beam or exploding briefcase to help James win 16 straight passes.

It was certainly one of the highlights of my life.

I was sure I was gonna win every time I played the tables in Las Vegas.

Of course, I was a stupid 22-year-old kid.

Little did I know.

I was just learning that the two sentences that built Las Vegas were:

"I feel lucky."

"I got a hunch."

But I was a lucky gambler that night.

Extremely lucky.

And my success that night also probably had much to do with my becoming a professional poker player.

Yep. Something else you didn't know about me, huh?

But it's true.

Starting in the late '80s, and over a period of about five or six years, I was one of the best poker players in the West and—undoubtedly—one of the best in the entire country.

Think not?

Well, chew on these numbers for a minute.

In 1990, I entered 73 tournaments and made the final table 65 times.

Sometimes up to 500 people would start in the tournament. The final table is the last 10.

I would say average tournaments were 100 to 200 people. But there were a lot of tournaments that would have 50 tables of 10 each.

I won a lot of money.

A lot.

Chapter Eight

I don't think I'm going to tell you exactly how much because I've already worked that out with the IRS and I don't want to have to go into it again with them.

But let's just say "a lot" means six-figure type of "lots."

I loved making the money, of course, but in a way it truly was beside the main point of playing poker.

The money was the way you kept score.

Fine.

But the main point of playing poker was the challenge the game offers.

The excitement.

The scene.

The action.

Remember those words I've used to describe much of the rest of my life? They applied big-time to the world of competitive poker.

I was always striving to improve myself.

And I found out a truly fascinating thing about the game.

I could tell more about a person's character from playing poker than almost any other thing in life.

I found out that the guys that would cheat at cards would cheat at life.

I found out that guys who used to win all the money in the card games were more successful in other parts of life.

They were brighter. They used their heads.

I found out the guys who had real courage and the guys who were chicken.

I could sit there and be friends with a guy for two years and go out with him socially—him and his wife and his family. But I could find out more about his real character in one night of playing cards with him.

Whether he was stupid or whether he was wise. Or whether he was honest, whether he was dishonest. Whether he had courage or whether he was a coward. Or whether he had brains or was a total fool.

What interests me about poker is that it's a lesson in how to play people.

It's learning how to play the whole world.

To be good at poker you must have three things:

(1) To be good at mathematics. You must remember cards that have been played and laws of statistical probability.

(2) To know the strategy. The classic hands to hold, the classic hands to fold in the classic situations.

(3) To know psychology. This is the most important aspect of all. You must be able to read the people in the game—their strengths and weaknesses of character. You must be able to understand and conceal your own strengths and weaknesses.

And then one of the other things that really turned me on about poker

after I started playing, was the colorful people that I met.

As you know by now, I love characters.

You don't meet guys like Wild Bill every day.

But I did, nearly every day, in poker.

Cigarette Mary.

Visor Mary.

Denny the Dog.

Then there was Buddha. He had a big old shaved head, was a huge Seahawks fan and raised on everything.

There was Eskimo John.

And The Rabbi, whose actual name was David Rabbi and was kind of a sleaze.

Then we had Table-Top Tom.

And we had Hans the Tuna, one of the greatest tournament players ever. He was steady, he could read people very well and was excellent at managing his money.

We played with people so colorful they'd have made Damon Runyon sit up in his box.

I'm tellin' ya, the people you played with, was the game. I loved it.

These people were the characters' characters.

Playing against them just fed right back into my joy and fun in observing people.

And then the cherry on top of all this wonderful dessert-tray of zany humanity was easily the most amazing and interesting person I got to observe playing poker.

Rebecca.

My wife of 15 years.

That's right. We got to do this together.

We were living in Rancho Mirage when we dived headfirst into the world of poker.

I dived first. I got into poker by just starting to observe the way people played in casinos.

And then I got OK.

And then I started entering some small tournaments. I just went in and signed up. That was it.

And after about six months, I got really good.

And then after about a year, I think I got great.

I played a lot of tournaments in Las Vegas. Then at the card clubs in Los Angeles, at the Bicycle Club and the Commerce Club.

I started playing at the first Indian reservation in California that allowed live poker. It was in Indio.

And the coolest thing of all, Rebecca joined in. And she started getting

Chapter Eight

really good at tournaments, too.

One year, there were four major tournaments in Indio. They lasted two days. Rebecca and I won all four of 'em.

She won two and I won two. It was in 1990.

When other players saw us in a tournament, they knew they were up against competition.

When the tournament started, they said, "Well, we know a couple people who'll be at the last table."

And that was a given.

On those occasions when we faced each other at the final table, it was tough competition.

Down and dirty.

Am I willing to beat her butt?

Oh, most definitely.

You bet.

Is she willing to beat my butt?

She loves it. Loves it.

She tries to fake me out of my sneakers.

She's good at it, too.

She knows me, knows my personality and my thinking so well, she can play me.

She's got me good a couple of times. You bet she did.

In fact, Becka's got the biggest trophy in the family. Six feet tall or something.

She won that one at Indio. I think it was a $25,000 tournament.

It was called "Stairway to the Stars."

We were playing Texas Hold 'Em.

We'd enter everything from $10 and $25 tournaments to $5,000 tournaments.

A $25 tournament means you've got a $25 buy-in, but you could win $1,000.

Most of the local, week-night tournaments that we used to play in, it was anywhere from $1,000 to $2,000 to the winner.

Not monster-high stakes.

We're not talking Sting money changing hands here.

We're not talking actual James Bond "Casino Royale" stakes on a nightly basis.

But still, significant sums could be won.

And it was fun.

That was one of our social activities. We met a lot of wonderful people over the years.

Becka and I are soulmates.

I have been so lucky to have found her.

Poker was just one thing we shared. But I'm glad we did it as a couple rather than one or the other of us getting into it alone.

And I'm glad we both felt the same way about the game.

We didn't let it consume us.

We didn't let poker take over our lives.

But we also cared deeply and passionately about winning.

Most people are recreational players and they don't really give a hoot, or have the pride, in winning and losing.

It's an avocation.

We take it a lot more seriously.

For me, it's just because of my competitive nature.

And I think it's the same for Becka.

I mean, one of the few nicknames I've ever had, besides "Lumpy," I got from poker.

One guy called me "The Iron Duke."

And it kinda stuck.

Because I was pretty damn hard to beat.

He was just so frustrated playing me.

He says, "It's like goin' up against an Iron Duke."

And I didn't want to say to the guy, "You schmuck, I don't bluff."

But I liked to make everybody think that I did.

I mean, once in a while, you play loose hands.

But it's an acting job.

Being a great poker player is no different than being a lawyer, which is also an acting job.

You're trying to convince somebody to do something.

What you want to do, if you've got a great hand, you don't want them to fold.

You know?

And if you've got an average hand, you want them to fold. So all it is, there's the art of convincing somebody.

I didn't learn these things until I got older.

Going back to that night at the chemin de fer table with the Asian women and the 16 straight passes?

I was a schmuck.

I was just a lucky schmuck.

When I was a kid, I was a lousy card player. But I got smart as I got older.

I didn't say I was always smart.

I had some lessons to learn along the way.

See, that's the thing that separates poker from other games in the casinos.

Poker is not really gambling.

I hate gambling.

Chapter Eight

But I love poker.

Because when you do it right, there is no gamble involved in poker.

It is the one game at the casinos that is largely technique.

That is because of one very important difference from all the other casino games.

You're playing other people

You're not playing against the house.

When you play other people, you have a chance to win with your brains and your guts and your strategy and your ability to read people and the willingness to know yourself.

When you play the house, you have no chance.

No chance to win, whatsoever.

Most people don't seem to understand this.

And it never ceases to amaze me.

They just keep on gambling.

And, inevitably, losing.

Do you know that in a game like "Let It Ride" the house has a 30 percent advantage, and a game like "Caribbean Stud" the house has a 24 percent advantage?

Yet people play these games and expect to win.

You can't, on any continuous basis.

And slots.

I can hardly talk about slots without getting angry.

There's never been a machine made that was ever set to lose.

They never were, and they're never gonna be.

And yet people stand there all day and night moronically pulling this imbecilic arm.

Becka does this.

She says to me, "I know it drives you crazy. I don't care. I enjoy it."

But she does know what I'm saying is true.

"It's a sucker play," Becka will say. "But at least I know this when I'm doing it. I treat it like an evening of entertainment. It's gonna cost me X amount, just like a good show or something. I know the game is rigged so I can't win in the end. A lot of people don't accept this, though, and throw all their money away into the slots."

OK. But I still detest the machines.

I consider the machines an insult to my intelligence.

Especially the machines that talk back to me.

"Oh, come play me."

"I'm gonna hit right now."

It's like some whore luring you or something.

An ugly whore at that.

Because the enjoyment is going to be minimal and infrequent.

It's absolutely ludicrous.

Poker machines are no better.

This, too, is not real poker.

Machine poker is rigged so the numerical odds are in its favor.

You can't overcome this with psychology or cunning, two of the biggest tools you have in a real poker game.

Poker machines are hypnotic.

They can actually hook you like dope can.

That's why the machines are there.

That's why the stock in International Game Technology has done so well.

I do happen to own two poker machines.

I keep them in my den.

I will play those because I own them and I am now the house.

I have the key to the coin chute at the bottom.

As long as I can get my coins back, I can be hypnotized for nothing.

That's how you beat those games.

You own them.

I mean, of course, you can have fun with them. I admit that. That's why so many people play them.

You can have fun with a broad, too.

But it's the most expensive thing you'll ever have in your life.

You're gonna pay for it.

One way or another.

All right, so I just offended you.

But I'm still stating a fact, even if it's a slimeball, sexist-pig statement.

I'll own up to it.

In the meantime, I am telling you that you cannot let these gambling devices whip you with their Svengali approaches on your psyche.

Because they're gonna kick your butt every time.

"I've got a hunch."

"I feel lucky."

Remember the two sentences that built Las Vegas?

Say those two sentences to anyone in Vegas, and they will send a limousine for you.

All you have to do is say to them, "I feel lucky."

And they're like: "We'll be right there, Mr. Bank. Your room will be ready. How big is the credit line?"

I want you to think about this.

These people actually come out and tell you that you are a sucker and you're still gonna go there and play their stupid games?

How do they tell you that you're a sucker?

Chapter Eight

Everywhere.

It's all over the TV, in the magazines, in the newspapers.

It was in *USA Today* that there's a bounty out right now for any computer hacker who can invent a game that is more hypnotic than the ones currently being played.

So they can draw more suckers to the machines.

The guy who invented Let It Ride now franchises it to all the casinos.

I understand he's making over $1 million a month.

I think he was a truck driver and he figured it out at a truck stop one night.

All you have to do is come up with another interesting game form. You've got a 30 percent advantage.

There's no way you can lose.

It's the same no matter what game you play.

You hear about people who have a "system" to beat the roulette wheel. Please.

There is no successful mathematical roulette system in existence to man.

Or woman, for that matter.

It cannot happen.

Period.

The end.

If you're approached by someone who has a "roulette system," run, do not walk, the other way.

Now, I say no game is really fair against the house at the casino?

Well, OK.

There is one game, we all know, where you can even the playing field just a bit.

And that's all you can do.

Virtually even it.

The game is blackjack.

Can you beat a one-deck blackjack game?

Yes.

But do you have any idea what an infinitesimely small advantage it is?

If you count cards, if you use money management and the basic strategy...if you use those three things expertly in a short-deck blackjack game, you have about a 1.5 percent advantage.

Now, in a blackjack game, for you to have that much of an advantage, you have to put in an 8-hour day and maybe you win $150.

You can work that hard in a lot of other jobs and do better.

But that is the only shot you got.

Except poker.

There you can clean up, if you know how to play.

And that is because—repeat after me, because it's true—you're not playing against house odds...you're playing against other frail human beings.

That's why a lot of casinos in Las Vegas (A) do not offer poker anymore, because it takes up space which could be occupied by machines, and (B) the ones who do offer poker, do so only as an accomodation to their customers.

And they're holding their breath like hell that your wife is playing those machines morning, noon and night while you're playing poker.

Or that when you walk away from the poker table, you're gonna take leave of your senses momentarily and drop off some money on Let It Ride or Caribbean Stud or some moronic game like that.

That's the only reason poker tables are even in Vegas anymore, and why they are disappearing.

I mean, I admit Vegas is still a cool place.

But I both love it and hate it.

I hate watching people throw their money and lives away.

I see future Gamblers Anonymous members by the busloads there.

There will be bankruptcies. There will be divorces. There will be suicides.

All three will come out of the games people play against the house any night you are there.

Greed.

It is absolutely the root of all evil.

But I understand the pull of Vegas.

I truly do.

I have gone to the craps tables and picked up the dice and had a lot of fun.

But I make my money hopefully by investing my clients' money in a proper way.

I do not make my money by walking up to a craps table and trying to hit 10 sevens in a row.

Or by going over to a slot machine and trying to get three sevens to come up.

Or by going over to a blackjack table and trying to pick up twenty-one, 25 times in a row.

I like the ambience of Las Vegas.

Sorry to say I love the food of Las Vegas.

(As you could tell by looking at me at this point in my life.)

But I do.

That's a big highlight.

The whole scene is a beautiful place.

The showgirls.

The shows.

Rebecca and I both enjoy it.

Chapter Eight

It's like a second home to us.

But you don't have to be a gambler and you don't have to be a sucker to enjoy Las Vegas.

Not with all there is to do there now.

Omigosh, the places there are, one after another.

Siegfried and Roy are marvelous.

EFX with Michael Crawford is arguably one of the greatest shows you will ever see in your life.

These babies aren't cheap.

Sixty-five bucks a ticket.

I mean, 130 scoots to see a two-hour show. Not even two hours. That's a lotta scoots.

Then you go have an expensive dinner. You're talking about a $300 evening.

That's a lot of money.

But it doesn't have to be that way.

For 30 bucks they'll put on this really nice joust at Excalibur and it's fun.

Hell, I even shelled out 29 bucks to see Pauley Shore.

I know, a lot of people think his humor is too idiotic. But remember, I love idiots.

Something about the guy cracks me up.

I don't know what it is.

I guess I'm warped, huh?

But like Baskin and Robbins, there's a flavor for everyone in Vegas.

There's lots of shows you can go to in Vegas for 25 bucks or less.

And there are tons of great dinner values.

For 100 bucks you can have a marvelous evening of dining and dancing and shows and frivolity.

Maybe during the daytime you want to lay out by the pool at the Mirage.

Slide down the water slide.

Sun your buns.

Work out.

Go hit that maddening little white ball on a fantastic golf course.

Have fun.

Just don't let Vegas have you for lunch.

Stay away from those machines.

If you're gonna play a game, play poker.

If you get good enough, you can win.

No matter how good you get at the other stuff, you can't win.

It's that simple.

Hey, you're talkin' to the Iron Duke here.

The Duke knows what he's talking about.

But even if you do get good at poker—even if you get better than Denny the Dog and Cigarette Mary and Wild Bill and Newman and Redford in "The Sting" and even if you're the baddest one poker-playin', grub-stakin', pot-takin', Cincinnati Kid, Cool Hand Luke and Bret and Bart Maverick all-rolled-into-one on the planet—I want you to remember one thing.

My wall.

On my wall I keep a framed poker hand.

As anyone can plainly see, it is a nine-ten-jack-queen-king of clubs.

That's right, a straight freaking flush.

A sure winner every freaking time.

I lost with that hand.

It was after I got really good as an adult poker player.

I was what is called a "proposition" player.

Or you could also call me a "shill."

I was working at the Normandy Club. My job was to sit in and take up a seat until a live player came along to fill out a table.

And that was the hand you see framed on my wall.

A straight flush.

A loser.

I had nobody to blame but myself.

I was dealing and I dealt myself this hand.

Pat.

That's correct.

The first five cards I dealt myself.

Straight flush.

I dealt this kid in the game a three-card draw.

He drew three cards and I had a pat hand.

He beat me with five aces.

Yeah. That's right.

Five aces.

Four aces and a joker.

It's the best hand I ever lost with.

Luckily, I only lost $128.

If I'd had the deed to my house and my car and all my life savings I would have lost them, because I would have bet them on this hand.

Fortunately, I only lost what I had on me at the time.

I keep that hand framed on my wall to remind me of one thing.

There is no such thing as a sure thing.

And now, maybe the next time you're counting on changing your life with a run of luck at the gaming tables—even if it's poker where you can win, and where your skill can come into play—maybe you'll remember.

Lumpy's wall.

Chapter Eight

Remember those five clubs in a row.

And don't bet your house or your car or your wife or your kids on a hand of cards.

Take the game of poker for what it can be. Just a little entertainment.

Let that ride.

Let it go at that.

Take the money and take your wife on a cruise and be a real Caribbean stud.

Don't gamble.

Or, you can do what Beeky and I do.

I call her "Beeky" whenever I want to hack her off.

I mean, I love that nickname "Beeky."

I think it fits her.

But for some reason she doesn't.

Whenever she hears me, she says, "Don't call me Beeky."

Sort of like someone else you may have heard once upon a time going, "Don't call me Lumpy."

Anyhow, do what me and Beeky do.

Gin.

Yep. We have what has to be the world's longest-running gin rummy game. Or at least a contender for the title.

It's 16 years in the making.

We play everywhere we go.

Anywhere we travel.

To the park.

Just sittin' at home.

The next thing you know, the cards may come out.

We have a running tally.

And we keep the sheets.

We've got boxes and boxes of score sheets around here.

And they will always be with us wherever we go, forever.

A quick glance at those scoresheets will tell you one thing.

It will tell you who is ahead in this world's-longest-running gin game.

That's right, baby.

The Duke.

Me.

I am up, something like 2,137,428 points (I expect payment, in full of course, some day).

But me and my baby playing gin rummy?

Now that's a sure thing.

Oops.

Gotta go now.

I think I hear Beeky...I mean Becka...comin'.

Desperately Seeking Mayfield

awn.

The No. 2 tee box at the Springs Country Club in Rancho Mirage, California.

Back of our house.

Rebecca and I are draped across some lawn chairs on the tee. Blankets wrapped around us.

Scraping the crust from our eyes, which must have looked like four badly raked sandtraps, after being awakened before daylight by an earthquake.

I looked at Rebecca.

Rebecca looked at me.

California had taken another huge divot out of our psyches.

"What the hell are we doing here?" I said.

"What are we doing here" she said.

At that very moment we decided to move.

What kind of a place is the second hole at the Springs Country Club to make a decision about where you are going to live?

Well, let me tell you, it's a helluva good place to make that decision when you're afraid to go back into your house.

We couldn't sleep in our house because we were just a little bit afraid it would fall down on us and squash us flat.

We were afraid it would make Bankcakes out of us.

I mean, this earthquake wasn't the big one.

But it was a big one.

One of the biggest.

To be more precise, it was two.

These were the twin earthquakes, Landers and Big Bear, which cracked Southern California like a hardboiled egg on the stove a few years too long.

The first measured 7.5 on the Richter Scale. The second 6.9.

Which is shake-rattlin'-and-rollin' pretty good.

And California's temperamental geology had been serenading us to sleep with "We will, we will rock you" for years now.

Too damn many years.

We decided we couldn't take it anymore.

Just like we couldn't take the fires anymore.

Or the mudslides.

Or the riots.

Or the freeway shootings.

It was like living with the Four Horsemen of the Apocalypse in your guest bedroom.

Every morning you'd get up to the announcement that yet another holocaust was being visited on Southern California.

Suddenly, this place in which I was born, this cool jewel of a place I grew up in, this place I loved working and partying and planning and dreaming in—this place that I thought was the place on earth...

...well, it wasn't me anymore.

It was like a 5,000-year-old gypsy curse had been placed on it and we were doomed to dance endlessly with disaster every day.

You get up one morning and the people of Malibu are standing in the Pacific Ocean, and it isn't because they're trying to fix those annoying tan lines.

They are hoping they don't die because the hills across the Pacific Coast Highway are Dante's Inferno, a blaze sweeping through the dry chaparral and overpriced homes, bearing down on the beach.

And the sea is their only hope of surviving as a funeral pall hangs with blinding blackness across the Malibu Hills.

You wake up another morning and watch the police beating some citizen senseless on national TV.

Another morning and citizens are pulling fellow citizens from their trucks in the middle of intersections and beating the hell out of them.

Suddenly we were a marred masterpiece painted by John Milton.

We were paradise lost.

Suddenly we weren't out there a-havin' fun in that warm California sun, to contradict the old Rivieras song.

So Becka and I decided to move.

But where?

We found that what we really wanted was to move to the most wonderful spot on the planet.

The most peaceful.

The most blissful.

The safest.

The sanest.

The sweetest.

The goodest.

The happiest.

Go-luckiest.

Bestest place on earth.

Mayfield.

Yep. I'm speaking of Cleavertown.

The place where the Cleavers raised their family. And the Rutherfords raised theirs, I might add.

OK, so there might be an Eddie Haskell or two in Mayfield. But it still was the greatest town ever created.

So what if it was mythical?

So what if it was made-up?

So what if it was a figment of some writer's imagination who thought it up only to sell soap and keep a sitcom on the air for a few weeks out of the year?

It wasn't that way to me.

Mayfield was real.

Mayfield existed.

It existed in my mind and heart. And the minds and hearts of Hugh and Barbara and Jerry and Tony.

And millions of viewers each week, all the way through decades of syndication and movies.

You believed Mayfield was real, you guys out there in livingroom-land.

That's why you tuned in year after year, because you knew there was this America out there somewhere...maybe everywhere, really, maybe just as close as the trapdoor where you hid it inside your soul and your spirit.

In spite of overcrowding and crass commercialization and future shock and rampant crime and the great racial divide and poverty and hunger and voter indifference and the dumbing-down of education and recreational drugs and the national debt—and in spite of painful irregularity, George Steinbrenner, unsightly blemishes, Dennis Rodman, daughters telling mothers which douche to use, offending underarm odor, the heartbreak of psoriasis, Tammy Faye, Don King and the male itch—in spite of all these problems and plagues and pestilences upon all our houses, still....

We still believe there is a Mayfield.

Or we want to believe it's real.

So Becka and I went to live in Mayfield.

We had only seen three Mayfields in our lives, basically.

One was Pittsburgh.

Two was Cincinnati.

Three was Kansas City.

Chapter Nine

We went for door No. 3.

Kansas City, Missouri.

We moved there in 1993.

We loved every minute we were there.

Kansas City was Mayfield in so many ways.

Friendly people. People raising their families. People leaving each other alone. Easy-going people in a laid-back town. A rush hour that lasted about 14 seconds. Housing that was way-y-y undervalued.

The Royals. The Chiefs.

Good major league franchises on which to shower my neverending affinity and affection for sports.

The University of Kansas basketball just minutes down the road. One of the true blueblood college programs in sports history. Roy Williams, one of the great contemporary coaches, an honest-to-God legend-in-the-making.

Of course, I could continue to fixate on my beloved Dodgers and even more worshipful UCLA Bruins. And I did live and die with them from afar.

But the Jayhawks, Chiefs and Royals were enough to get a fix for my sports Jones.

Becka and I lived in your basic mansion in Johnson County, just across the state line on the Kansas side of metropolitan Kansas City—one of the richest per-capita communities in the nation.

We were living in a nice, clean, unthreatening environment, safe from natural disasters (if you didn't notice the odd house or Auntie Em and Toto spinning by from one of the Midwest's notorious tornados).

Incidentally, I have hereby done my duty. It is mandatory when mentioning anything connected with Kansas, for there to be an obligatory reference to Oz and Toto and some ritual variation on the "we're not in Kansas anymore" line from the movie and stage play and all the rest.

National pundits and commentators and screenwriters and playwrights and funnymen just can't seem to get enough of these Toto jokes.

In fact, if the sum-Toto of all the Oz jokes about Kansas were laid end-to-end, they would almost reach across these comedians' big mouths...although not quite.

The average Kansan just takes it all in, noting the massive originality, cleverness and intellect it must require to come up with a Toto-Oz-Auntie Em reference for the 27 billionth time. The Kansan then rolls his or her eyes and, in quiet satisfaction, goes back to living in one of the coolest places in the country.

We had a great time in our four years in K.C., Rebecca and I.

I was a vice-president for a national brokerage firm with a branch located on the Country Club Plaza, one of the swankest, most stylish business-living-recreational areas you will find in the country.

Anyone who hasn't discovered this gem is missing a huge, best-kept secret, a fountain-and-flower-bedecked district that rivals even Rodeo Drive in my estimation for chic, smart stores, cafes, watering holes and galleries, all ensconced in a distinctive Spanish Mediterranean architectural style and exquisite landscaping.

As I mentioned briefly before, I was on the local CNN radio affiliate with my "Frank Bank on Finance" program.

I had a blast and it was very well-received, if I do say so myself.

Anyone who knows anything about radio or the market knows Frank Bank ruled when it came to assessing econonomic conditions and passing along sage insights to listeners.

I know that sounds egotistical.

Probably is.

I'm sorry.

Hey, what am I gonna do, lie?

I was great.

What can I say?

The show not only goosed my brokerage business with Prudential, but it got me to knowing scads of Kansas Citians, which I found to be delightful.

Then there was the food...always a pretty important issue with me—too much so, if you listen to my doctors. Which I should.

But it was just too hard to resist. Kansas City is the barbecue capital of the world, pure and simple. It is at the head of the class and you can stop taking roll right there.

Gates. Bryants.

These are the two giants on which K.C.'s BBQ reputation is staked, and they are well-deserved. But there are a half a dozen or more that are also better than anything in any other city.

And I've driven across this great country more times than I can tell you. I know what I'm talkin' about.

When it comes to the feedbag, this comes straight from the horse's mouth. Mine.

If you're ever in Kansas City, I also highly recommend you take in Stroud's. This is a pan-fried chicken place that isn't just finger-lickin' good. It's elbow lickin'.

You're gonna be in some great goo up to your neck and you're gonna lap up every last drop.

But my feelings for Kansas City went much further than my stomach.

They went straight to my heart and soul.

I guess, as much as anything, I discovered in Kansas City that I'd always longed to live in Mayfield.

Chapter Nine

I had been seeking Mayfield ever since I burned out on the Cadillac days.

Ever since the frenzy of the Hollywood Boulevard prowls and the Sunset Strip searches and the Haight-Ashbury forays and my ridiculous six-second marriage and my walk with the fame-and-name game.

All through that I had really been looking for the haven and refuge of Mayfield and trying to raise a family and trying to be a good neighbor and a good parent like Ward and June.

I didn't do that so well in my first marriage. Even though I felt like I tried and it lasted 15 years, I just didn't do a very good job as a husband.

We had two great daughters together, Julie and Kelly.

I was a liberal dad, but if you screwed up, you got the Ward Cleaver speech, what else?

I knew those talks by heart and I thought they worked well.

I just ripped it out of page 112 of the Father's Manual: "Hey, now, it's time to sit down, be quiet and listen."

But I didn't always pull it off as well as Hugh Beaumont. I'll admit that. I couldn't make my own June happy either.

But no hard feelings. We split.

And then I met Becka.

We had the most incredible affair. Better than any romance novel.

It started one night at a party in Tarzana.

And that was the night we went "Booiinng!"

I came around this corner and saw her.

I looked at her.

She looked at me.

Bells rang and volcanoes erupted and violins played and here-to-eternity waves crashed around us.

The whole 99 yards, like in the movies.

That was us.

I saw Becka and, I don't know, there was either a look on her face, the way she moved—something happened.

And I just went:

"Omigod.

"This might be the one for me."

And we just sat and talked and talked and talked forever and ever.

Becka said she felt the same when she saw me.

She felt kinda like a female me. And I kinda felt like a male her.

It just kind of laid in on both of us, and it was wonderful.

Before we bumped into each other, I was just sittin' at this party havin' a drink—I think I was watching either a baseball game or a football game on TV. It mighta been a baseball game.

This was right around my 39th birthday and they probably had a dozen people over there.

It was kinda like what happened almost every night of the world in Tarzana.

Tarzana was this big social whirlwind. It never ended.

Every night someone had some soiree or get-together or dinner or barbecue or just-plain party.

Always.

Food and drink and whatever grass or appropriate drug was out. Which was the reason I looked down on the whole thing, because that wasn't my bag.

Literally.

I was flying straight.

I didn't like drugs.

And I didn't like the whole scene in general after awhile.

These parties were all about impressing each other with our status and our toys and our achievements and our baubles, bangles and beads.

That permeated our lives all the time.

Did I tell you the story, after my dad died?

My first wife and I had this big, long old house on Van Alden in Tarzana.

It was like a half-a-block long.

And my Uncle Al comes back from the cemetery. We had everyone come over to my house after the funeral.

My Uncle Al says, "I didn't know what house it was. All I saw was Mercedes-Benzes out front and Rolls Royces and Ferraris."

I said, "Well, that's how it is around here, Uncle Al."

And he says, "Well, I'm driving..."—ah, hell, I forget what he was driving. But he made some comment about it...and about whatever his normal, puny little nondescript car was.

And you know what? I've never forgotten the idea behind that remark.

It was like, the pretentiousness of all of us in my neighborhood.

It was just totally '80s.

It was almost like seeing Michael Douglas in the movie "Wall Street" when he said something like, "This is the greed generation. This is the Me Generation. And greed is good."

I don't remember the exact line, but I remember the intent, if not content, of it.

We were all just plain greedy.

That was what was driving us.

And it was reflected, perhaps most of all, by the lemming-like accumulation of the cars we were driving.

I was caught up in that. I'm just as guilty of it as anyone.

Chapter Nine

But I don't think it was really me.

And I didn't like it.

All we did was stand around exchanging incredibly banal observations about what we were spending and all the labels and how to buy the next Rolls or how to buy the next Ferrari or Mercedes.

The designer vacations or summer homes or boats.

What happened was, there was so much pretentiousness that the real feelings got lost.

That's what was sad.

Maybe that's partly why my first marriage fell apart.

Whatever we could spend, whatever we could grab, whatever we could flaunt or flash around—it was like getting caught up in a spider's web.

And you kept getting deeper and deeper and deeper until you weren't going to get out of the web. Not and feel alive.

It was a competition.

I didn't want to compete in this manner.

I mean, I still had my big house.

And we were a two-Mercedes house.

We had the 450SL and the big sedan.

The color of the SL was red.

The color of the sedan was chocolate..

For a playtoy I went out and got an old classic Corvette Stingray with two tops.

We had so much status junk.

We had motorcycles.

We bought golf carts for our second house.

Almost got a boat.

My friend, Anita May, talked me out of it.

I was almost the proud owner of a big old Uniflight out at Marina Del Rey.

But then, Anita said her dad had made the statement to her one time: "Show me a boat owner and I'll show you a boat for sale."

That got me just in the nick of time, because I was getting ready to buy a boat for about 50 grand.

This boat was going to be like a 35-footer.

That doesn't quite qualify as a yacht. But a junior one.

Helluva boat, man.

Sleeps eight or 10 people.

Not too shabby.

Yeah, I could have run around like all the other Thurston B. Howells and had Skippers and Little Buddies hopping-to-it all over the thing.

But I got away from that.

As all my fellow would-have-been yachters might have put it, "Thaaank Gawwd!"

Didn't ever come close to the airplane thing.

Why should we?

None of the gunk we'd bought up to then meant anything.

None of it mattered an iota.

It was all just for show. To out-accumulate the people next door or down the block. To put a sheen on the surface while everything inside felt like rough-grit sandpaper.

All this was why my first wife said life was so shallow.

(Incidentally, in case you're wondering why I keep referring to her as "my first wife," she asked that I not mention her in this book. So I'm honoring her wishes—by not naming her. I admire her and respect her, so this is fine by me.)

Anyway, my first wife said that one day she was gonna write a book about our lives.

It would be called "The Shallow Pond."

It would be a great title.

I hope she writes it and makes a million.

The one excess that worked into anything good at all was our second house.

It was in Rancho Mirage.

That's how I got down there.

By that time, my first marriage had taken a turn for the worse. Becka and I had met and we began living in Rancho.

Why was I drawn to her like magnetic true north on the compass?

Beauty alone?

Absolutely not.

Becka has that in great abundance.

But that isn't it.

It's her warmth.

I mean, Becka is extremely physically captivating. And I remain enormously attracted to her.

But that had nothing to do with it.

Everything had to do with her warmth and the way she would talk to me.

She was like my coach and my team player at the same time. She was like my cheerleader.

From the very first moment we were together, she was going, "You can do it. You can do anything."

She said, "You're kinda like a hero guy. You gotta be that way, Frank. You're always gonna be that way. That's your lot in life."

And her belief in me kept me going.

Chapter Nine

There are times, you know, when you don't believe in yourself.

Even someone like me, who had been striving so hard to develop a healthy ego since adolescence—and succeeding quite often.

But through all the errant ways of ego-stroking, I was missing something huge in my life.

Becka was it.

We just sat on this couch and got so close the first time we talked.

We said we both were the type of people who could give love. But we needed love back.

We had both just split up with our spouses, and we both just babbled on.

We must have talked five, six hours.

We didn't go to bed together that night.

That came a few times later.

We got very solid in this thing.

I mean, when we did dive into bed, it was the most incredible thing for both of us.

I promise you.

I'd never felt anything like it.

It rekindled my youth.

It was torrid.

What it did, it brought me back to that huge sexual appetite of my youth. Which had sorta been dormant.

And I truly did not know it still existed at that point.

I probably had left my sexual drive back in Haight-Ashbury. It was probably leaning up against that lamppost on the corner I told you about earlier, panting for breath like a whipped puppy. Or over in a corner, passed out in some nameless coffee house.

I'd probably burned that baby out quite a bit on Cadillac with the towels and the togas and the musical partners.

But it had gone kaput in San Francisco.

But Becka woke up everything in me.

She's my soulmate.

She's my best friend.

She's my gin partner.

The gin sheets bearing the scores of our 16-year game—however long it gets to be—will be buried with the first one of us who dies.

The current decks of cards we're playing with will be buried in there, too.

We have been through cases and cases and cases of cards.

When we went to Europe one year and traveled all over everywhere, we played in every city.

We'll go to Las Vegas sometimes and we'll say, "Hey, let's go up in the room and play a couple sheets."

Wherever we're at.

We just refer to it as The Gin Game.

I mean, when I hit two million points in the gin game in Kansas City, I was gonna hire a skywriter and put a big ad in the paper.

I was gonna write the score in the sky and say, "I love you, Beeky."

Becka's a good person.

I found my One, without question.

It wasn't all smooth, though.

There were a lot of problems with my children and hers.

Becka and I both had two daughters. So we have four daughters between us.

And I think the problems are healed now.

Originally, my kids probably resented my taking another woman. And hers probably did the same with her about taking me.

In the beginning there were no how-to books on step-parenting, and we kind of trialed-and-errored.

But I think our kids all know that we love them now...and always did.

Maybe one of the kids felt they didn't want to call me Dad. Or another one didn't want to call Becka, Mother.

Which is fine.

That's cool.

These were all pretty basic things, the kind of animosity being built up.

And, you know, when we felt that animosity being built up, we figured, well, we've gotta let loose of the whole thing.

Otherwise you build up this big, huge, impenetrable wall.

We had half a wall built, and we finally just kind of let the kids go and have their space for awhile.

But we still stayed with them—every single second of every single day—in our hearts and minds.

I was always my kids' biggest cheerleader.

And, as it turns out, we came out with four really good kids.

Julie's 26. She's gonna become a teacher. She's a graduate of Arizona State. She's my oldest.

Becka's oldest is Michelle. She's working on her doctorate. She already has her Masters in early child development. Oh well, I guess there'll be a doctor in the family after all.

Kelly just graduated as an English major from San Francisco State. She's my baby. She's 21. Kelly's gonna go into showbiz. Not on the front end of the camera. On the back end.

She wants to write. Or possibly be a casting director. Something in that vein. She enjoys the business.

Chapter Nine

Her boyfriend Mike, whom we love like a son-in-law already, is a great kid. They live with each other...actually with us, right now. They just moved down to Southern California, where we relocated a few months ago.

Mike was Kelly's best friend in the eighth grade. And they've been best friends ever since.

They love each other, a lot like Beeky and me.

I love it.

It's a good situation.

I thought I'd never allow another guy near my girls.

But it's cool.

Then there's Joanne, who's Becka's youngest. She's 23.

She now works for a Lexus dealer in the San Fernando Valley. She's in the business end.

Julie and Kelly are my kids with my first wife.

Michelle is Becka's kid with a guy named Paul.

And Joanne is Becka's kid with a guy named Elliot.

Whoa.

Elliot?

Did I say Elliot?

Oh, man.

That reminds me of one of our all-time favorite escapades as a family.

I think you can take this as proof our family finally healed and we all knew for sure that we loved each other to death.

Death being involved in this caper, actually, now that I mention it.

One day we got a phone call in Kansas City.

Elliot had died.

Becka went out to be with Joanne in California.

Meanwhile, back in Kansas City, someone would ask me where Becka was.

I'd say she was out in California because her ex-husband, Elliot, died.

And people would go, "Awww. That's too bad."

And I'd go, "Why? The guy was a jackass."

But anyway, Elliot had finally checked out of Heartbreak Hotel, otherwise known as his life.

I say that because this cat was a huge Elvis fan.

Make that HUGE Elvis fan.

All capitals, italicized and boldfaced.

HUGE —yeah just like that—Elvis fan.

He was one of those dudes who used to go around impersonating Elvis.

Elliot's house looked like an Elvis museum.

Every inch of wall space...pictures, juke boxes, posters, capes, tapes, mementoes.

I think he might have had a rhinestone refrigerator and kept crushed velvet in there.

Man, this guy was an Elvis freak.

And Elliot ran a video store in Moreno Valley out by Riverside.

This was in April of '95.

So now we get the call that Elliot has cashed it in. Becka gets on an airplane for the West Coast.

We had been asked to this guy's house for barbecue...well, actually, it was the dork who's writing this book with me, Gib Twyman.

And his wife at the time, Sherry, and their two kids, Matt and Emily, are there.

So is another complete idiot, Steve Cameron, who did this sports show on the local CNN radio affiliate, called "From the Cheap Seats" with Gib.

And so is the owner of the radio station, Bill Johnson, and his wife, Susan.

So I had stayed behind in K.C., representing our family at this barbecue.

And that is where I get a call from Becka and Joanne and Michelle, who also has flown to California from Wisconsin. The three of them are out there in Joanne's apartment.

And they were wondering what to do with Elliot.

They tell me on the phone that they've already decided they are gonna cremate him.

And I say, if that's the case, then there's only one place for Elliot.

"Graceland," I said.

Big mistake.

The minute I said it, I knew I'd stuck my foot in my mouth.

I knew it.

Because the minute I said it, all three of 'em lit up and said,

"That's it!"

And I said, "No. I didn't really say that."

I said, "No. This is Joanne's father. What kind of dumb thing is that? Graceland? Dumb idea."

But they said, "That's exactly where Elliot would want to be."

I get off the phone and tell everyone at the barbecue about this Elliot thing. I say I can't believe what I'm getting myself into.

Bill Johnson says he'll hire a helicopter to zoom over Graceland and bombs-away Elliot on Elvis.

Cameron (you gotta wonder about this guy) says he knows some shady character who's supposed to have some mob ties. This guy can maybe smuggle Elliot into Graceland in the dead of night.

Wild ideas are floating all over the place, thanks to a little help from my weird friends.

Chapter Nine

Well, sure enough, they give Elliot the burn job.

And Elliot turns into this little box.

First of all, they have like a funeral ceremony in his video store. They held it in the Elvis aisle, naturally.

And then Joanne comes back to Kansas City with Becka. They've got Elliot with them in the box.

He's gonna stay with me and Becka until we can figure a way to slip him into Graceland and douse him on Elvis' grave.

So we put him in a room on the third floor of our house.

In a little cabinet up there in one of our closets, but that didn't hide him as far as I was concerned.

Gave me the friggin' creeps, man.

Guy's up there every night when I go to sleep.

Lookin' down on us.

Up on the Elliot Wing of the Bank's house.

Got his own suite.

His own space.

Hangin' out in my house.

Everywhere I go in the house, I know Elliot's watchin'.

Hey, I don't mean to be cruel, to quote Elvis.

But the sucker was givin' me the willies sleepin' upstairs in our house.

I had to get him outta there.

Ease Elliot on down the road.

First, I decided on a little daytrip.

Get Elliot used to the idea of leaving for good.

Elliot was in this bronze box. It's, oh, about six inches tall and four inches square, something like that.

But it was just the perfect size to put a headset on.

I decided to visit my two jerkface friends who were doing their dumb sports show on the local CNN radio affiliate.

They used to invite me on the air from time to time because we're buds and they know what a sports freak and fantastic guest I am.

So one day I waltz into their studio at the Downtown Mariott Hotel.

And I'm packin'.

I decide to bring Elliot with me onto the show.

And the one guy who always has a smelly stogie and was always polluting the hotel with his smoke, Cameron, he goes, "Well, you won't believe it, we've had a lotta guests on this show, but this is the first time we ever had a dead guy."

"With the exception of my partner," the other guy, Twyman, this all-knowing, omnicient mayonnaise jar, pipes up. "Actually, dead air is probably preferable to listening to us anyway."

But anyhow, we all look down and there is Elliot with the headphones on his box.

And every now and then we'd all ask Elliot a question or bring him into the conversation about Brett Favre or Mike Tyson or something.

And if Elliot didn't answer—and I don't think he ever did, if memory serves correctly, we'd just go, "Thanks for sharing those thoughts, Elliot. They were better than anything we've come up with."

Or we'd just go, "Elliot can't speak right now. The topic obviously has left him speechless with emotion."

Well, that primed the pump for Elliot taking a hike for good.

A few days later came the big moment.

Elliot was goin' to Graceland.

I thought it was time for him to move on.

Now, this was in August. Joanne comes back from California. And we all hop into our car and we drive from K.C. down to Graceland.

Here it is, me and Becka and Joanne and Elliot.

Elliot is riding shotgun as he heads for his last roundup, sorta underneath Joanne's shoulder.

See, we'd de-boxed him and we baggied Elliot.

We ziplocked that sucker.

You know, the one where you turn the bag over and the fish won't fall out?

We didn't want this lunkhead, Elliot, to fall out.

If he was gonna sleep with the fishes, as they say in the Mafia, we didn't want him to leak out of the bag. We wanted him to be all buried in the same spot.

So we've got him in a good ziplock.

Now, we get to Graceland and it's kinda like an armed fort.

It happened to have been the weekend of the anniversary of Elvis' death.

And there's freakin' teddy bears all over the place. All over the sidewalks. The walls.

You can't walk two feet without stumbling over a teddy bear. Or some other endearing, totally cheesy Elvis artifact.

Which is good.

We sorta tried to do this deal while everything was hectic.

If it was quiet, I never woulda been able to do this.

So now we join the official walking tour of Graceland.

Like I said, it's August. In case you didn't know, Memphis, Tennessee, the Elvisburg where Graceland is, is approximately 1,003 degrees in August.

Hotter'n two hells.

I'm carryin' this baggie.

Chapter Nine

I'm tellin' ya. Even in death, Elliot wasn't any flyweight.

He musta weighed 10 pounds.

That's a helluva lot of ashes.

I mean, we tried to make it not noticeable that we're carrying this dead guy around with us.

Becka originally is carrying Elliot around in her purse at the start of the tour.

And before we get to Elvis' grave, we decided maybe to start spreading Elliot around on some of the plants and flowers, you know.

I told you the guy was full of it.

He made good fertilizer.

Graceland shoulda been grateful.

But we still weren't exactly sure they would have expressed their open appreciation for some schmuck from California having his mortal remains dusted across the King's grounds.

We're like Hansel and Gretel leaving crumbs of Elliot all over the place.

So now we get to the gravesite and there's these two guards.

There's also a little grandstand packed with people, sitting there staring at the great man's grave like, well…they're all shook up.

Maybe it's the audience, maybe it's my family's spurring me on—maybe it's my strong desire to get this the hell over with.

But I am suddenly inspired to give a pretty decent burial-scene performance, if I do say so myself.

I climb over the wrought-iron fence.

And now, I look very, very pious.

I am very sad.

Now I am down on my knees, crawling to the grave, goin', "Elvis…Elvis…Elvis."

I am in serious deep mourning.

I was nuthin' but a houn' dawg.

Cryin' all the time as I crawled, bereft, toward the grave—glancin' over my shoulder a time or two to see if the guards are buyin' it.

Shoot. They musta had nuts all the time bellyfloppin' on Elvis grave.

Whatever. Because the guards didn't have a clue what I was doing.

I just kept inching forward on my hands and knees.

"Elvis…Elvis…Elvis."

And finally, very solemnly, I put my left hand on Elvis stomach. I think he would have liked it that way. I think the left hand is the hand Elvis used to punch with when he did those karate chops during one of his songs.

And right in the middle of the grave, right where the King's stomach is, with my right hand, I got the baggie on the ground.

I got my finger in there, I open the baggie, and I'm takin' the ashes out.

And I'm spreading the ashes all over the green, green grass of Elvis' home.

"E," I said, "meet E.

"King. This is a loyal subject, Elliot.

"Came all the way across the country to be with you.

"He's all shook up now. All over you, Elvis.

"Enjoy, you two hunka-hunka-burnin'-loves.

"Amen."

Or something along those lines.

And now Joanne and Becka are goin' ape.

They're snappin' pictures.

It wasn't a real pleasant thing to do, I gotta tell you.

I've really done nicer things.

I'd rather make fudge, actually.

Better that than have my wife's ex-husband smeared all over my pinkies.

I mean, I got the baggie open enough to shake the dude out. But I still had to take the ashes and rub them into the ground.

It was kind of a mess, you know.

Funny, I couldn't wash my hands enough afterwards.

Made it hard to eat ribs or sushi for awhile.

You didn't want no finger-lickin' food.

But, anyhow, I figured, OK. I really did my duty.

Elliot is now with his idol.

Joanne and Becka were happy.

And I didn't have to do the jailhouse rock.

I was really getting ready for arrest No. 2 in my career as a criminal.

I thought they would try and nail me on this.

I figured the worst that could happen, is Elliot is with Elvis, but I pay maybe a $300-$400 fine.

But it never happened.

That was the Elliot and Elvis union.

But, to tell you the truth, it's one of the coolest things I've ever gotten to do.

That is because it was the least I could do for my daughter.

Because I love her so much.

I love her so very much, just like all my daughters.

And I would do anything for them.

As I think I've pretty well proven by now, making a complete fool of myself, crawling around on my snout like some blue-tick hound in Tennessee.

Anyway, I think we found a serious piece of Mayfield that day in Memphis, Tennessee.

Chapter Nine

It's the kind of ticklish situation you could have seen Ward getting into with the Beav.

I like to think we did it the way the Cleavers would have.

We stumblebummed around not knowing what in God's name we were doing for awhile.

But we stuck together.

We loved each other.

We did the best we could.

We got the job done somehow.

All before the last commercial, just like the Cleavers.

In the meantime, I have to say maybe Joanne also should consider a job as a director. Because she did inspire her dear old stepdad into the acting job of a lifetime.

Talk about your Academy Award performances.

I was thinking about giving myself an Oscar and an Emmy.

Best Performance by a Stupid Broken-Down Hammy Ex-Actor Sprinkling the Mortal Remains of a Weirdo Ex-Husband of My Wife and Father of My Wonderful Daughter Across the Tombstone of a Former Pelvis-Thrusting Rock n' Roll Singer.

I humbly accept these awards in honor of my loved ones and E.

Thankyouverymuch.

Chapter Ten
Frankly Speaking

Ryan O'Neal put his hand on my chest and shoved me aside.

Complete jerkwad that he was.

He thought that was the end of it.

He was wrong.

O'Neal and I were guests on "The Nanette Fabray Show" with Nanette Fabray and Wendell Corey.

The two of us, Ryan and I, were supposed to be on the Beverly Hills High School football team.

My friend, Earl Bellamy, was the director.

Ryan and I were supposed to walk in the front door.

Earl says, "Frank, you come in first. Ryan, you come in right after him."

So the camera rolls.

Earl goes, "Action."

And Ryan takes his hand, pushes me aside and walks in first.

"Cut," Earl says. "That's not the way I had the scene planned out.

"OK, let's go back to our marks."

So OK.

We close the door.

I look at O'Neal.

I go, "Hey, pal, didn't you hear the director?"

All of a sudden, he takes both hands, puts them in my chest and shoves me again.

He says, "I'm the guy who's gonna go in first."

And I look at him and I go, "No. You're the guy who's gonna go to the floor first."

So he gives me a little push.

I give him a push back.

I haul off on him.

It was never a question about who was going to win this fight.

This was the only question for Ryan O'Neal.

Do you want one lump or two?

Lumpy is just the man to provide what you need.

It turned out one punch was all that was required.

I wound up goin' in first.

Hey. Didn't you ever learn anything watching "Beaver" episodes?

Don't mess with Lumpy.

I never talked to this pompous peacock, O'Neal, again as long as I lived.

O'Neal was a total putz.

And everyone knew what happened.

They came up to me and said, "Frank, you're not the only guy who's had trouble with him.

"He was a jerk from the word go."

But he was under contract to Universal and they had to use him.

And yet they didn't have to use him to walk all over me.

I got a fairly good shot in on him. I mean, I didn't break anything.

It wasn't that kind of a hit.

But I certainly mussed him up nicely.

The experience illustrates one of my basic beliefs in life:

Acting ain't all it's cracked up to be.

In case you hadn't noticed, that's what you're gonna get in this chapter.

The World According to Garp—Frank Bank version.

Here's where I get to tell you what I think.

About anything.

Whatever's on my mind.

Hey, it's my book.

You want to tell me what's on your mind, write your own.

I get my hands on a copy, I'll read it.

I love reading anything.

I might learn something.

But right now, here's where I get to be a self-centered blowhard and it's your turn to read.

You might learn something.

Besides, they're paying for this. I owe you. It's the American way.

Anyway, one of my fundamental beliefs is that I wouldn't exactly want my kids to get into acting.

There are way too many people in the profession who are a few ants shy of a picnic.

You see a lot of broken psyches and chewed-up lives.

Why would I wish that kind of torment on someone I loved?

I will have to say that most of my time at Universal was wonderful.

Besides Brando, who stands as something of a towering Matterhorn of arrogance, I only had one other unpleasant experience at Universal.

It involved another fat man whose ego was so big it must have slid down to his belly. He must have been keeping something huge in there somewhere.

I speak of Alfred Hitchcock.

Yep.

The master of mystery himself.

The sultan of suspense.

The Jabba the Hut of jerks.

The dispute was kinda over my car.

Kinda over a parking space.

And kinda over nothing.

Other than Hitch being a bitch and wanting me to know he was Mt. Rushmore and I was head lice in the grand scheme of the entertainment world.

Remember this one Corvette I told you I used to have?

It was that metallic turquoise, you know, 1958 or '59.

Really cool car.

Ran like hell.

Four-speed, fuel injection.

This car rocked.

Well, every Friday afternoon, see, it was a regimen.

We would finish shooting. We usually parked our cars very close to Stage 17, where we shot "Beaver."

And with traffic starting to hit at 5 o'clock, it's going to be bumper-to-bumper on the Hollywood Freeway, going over the canyon and all that other good stuff to get home.

And before I left, I had to stop by the casting office and get next week's script.

It was close to the front gate. There are just these few rows of parking spaces.

So I get into my car.

I drive up to the front gate. I pull into this parking space.

I leave my engine running and put the parking brake on. Because I'm right near the guard gate.

I'm not more than 30 paces from the gate. They can see my car.

I remember this guy, Scotty, who was still the regular guard on duty until he died about a year ago.

He was a fixture at Universal.

I said, "Scotty," and I just sort of waved.

He knew I was going in to pick up my script. He knew my wave meant: Please keep an eye on my car. I left the engine running.

You know, why bother turning it off? I'm gonna be out in 7.5 seconds.

Chapter Ten

I didn't even open the door.

I bailed over the car.

That was the cool thing to do anyway.

It wasn't just for speed.

It was for something way more important.

Looks.

Style points.

Never open the door. Never.

That way when you came back, you could bail over the side and then sssliiide in.

Gotta slide in.

Gonna have to deduct points if you don't come over the side with that good glide and slide.

So I run into the office.

And I'm going, "Hey, Ione"— that was the script lady's name, Ione— "where's next week's script?"

Nice lady.

She'd been there forever.

And she goes, "Oh, hi Frank. Here."

She hands me the script. That's how long it took.

OK. Maybe it wasn't 7.5 seconds on the nose.

Maybe eight or nine seconds.

Ten more steps out of the casting office, back to my car.

I'm ready to glide, slide and ride, Sally, ride.

And there behind my car is this big black, hulking limo.

Right up on my bumper.

Great. Just what I need.

Some self-important yutz gumming up the works just as I'm trying to make my escape and go out and play chicken with the rest of the easy-ridin' Angelinos out on the freeways.

I walk over to the limo.

I go, "Uh, excuse me, I'd like to get out."

All of a sudden the back window of the limo opens up.

It's my good friend, Alfred Hitchcock.

He leans out the window.

He starts giving me a load of crap.

He says, "You must be an actor, because you can't read."

Which is kind of a good rip, when you think about it.

I don't know whether the 10 or 15 seconds he was waiting were enough for him to come up with something that cute.

I don't know if his mind works that quickly or what.

Maybe so.

Frankly Speaking

I mean, any guy who can make "Northwest Passage," one of the all-time great movies—or any of the other dozen great ones—must have a hair-trigger on the machine-gun mind up there.

He must be the Dan Marino of deep-thinking—you know, quick release and all that.

You're ready to get in Hitch's face, but he just fires off a quick salvo before you can reach him.

Direct hit. Score.

Hitch escapes the hit, unscathed.

But, frankly, I was in no mood to think about what a great director he was or how quickly he could rip off a one-liner.

I mean, if he hadn't been saying that to me, I mighta laughed my butt off.

But he was saying it to me.

And I didn't need the aggravation.

My fellow Angelinos were already out there revving their engines, willing and able to provide all the aggravation I needed on the L.A. Grand Prix, otherwise known as the drive home.

So as it turned out, what Fat Al was saying to me didn't strike me as being so funny.

Fact was, it was irritating as hell.

I mean he started really ragging on me.

I was parked in his space.

It was like I was the donkey and he was the all-important director, you know?

He was very deliberate and very condescending.

But you know what?

I was building up a good mad myself. And then I just wasted it.

I wound up to take a mighty blow back at the old coot, and I just whiffed.

Nothing clever came out.

No heavy artillery returning fire.

All I could do at the time was look at him and say, "I'm really sorry, Mr. Hitchcock. I was only in the space a few seconds and I do apologize because I know how I feel when someone takes my space."

And I said, "It'll never happen again."

And the guy told his driver to back it up.

He let me out.

Just retelling the story I am more aggravated than ever.

I didn't fire back on Hitchcock at all.

I just took the tongue-lashing meekly.

I wish I'd have said, "Gee, Mr. Really Terribly Significant Director Person and All-Around Genius, I'm sorry you're such a pompous butthead and your car is probably broken down from trying to haul your tub of lard all over

Chapter Ten

town. So naturally, you need to get it parked in the next seven seconds. Thanks for throwing your weight around. I guess that's why you're roughly 300 pounds, so you'll have a lot of it to toss.

"But now I gotta haul and get out on the freeway. So have a nice day lording your egocentric self over everyone you meet."

But I didn't.

I just rolled over.

I let him be an idiot with impunity.

As I get to the front gate, Scotty is sitting there doubled over laughing.

And he goes, "That beeetch, Frank." Which is Scotty for "bitch." And I said, "You know what, Scotty, the guy was right, I was in his space."

The truth is, of course, that was so.

I mean, I had hogged the guy's parking space. So I was in the wrong, even if for a millisecond.

But looking back on it, I still feel it's a bigger example of Hitchcock being an overbearing donkey than my being an inconsiderate whelp.

Again, it's my book.

Why shouldn't I make me look better?

In his book, Hitchcock could have prettied himself up and made me out to be a bigger ninny.

If he'd even bother.

Which I seriously doubt.

You have to think Alfred Hitchcock did not spend his latter years conjuring up Frank Bank memories.

In any case, they really should have had a space for "Parking, Five Minutes Only."

But parking was at such a premium. And everything was such a political move on that lot.

I mean, if you had a good parking space, you had to be God.

And, actually, I guess that's part of what I'm talking about the whole acting thing.

So much of it boiled down to superficial garbage. People getting excited about absolutely nothing.

What did we just spend the last few minutes discussing?

Parking.

That's a burning world issue.

See what I mean?

When you're in the entertainment industry, your parking space is what you think is a world-shaking concern.

And that's why I think so many guys and girls had trouble handling the fame thing.

Example.

Right next to Beaver, they always filmed "The Virginian," and they had a guy who greatly illustrates what I'm talking about.

Doug McClure

Doug was on "The Virginian."

Doug was a cool guy.

Doug just died not long ago, very young.

He didn't have a real happy life. He did "Virginian" and "Checkmate" and after that he was scrounging for a job for 25 years.

I don't know what happened.

He was God's gift to women.

They would go crazy for Doug McClure. Big smile and the blond curly hair. Doug was a great-looking guy.

And he was a real nice guy. A lot of these guys, they work in that one big show and they can never repeat it. And they spend the rest of their lives trying to duplicate it.

They're Al Bundy.

It's the truth.

You know, Warhol says you get 15 minutes of fame. Well, I've hogged up the spotlight for some reason, but he ain't too far off base.

There is an upside to fame. The flip side is the good that you can do if you're famous.

It's the weight you can carry.

Not the kind Hitchcock liked to throw around. It's the juice you pour into the positive side of things.

It's certainly not fair that entertainers have this weight, but as they say, life's a bitch and nothing is fair.

But if you use fame in the right way it can be a wonderful thing.

If you disregard the fame and you don't care about other people and only care about yourself, then fame sucks.

And you don't deserve the fame.

I don't think Sinatra deserves the fame.

Sinatra's a mean-spirited, self-centered man.

Treats people like dirt.

I think Bill Cosby deserves the fame.

Arguably speaking, Cosby went through a period when I thought he was a hypocritical guy.

Hard to put my finger on it.

It might have been a racial thing Cosby was reflecting earlier on in his life, and I'm not a racial guy.

But I think he was into a black superiority type of thing.

I don't believe in black superiority, Jewish superiority, Catholic superiority, or any other kind of superiority.

Chapter Ten

I believe in: You gotta be cool.

Sammy Davis even went through it for a little while, but he rejected it in a little while.

He had a real turnaround.

And I look at Cosby at a later date and I have to admire him a lot.

I thought the original Cosby show was so wonderful.

How about the fact that he had his kids speaking English instead of Ebonics?

I mean, when you listen to Rafer Johnson and the really cool way he spoke—or when you listen to French blacks, like Yannick Noah—you know.

Ebonics is all garbage.

Ebonics is not black language. It's a lazy American dialect.

But anyway, I think Cosby is a very, very good example of the American dream. I think he has used power very well. I think he has used fame very well.

He used it as a teacher. He set a good example for future generations. And I admire that.

Now look at Richard Pryor.

Here were two black comedians who started out five years apart. Pryor has had a much sadder life because of the MS he has now. But if you look at Pryor at his zenith and Cosby at his zenith, I think it's night and day.

It was a very sad situation with the drugs and all the other stuff for Richard Pryor.

But I'm talking about two very, very popular comedians, both basically doing the same kind of comedy, really hitting fame under the same guise.

But one being a totally admirable person who you would be very, very proud to emulate.

The other one, you wouldn't be proud to emulate—Richard Pryor.

I love Cosby's new show and my heart breaks for him with the death of his son, Ennis.

Now, Cosby's movies were pretty bad and it's hard to figure why.

In fact, he made the all-time worst movie I think in history, next to "Attack of the Killer Tomatoes" or something. What was that called, "Leonard 6"?

But Cosby is a good guy.

I like good guys.

I've always liked heroes.

Going all the way back to childhood, I always liked Hopalong Cassidy.

I always liked Roy Rogers.

Gene Autry.

I love Sean Connery.

I like all the good guys.

I couldn't vote for Bill Clinton, OK?

He's not a good guy.

I couldn't have voted for John F. Kennedy.

His charisma may have been incredible, but I knew he wasn't a good guy.

Even before the Marilyn thing came out fully before the public, I'd heard stories. I knew John F. was a far cry from his image.

I mean, I knew Kennedy was gettin' it on with Monroe from my friend, Chuck.

Chuck used to be a guy who regularly drove Marilyn out to Peter Lawford's house on the Pacific Coast Highway—it was right down just a little ways from Knights Beach, in fact, not far from the Santa Monica pier.

And Chuck drove Marilyn out there so she could make it with Jack Kennedy.

This came to light when we used to park cars at this place in Beverly Hills called Romanoff's.

And it was just like that show Edd "Kookie" Burns did on TV... "77 Sunset Strip."

You know the song, "Kookie, Kookie, lend me your comb?"

That came out of that show and the show came out of the experience we had parking cars at these places.

Like we'd park them over on Restaurant Row at the Islander.

We'd go over to The Bistro and park cars there.

It was a happenin' scene.

In fact, pretty much like the TV show where Kookie was always pickin' up broads and meetin' and greetin' the rich and famous.

Oh, yeah.

That's what it was like.

Many's the night some chick would come out and I'd say, "Hey, I'll take you home."

And I did.

Romanoff's is where I first met Sinatra.

I had thought he was really cool watching his movies.

I wanted to be a Rat Packer and be hip like Frank and Dino and Sammy and Joey and all those guys.

But when Sinatra was hanging out at these places in Beverly Hills, I found out he was one of the world's great slithering slimes.

Lawford was a fairly nice guy.

Lawford would sit out front and shoot the breeze with us all night.

And it was from parking cars and meeting Lawford that Chuck got to drive Marilyn out to be with Lawford's brother-in-law, Jack Kennedy.

Chuck would look at me and say, "I gotta go pick up Marilyn and take her out to Lawford's."

Chuck got there and he'd see Secret Service guys. Big guys with 18-inch collars, you know?

And you could see 'em lurkin' in the bushes.

And Kennedy used to arrive by helicopter a lot.

And Chuck would wait outside two, three hours while Marilyn and Jack were in there.

All right, I guess you can say Chuck never actually saw what Marilyn and Jack were doing in there.

But I guess we can safely assume they weren't talking the balance-of-trade deficit and normalization of Sino-Soviet relations.

You'd have to assume it was state-of-their-union addresses. Or undresses. Wouldn't you?

On a somewhat eerie note, because of the whole car-parking thing, I think we figured out that the last person Marilyn ever spoke to quite possibly was Joe DiMaggio, Jr.

Joe DiMaggio, Jr., used to hang out at Romanoff's.

He wasn't one of my buddies. He was buddies with a couple guys I knew there.

But I do remember that when she died in August of '62—the day after that, my friend told me, "Joe Jr., was talking to Marilyn last night."

I said, "Really, what time?"

He says, "Around 9 o'clock at night."

He said, "She died around 10 or 11, didn't she?"

I said, "Yeah."

He said, "Wow. Wow."

But anyway, I have no admiration for Jack Kennedy.

Not just the Marilyn thing.

Obviously I've been a womanizer myself, so I can't point any fingers.

But I still just think, looking at his entire life, he was one of the most ruthless men of the 20th Century.

Of the presidents I look up to, my hero of the last 30 years has to be Ronald Reagan.

Ronald Reagan is not the smartest man who ever lived, and he'll be the first one to tell you that.

But he was just like The Gipper.

He tried.

He constantly tried.

And every time he truly wanted to do the right thing.

His heart was in the right place.

I always felt that.

So whatever he did, I voted for him.

He was my leader at the Screen Actors Guild.

He was the president of the guild and he got me new contracts and he did a great job.

He was my governor for two terms. He was the best governor California ever had.

Because he left the state with no debt. The state had grown tremendously—you'd never seen such growth in your life. And we became a major force in the world economy while Ronald Reagan was governor.

Not the Browns.

Ronald Reagan.

Not when George Murphy was senator.

Ronald Reagan was the man.

Ronald Reagan was not just an actor.

He was way beyond that.

He was a man.

By and large actors have trouble with that one.

Being sound men.

Or sound women.

They are insecure.

They want everyone to like them.

I'll give you a good test.

You can walk up to an actor—an up-and-coming young actor—and you can go, "Heyyy, Joe, how are you? Remember, we met at a party over at Fox?

"And da-da, da-da, da-da."

And you know what he's gonna say?

"Yeah, how are you?"

Even when he doesn't know you from a box of rocks.

Ninety times out of a hundred that'll be his reaction.

Some totally surface response.

Because of the insecurity.

Then if you turn out to be a schmuck, he's gonna come back at you and shine you off.

But by and large his first comeback will be some tentative B.S. because of that insecurity.

They want to be loved.

That goes for all of us, of course.

It's human nature.

But for people in the arts, it's magnified a millionfold.

You are changing your personality. You are becoming somebody different every week.

Unless you're me, who was Lumpy, and then I was Lumpy every week.

But I had done so many shows around the Universal lot, I also had been a different guy at times.

Chapter Ten

So if you prepare for that, usually you were that different guy the night before you go to the studio, and you try and wake up as that character.

And I would try all the way to the studio to get into my role, because I know I'm gonna spend a lot of time as that character. So you want to become that person.

In doing this repeatedly, it becomes fairly easy to forget who you really are.

If you ever knew.

Why do you think a lot of these people turn to drugs?

Turn to suicide?

Turn to alcohol?

Because it can just be a terrible pressure as an actor.

I mean, I saw some of the leading child actors that were my contemporaries become drug addicts.

One girl who was a big, famous star, turned to prostitution because she couldn't get a job.

These other guys wound up on heroin.

Their lives were so jacked up.

After they were a star...once they got cancelled...they never got that next big vehicle.

For child actors, I think it's so much tougher than people who got into the profession later.

As adults, we spend our entire lives dealing with rejection.

It's persistence in overcoming this which makes a lot of people successful.

But if you're starting off with major rejection that early, it's just more of a mountain to climb.

But not every actor goes into the toilet.

There are lots of healthy ones.

They're normal people—or as normal as any of us is likely to get.

How do some of them stay away from drugs and other abuses?

Maybe they find more valuable things in their lives than acting.

That's the way I feel about it.

Maybe you find love.

Maybe you can find books.

Other arts.

Painting.

Singing.

Some people find religion, OK?

I always tell people I'm the luckiest guy in the world. I truly believe that.

I've haven't just had my time.

I've been having my time, forever. I haven't had great periods. I've had one hell of a great life.

Frankly Speaking

I mean, I wound up making more money than I ever dreamed I could possibly make, being more successful at a job than I ever dreamed I could possibly be.

And guess what, that job wasn't being Lumpy.

Or any other make-believe part.

That job was the self-satisfaction of becoming a great financial analyst.

The other things that saved me were my families.

Both the one I have now and the one I had growing up.

I can't emphasize enough how great Leonard and Sylvia were.

I had two of the greatest parents anyone could ever wish for.

They were not rich.

They were not the smartest people.

They had all heart.

They loved me incessantly.

I told you my dad was my best friend. And that we were sports junkies.

Well, as shallow as that may seem, our shared love of sports just seemed to make our relationship so easy to take.

It smoothed out a lot of rough places.

It gave us common ground.

Even though, yes, it was just a bunch of people running around in funny-looking clothes engaged in a basically meaningless pursuit, when placed on a world scale of any real significance, it still gave Dad and I bond.

And that bond meant everything.

It wasn't built on sports alone.

Hell, no.

There was lots of stuff about acting right and working hard and trying to be a decent person and all that kind of thing.

But sports just gave us a peace between us.

All we ever did was talk about baseball and football and basketball.

I'll never forget one night, we were listening to the Lakers on the radio.

It was during a Passover seder.

When Pops Selvy missed this really famous shot, Dad spilled the wine on the table.

We were so shaken.

That was the shot heard round the world—or what passed for it in our own little corner at the time.

Selvy, in the last second of the seventh game of the NBA finals against the Boston Celtics, throws a ball up.

It's the winning shot.

It's in the basket.

It rims the basket.

It comes back out.

Chapter Ten

It was in and out, and it cost the Lakers their first world championship in 1962.

So Leonard the Sport spills the wine.

It's this traditional seder and Leonard says, "Son of a bitch." Leonard was livid.

I was livid.

And then my mother's going, "Len. It's Passover."

He goes, "Yeah, I know it's Passover. But the son-of-a-bitch missed that shot."

And my mom goes, "Len, don't get your balls in an uproar."

My mom always told my dad that whenever he blew his stack.

And my dad goes, "Yeah, Sylvia. But my balls need to be in an uproar. The son-of-a-bitch missed the shot."

And the thing is, I understood.

I was on a perfect wavelength. With both of them.

It was a sacred moment, the seder.

I got that point.

Mom was right in getting the message across.

But, hey, the son-of-a-bitch did miss the shot.

And I understood that, too.

I'm sittin' there pretty much in total agreement with my dad on the matter.

How often do you get that growing up.

Yeah, Dad.

Right on, brother-man.

Hey, we had a right to be hacked.

Even at a seder.

Hell, Moses would have spilled the wine.

Abraham would have been upset, too.

I believe God understands this.

And I mean, we had plenty of opportunity to be pretty torqued at the local talent on our sports teams at the time.

We were big Ram fans, too.

The Rams.

My cousin, Sid Gillman, was the coach.

He was married to Bailey Bank. She was a cousin of mine. Actually, she was my father's cousin, but that made me a second or third or whatever cousin.

Close enough kin to inject additional suffering into the Rams picture.

The last fond remembrance of the Rams I have was the championship game of 1950 against the Cleveland Browns.

With Tommy Fears and Elroy Hirsch at the ends, Bob Waterfield and

Norm Van Brocklin as quarterbacks, Vitamin T. Smith and Tank Younger and Stan West on the line.

This was our team.

Not too shabby.

We were up against big Otto Graham—only quarterback I ever saw, wore No. 60. Then he changed it to 14 at the end.

But they had Marion Motley...there were some pretty good players in that game.

The Rams broke my heart for 32 years. You know, you talk about being a Cub fan...the way we went through the '60s and '70s when we had George Allen, we were knockin' on the door every single year.

We had such incredible players. I mean, the Fearsome Foursome is the greatest defensive line in the history of football, and we couldn't win a goddam championship because we couldn't beat the Vikings and the Cowboys.

Every year.

I met Merlin Olsen of the Fearsome Foursome, and you talk about a vicious football player who looks like the biggest pussycat in the world.

When Merlin Olsen tackled you, you stayed down. He had a set of mitts on him and he slammed you.

I have his jersey from the 50th anniversary of the NFL. He was named to the top 50 team in the NFL.

So I've got Merlin Olsen's No. 74 jersey that he wore when we lost to the Cowboys in the championship game.

I bought it at auction on public television—California Educational Televison. KCET. I bought it for 80 bucks. You know how many thousands it's worth now? I would say somewhere between $5,000 and $10,000.

If I had it autographed...you know, Merlin Olsen's agency is down here in Ventura. I know he'd autograph it for me if I took it in. He's a sweetheart of a man.

Right Merlin?

The Lakers were better to us fans in so many ways.

We were truly blessed.

We had Elgin Baylor. We had Jerry West.

Elgin was god.

And Jerry was god, jr.

And you know what?

They took turns being god and god, jr.

Chamberlain and Russell and all those guys were in the league then, and they belonged on any all-time team.

But we had Zeke From Cabin Creek—Jerry West. At the end of the game, you would rather give the ball to Zeke than put your money on a horse that was going to win by 20 lengths.

Chapter Ten

Because Zeke was the greatest clutch shooter in the history of basketball. He was un-be-lievable. He was ice. I mean, they called George Gervin the Iceman, but he wasn't squat next to Zeke.

Oh, God, Zeke was it.

Too bad he wasn't around to take that shot Pops Selvy took. The Lakers would have won a title right then and there.

And Sylvia wouldn't have had to get the wine out of the tablecloth.

The Dodgers, of course, were a whole different matter entirely.

Here, we Angelinos had it as good as it ever gets in this world for sports. We had Sandy and Don.

It didn't really matter who else we had.

We had Koufax and Drysdale.

We had some other good players, sure.

But as long as we had Sandy Koufax and Don Drysdale, it didn't really matter what weak sisters you brought out there.

You were going to lose to us. The Dodgers.

Sandy truthfully only had seven or eight great years, but that's all he needed, boy.

I guess of all the sports—and I love sports so dearly—the greatest sports duels I think I've ever seen were the Sandy Koufax-Juan Marichal pitching duels.

They were the treat of a lifetime.

How I hated that man, Marichal.

The 32 different arm angles, the leg kick. His kick was all the way to Venus.

And what a scumbag. He went after Roseboro, our catcher, with that bat that day.

And you know what? He got the short end of the stick for it. He got what he deserved. History has never treated him with the respect that he deserved.

In a way that was wrong.

See, Bob Gibson got in right away into the Hall of Fame.

Juan Marichal, who had to wait to get in, was 10 times the pitcher Gibson was. I know Midwest guys don't like to hear that. I'm telling you, Marichal was better than Gibson.

And I hated him.

He was a Giant.

I was a Dodger.

When I saw No. 27, Marichal, hit the mound, I'm sitting there going, "OK. Maury Wills will bunt, get on first base. He'll steal second. Charlie Neal will lay down the sacrifice to send him to third. And Frank Howard'll hit the fly ball to bring him home.

"The Dodgers win, 1-to-nothing, with Koufax."

That's how we won the pennant in 1962.

Sandy did it.

And in '63. I mean, every time Sandy pitched, you expected a no-hitter.

He used to put 10,000 people in the stands wherever he went.

He was the greatest gentleman, the most incredible pitcher, I have ever seen.

I have never seen a pitcher with control like he had, with speed, with finesse.

They've tried to name the greatest athlete, and people argue, like, Jim Brown from football. Or Wilt Chamberlain in basketball. Or you could say Magic Johnson.

But for command of a sport, to be the most dominant force in your sport, Sandy Koufax to me was the greatest athlete of professional baseball, football or basketball.

Not swimming, because Mark Spitz holds that slot down with seven world records and seven gold medals.

Yeah, right, Carl Lewis in track and field. But, look, it took Carl Lewis 50 jillion Olympics. Spitz did it in one. With a death threat over his head.

But no one holds a candle to Koufax in my mind.

You had to see Sandy to believe him.

I was in the stands for two of the no-hitters.

The second no-hitter I was sitting in about the 10th row behind home plate.

I'm tellin' you, I saw the dust coming off Roseboro's mitt—every time that ball hit that catcher's pocket like a rocket.

I wanted to go, "My God, his hand must be throbbing."

Sandy must have been going 102 to 105 miles an hour, and each one of those pitches was dead at the crack of the knee on the inside or the outside portion of the plate.

And he would sit there and he would throw a rainbow curve that looked like it came from Cleveland.

You couldn't pick this son-of-a-gun up until it was past you.

It wasn't even fair.

These guys were missing the ball so bad.

And Sandy was effortless.

He didn't break a sweat.

He was just so good.

I have Sandy's uniform framed and autographed in my den.

If I had to carry something out of a burning building, I would yell at Rebecca (well, at least, I'd make sure she knew how to get out) to take a few pictures of the kids.

Then I would run downstairs to the den.

Chapter Ten

I'd tell Sophie, our long-haired dachshund, "You better follow me." Same for Mr. Benny and Neemer, the cats. "You better follow Sophie."

And then I would grab that autographed uniform of Sandy off the wall and carry it out of the burning building.

It means a lot to me.

I bought his uniform in 1969.

It wasn't autographed but I knew it was authentic. It was the Rawlings uniform. It was before everyone and his brother started making jerseys.

In fact, I was talking to this sports memorabilia guy one day and he mentioned he had a Don Newcombe uniform and a Sandy Koufax uniform and a Duke Snyder uniform.

All three Dodgers, among the greatest of the greats.

Why I didn't go after all three of them, I'll never know.

But all I do is look at him and ask, "How much you want for the Sandy uniform."

"I don't really think I want to sell it," he said.

I said, "I'll give you a hundred bucks for it."

He says, "Nah."

I know he's playin' me—remember, not too many people beat me at poker. But I don't care.

I want the jersey.

I said, "I'll give you 200 bucks, and I'll give you cash so you won't have to report it."

He said, "OK."

So I gave him 200 bucks.

And I had the uniform in my closet for years. I didn't get it autographed by Sandy until five years ago.

My daughter Kelly's girlfriend at school...her dad owned this chain of stores. Still does. I think it's the biggest chain of sports memorabilia in the country.

They're all over the place.

And Sandy appeared there. Sandy is under contract...he would have autographed it for nothing, but he has to charge $85 because of the contract.

So I said, "Hey, that's cool. I understand that."

I'd have given him a thousand for it. I didn't care.

So when I was in Kansas City, I took the jersey over to this great framer in Lenexa, this suburb on the Kansas side.

The woman looks at me and says, "We just did two George Brett jerseys in the last two weeks."

I said, "Well, there's No. 32. I want it very special."

And she put a beautiful Dodger blue background on a gorgeous pine frame. And it's just a tremendous piece.

I bought a Joe DiMaggio autographed picture and I think I got a pretty good price for it.

I paid $400.

DiMaggio was very, very shy on handing out autographs.

I have an autographed picture of Ted Williams made up.

Ted was a big hero.

I consider Ted the greatest hitter I ever saw with my own two eyes.

Ted was this very tall, thin, elegant man, wound up like a swiss watch. And he would go through that ball and follow through with the most incredible, sweetest swing I have ever seen.

In talking about these people, it may strike you as misspent emotion.

Maybe so.

Maybe I should have invested my heart and soul in something more meaningful.

Well, I did. My wife, my kids, my job.

But after that, why get worked up about fun and games?

It's just the way I am.

I think these people display an artistry that touches us in beautiful ways.

Horses affected me that way.

I cried when Native Diver died.

I went to his funeral at Hollywood Park.

I swear to God.

To this day, I have a Native Diver sweatshirt.

He was my horse.

Native Diver was the only three-time winner of the Hollywood Gold Cup.

I followed this horse whenever he'd run. I would be at the track to watch him.

He had guts.

He'd come out of the gates, open up a four, five-length lead, and then take a breather on the far turn.

The entire pack would catch up with him.

He'd look.

He'd see them.

And then he'd just take off.

It was like a kid, "Na-na-na-na-na."

And he'd win by five lengths.

He died on the way down to Del Mar.

He choked.

Something happened and they couldn't save him.

Everyone went crazy when Native Diver died.

And I cried like a baby.

Hollywood—Los Angeles in general—was so great back then.

Chapter Ten

It's gone downhill a lot, in so many ways.

Now that I'm back out here, I see the changes, some bad, some good.

I drive down Melrose, and it's the hippest street in the country now.

It was not hip growing up.

It was old and Jewish.

I drive by the original Johnny Rockets, and it reminds me of Sylvia.

She passed away at the Golden Age Retirement Center there.

I made a deal with Johnny Rockets to bring my mother food across the street.

That way she didn't have to eat the crummy food at the home all the time.

My mother loved burgers and stuff like that.

I drive from there over to Santa Monica Boulevard now, and all you see are 2,000 degenerates and the Pussycat Theater and the Pleasure Chest sex store.

Go down Sunset, and you get a couple hundred hookers.

Hollywood Boulevard, the scene of so many wonderful, unbelievable nights, is a trash heap now, tantamount to skid row.

But I'll never drive around these places without thinking of the good times.

Good?

Hell, they were great times.

I'll never, ever forget my days in the Knights.

They've never really become bygone days.

I never quit being a Knight.

I am president today of the Knights Alumni Club.

I was the Most Valuable Member once, an honor my fellow Knights bestowed on me my senior year.

There are hundreds of Knights out there.

We still see each other.

We've had reunions.

Enormous ones.

The club only lasted about nine years.

But at its height, it was the ultimate expression of that time of life for kids growing up in Southern California

The Knights meant, you know, I wasn't worrying about staying home and not having any friends.

Man, I had thousands of friends.

And they weren't fake friends.

They were good friends.

I earned them.

And they earned my friendship back.

I learned a lot of love and loyalty from my friends.

Even though a lot of times the stuff we did wasn't the most commendable or meaningful, the relationships meant something.

They meant everything.

If someone is good to you, then you gotta be good back to them. Those were our mottos.

There's like 200 Knights that have been in and out of that club.

If any one of them ever called me for a favor or ever needed me for anything, to this day, I would be there for them.

I'd go to the wall for them. Because they're my club brothers.

The experiences we had, they stick with you.

So does some other stuff.

I talked about some of the putzes in the acting field.

There were some princes, too.

I loved Slim Pickens. He used to sit out in front of the stages with us, telling us stories.

Slim was one of the neatest guys I ever met. He loved kids. He loved 'em. He was such a nice guy.

He'd talk about how we should grow up and respect our parents. And learn all we could from books. And don't put too much faith in show business, because it'll only break your heart, stuff like that.

I cried like a baby when Slim died.

He was a man, being nice to kids...he could have sat there and played Hollywood Movie Star or Veteran Hollywood Feature Character Actor all he wanted. But he sat there and took time out to come and sit with us. And we were kids then.

He was doing all kinds of movies at Universal. He was always around.

Slim was in everything. He was one workin' actor.

I mean, I used to see Slim at least twice a month.

He'd sit out there smoking cigarettes in his cowboy boots and cowboy hats.

And he did say, "Shee-ut."

He'd go, "Weh, bo-ahs."

Meaning, "Well, boys."

He had that Southern-fried accent you could cut with a knife.

You wanted to just put your head in his chest and go, "Take care of me, Slim."

He was so cool.

He was from "Tee-ex-as."

I don't know that for a fact, but I would have to guess.

He just told us to stay straight and walk the line and be a good person and do everything right.

And the good guys would win.

Kinda like Leonard.

Chapter Ten

Kinda like my dad.

There was a lotta Leonard in Slim.

You always had to be the good guy and you had to wear the white hat.

Slim was sweet.

And, of course, no one meant more than the cast of "Beaver."

Even back in the days of civil unrest, it used to cause me great unrest when rebels my age would dog Ward and June.

When they didn't respect June Cleaver's pearls, I said, "Leave me out. That's it.

"You wanna fight about it?"

You have to be true to your beliefs.

And I believe in Barbara and Hugh and Ward and June and Tony and Wally and Kenny and Eddie and Jerry and the Beaver.

I believe in "Beaver."

I believe it'll always live.

It'll always be a special part of the American tapestry.

Part of our self-portrait.

Part of our feeling about what makes us great.

There was a time when I didn't want to be known as Lumpy.

Even though I wasn't the big star of the show, it used to bug me when I'd go out and people felt like they could invade your privacy.

I grew a beard just for that reason. I was able to travel around pretty anonymously.

I remember one time I was at the top of the Washington Monument with my first wife.

These four kids cornered me.

They were really giving me grief.

They were goin', "Beaver's a big fag."

All that kinda stuff.

And they go, "Oh, Lumpy, you weren't so tough.

"You weren't so cool."

And I wanted to go, "You know, I could take you pitiful little punks and throw you down the stairs."

But I didn't.

I figured, "OK, I'm still a public figure." Even though I'd been out of "Beaver" for a year or two.

I grew the beard and I kept it for 25 years.

I did it so I wouldn't be recognized. I wouldn't have to go through any of that crap.

Whether it be good stuff or bad stuff, it wouldn't involve my life as an actor.

I figured, "I'm not in showbiz anymore."

Frankly Speaking

I want Frank Bank back.

But then I found out it's pretty stupid to run from all that.

Running into Becka helped.

I knew she loved me for being just Frank. Nothing else.

She always tells anyone, "I didn't marry Frank Bank, the actor. I married Frank Bank."

That sort of freed me up to love the actor that was in the past.

It allowed me to take full joy in the beautiful thing that "Beaver" was.

Today, I enjoy being Lumpy, just as much as I enjoy being Frank.

It's not an ego thing.

It's a comfort thing.

I'm comfortable with all the things that happened in my life, good, bad, ugly.

Lumpy was a good thing.

Call me Lumpy.

As to the bad stuff you've discovered in this book, I'm sorry for it.

Wish I hadn't been so callous.

Wish I hadn't been so selfish.

Wish I hadn't been so unkind.

But I'm also grateful for the good times with good people who feel like I've been good to them.

Because I've wanted to.

I wanted to wear the white hat.

Even when I was wearing cheese for a hat.

That happened when I had my heart attack in '96.

I guess I didn't tell you much about that yet, did I?

It was in K.C.

I guess it was a pretty serious one.

They said so.

Even though it never seemed like it was to me at the time.

It started so innocently.

Sunday night, September 30, 1996.

The Dodgers had just lost their third game in a row to San Diego. Now, each night I went down to the basement, to my big movie theater down there, to watch the Dodger game in peace and quiet.

Because I didn't want to disturb my animals. I didn't want to disturb my family, or anyone else.

Because I knew I'd be yellin' and screamin'.

Don't tell me I don't know what's important in life.

Anyway, as ludicrous as it sounds, the Dodgers lost three 1-run games to San Diego. All they had to do was win one game out of three to win the National League West pennant.

They lost all three.

Chapter Ten

I was so upset, I can't begin to tell you.

I came upstairs just in time to watch the Chiefs lose their first game of the year to the Chargers after they were 4-and-0.

I had a really lousy Sunday with the curse of San Diego and all that.

But I didn't know how bad it was gonna get.

It was gonna get worse.

Becka made dinner. She made this really good pasta.

Along about 9 o'clock, I started feeling very anxious. I couldn't sit still. Then I started feeling kind of a heatness, a burning in my chest.

It wasn't pain. It was heat.

And I figured, "Oh, well, it mighta been too much hot pepper in the pasta that I ate," because I always put lots of hot chili pepper on pasta.

So I said, "I'm gonna go upstairs to take a Zantac for the burning. And while I'm up there, I'm gonna take a Xanax. Because I'm feelin' really antsy. I'm really upset about the games."

So I do that, and I come downstairs and we're watchin' the news. About an hour goes by.

For some crazy reason, it wasn't clearing up. I could just feel this warmth along my chest, kind of like someone had laid a warm compress on me.

And all of a sudden, I sorta I broke out in a cold sweat. It's about 11 o'clock.

I said to Becka, "Well, I can do one of two things here. I could go upstairs, take another Zantac and another Xanax and crawl under the covers, cuz I got a big day at the office tomorrow."

But I said, "Here's what I'm gonna do, Beck"—and I don't know what possessed me to think about doing this, but I said, "I think I'm gonna go jump in the car and drive down State Line to St. Joseph's Hospital.

"And let them give me something, because they've got something a little stronger to get rid of this anxiety attack."

I mean, I'm really nervous as a cat.

That's all it was.

I wasn't hurtin'.

I wasn't having any heart attack.

That's the last thing I ever thought of.

First, Becka says, "We can't do that."

She wanted to call 911.

And I go, "Well, I'm not callin' 911. I don't want to wake up the neighbors on a Sunday night."

She couldn't drive me down there, because she'd just had foot surgery and she couldn't walk. It was all wrapped up.

So I said, "I tell ya what I'm gonna do. I'm gonna dial our home number on the car phone."

I went out in the garage and I called and I said, "Pick up the phone."

She picks up the phone.

I said, "OK, can you hear me?"

I said, "I'm gonna talk to you on the way down to the hospital and you'll see that I'm OK."

I said, "Beck. I can't hit anything. There ain't anything on the road at 11 o'clock on Sunday night in Kansas City.

I said, "I couldn't even hit a jackrabbit."

I'm drivin' down the street and I say, "OK, I'm passin' by the funeral home (maybe I shouldn't have mentioned that one). All right, passing by HyVee. OK, I'm passing by Barstow School. All right, here I am, I can see the hospital down here on the right. I'm turnin' on Carondelet Drive..."

I turn down the street. I see the ambulance entrance to the emergency room. Big red neon sign.

"Emergency Entrance."

There isn't a car in sight. There's nothing around this Emergency Entrance.

It's a big portecochere. I'm driving a big Chrysler LHS.

But I look in there and it says, "Emergency Parking Only."

And it says, "Other Parking for the Emergency Room" with an arrow to the right.

That was about a block and a half down.

I said, "You know what, some guy could be comin' in here hurt or something like that."

So I just turned and drove down a block and a half and parked the car.

I was wearing shorts and a T-shirt. I had my driver's license and my insurance card with me, and that was it.

I finally come walkin' into the ambulance entrance. And this guy looks at me and he goes, "You havin' chest pains?"

I said, "No. But I'm feelin' a little warmth up here in my chest."

And he just looked at me. He got like scared. He jumped up from behind the counter. He ran around and grabbed a wheelchair.

He looped around behind me and scooped me up in the wheelchair.

Now he starts running with me—and then he hits the wall just as these doors were gonna fly open. He gets straightened out and whooshes through the doors.

Somethin' out of "ER."

And the next thing I know, these two dudes grab me. And they pick me up and put me on this gurney, sittin' up.

So now I'm flyin' down the hall.

In about two seconds there's about four or five people workin' on me. They're puttin' all the pipes on me and checkin' my blood pressure and all

Chapter Ten

this stuff.

I'm trying to say to these guys, "I just want something to take away this heat."

And they put me on the EKG.

Then I see this one guy, who looks very Jewish, wearing a white coat and carrying a clipboard. I figured he must be the doctor.

He looks at me and he says, "Mr. Bank. Calm down."

And I said, "Calm down? This guy's just stuck me. I'm just here to get something because I've got some indigestion here."

He looked straight at me and he said, "Mr. Bank. We're trying to save your life. You're having a massive heart attack."

I said, "I'm what?"

I said, "Get real."

I still didn't really believe I was having anything except indigestion.

So then this other guy puts this needle in my arm. He goes, "Blood sugar, 430."

I go, "Get the hell out of here."

I said it a little worse than that.

I said, "My blood sugar isn't probably more than 120 or 130 right now. "

I said, "Do it again."

He does it again.

He goes, "460."

I said, "Get rid of this guy. He doesn't know..."

He interrupts me: "Mr. Bank. You're blood sugar is 460. It goes crazy when you're having a heart attack. Now shut up. I'm trying to save your life."

Now he's hangin' this bottle of stuff on my arm. Puts a needle in my arm. And there's this little bottle.

And he says, "Mr. Bank, that bottle costs $2,800. I'm trying to save your life with that."

It was called TPA.

Guess what's goin' through my mind.

"Am I gonna die?"

Nah.

"Am I in pain?"

Nah.

"Am I goin' through any fear?"

Nah.

What's goin' through my mind?

"I'm here for 10 minutes and I betcha my bill here's gonna be five grand."

That's what was goin' through my mind.

You gotta love it, huh?

I must really be sick...in the head, not the heart. Right?

But I was beside myself.

I felt like such a pigeon that they were really gonna clean my clock with the bill.

Well, the next thing I know, here come my cousins Tom and Deanna, along with Becka.

The doctor has called them at my house.

And Becka's sittin' there lookin' like a drowned rat. She's got tears in her eyes.

Tom and Deanna ain't lookin' like they just got done watchin' a Charlie Chaplin movie, either.

And Becka comes over to me and puts her arms around me.

I just looked at her and said, "Beek. Don't sweat it. Nothin's gonna happen here.

"I'm tellin' ya."

And she starts cryin', "I don't want to lose you." And "ta-da-tada-ta-da."

And I said, "I'm not goin' anywhere. There's no way I'm havin' a heart attack. Screw them."

I said, "But I'm feelin' a little bit better."

Needless to say, I was probably so stoned on the drugs they'd given me by then, I didn't know where the heck I was.

Next thing I know, they've got me upstairs in intensive care and Becka's with me. She says, "I'll be back in a couple hours, about 8 o'clock in the morning."

By this time I'm hooked up to all kinds of wires. This was all goin' on till about 4 or 5 in the morning.

So at 8, she says, "The kids are coming."

I said, "What do you mean, the kids are coming?"

"Well, I had to tell the girls," she said.

I went, "Yeah, but Julie's in Boston. Kelly's in San Francisco. Michelle is in Madison, Wisconsin. And Joanne is in Riverside County in California."

She said, "The kids are all coming."

"They are very upset."

So she tells me later the doctors had said, "You better get your family together."

So apparently they thought it was more than I did.

And I guess they knew and I guess it was.

So they got me stabilized. And I had a pretty positive attitude. Because I wasn't goin' anywhere. I knew that.

I don't know why.

Something just told me.

This was not my time.

Chapter Ten

I was too stupid to have any fear of death.

I wasn't afraid.

I was ignorant.

You know what?

Sometimes it pays to be ignorant.

So the worst part of this whole deal, now it's 8 o'clock at night and they got me all doped up, with pipes comin' out of me—in comes Julie and Kelly.

You have to understand something. My kids can be a little on the emotional side.

They lean over my bed and the tears start falling onto my face.

And you know what? I'm feelin' guilty as hell now. I'm goin', "Hey, you guys, what are you cryin' about? I'm here. It's over with. I'm fine. Look at me. I'm great.

"C'mon, let's go to the ballgame. C'mon, we'll go out to Stroud's. Or let's go over to Arthur Bryant's and get some ribs."

I mean, unfortunately, that's what got me there to begin with, but you know...

Anyhow, the doc comes in and he says they want to do this angiogram thing where they run a line up your coronary arteries, inject some dye and take a "picture" of your heart.

But they have to get me stabilized and they can't do it until Thursday. This is Monday night by now.

They said because of the heart attack, my heart had swollen and they wanted to give it a chance to go down a little bit.

By now, Michelle shows up from Wisconsin.

And she brings me this really cool cheesehead.

Cheesehead?

Well, if you follow the Green Bay Packers, you already know.

If you don't, I'll explain.

It's a big yellow plastic triangle that looks like a piece of swiss cheese, with a hole in the bottom so you can wear it like a hat.

Which the crazy loons who root for Green Bay do, en masse, each Sunday.

It's tacky to the max, and it's completely cool.

I really dug this cheesehead, because I was rootin' hard for the Packers by then.

Because I had this really good bet on them to win the Super Bowl at 8-to-1.

I had put a little bit of money for the Chiefs to win at 25-to-1. That was sentimental money. The real money I had put on the Packers at 8-to-1.

Everybody else was goin', "It's the Cowboys and the 49ers before the season began," but I said, "Nope. It's the Packers this time."

I thought they'd improved just enough to beat 'em and the Cowboys were getting self-destructive and I knew the 49ers were over the hill.

So I was in Vegas and I'd put this bet down on the Packers.

It wasn't huge. But about 150 bucks at 8-to-1. Hey, that was great.

So now I got my cheesehead on.

And now they start takin' me for tests the next couple of days. And, you know, they won't let you walk to the tests. So this dude comes in with the wheelchair.

And wherever I went in the hospital, I had my cheesehead on.

I didn't go anywhere without my cheesehead.

One guy says, "Wouldn't you like to leave that here? You'll be back in a few minutes."

I said, "I don't leave home without my cheesehead or my American Express Card."

So they didn't say anything more to me.

So now, I got to do this angiogram thing.

And I keep hearing the doctor going, "Tsk-tsk-tsk-tsk."

And I said, "Now, wait a minute. I don't ever like to hear anyone say, 'Whoops,' or 'tsk-tsk-tsk' in a doctor's office.

"Tsk-tsk-tsk is one of the two words or noises you don't wanna hear."

So now I'm layin' on the gurney here, and I'm lookin' at my heart on a television set. I'm layin' down, and they've got this dye in me and all this stuff.

So the doctor comes over and sticks his face in my face while I'm layin' on the gurney—freezin' my tush off, I might add, because it was really cold in there.

And he says, "Look, Mr. Bank, here's your main artery. It's 95 percent blocked."

And I went, "Uh-huh."

And he goes, "And here's this other artery. It's totally disintegrated."

And I went, "Wow."

And I could actually see...I mean, this artery was shot, man. It looked like detour down a bad road.

He sticks this thing up and he goes, "Then there's this other artery. You've got about an 80 percent blockage in this one."

He keeps goin' and finally, I said, "I get your point."

I said, "All right, what's the story?"

I said, "Am I gonna buy the farm or can you fix me?"

He goes, "Well..."

And I go, "Oh, the bypass."

And he goes, "Yep."

I said, "You think that'll work?"

He says, "Oh yeah."

And I said, "Well, I know you guys have got it pretty well perfected."

Chapter Ten

I said, "Let's go. Let's do it."

So I said, "Who's the best doctor?"

And I had heard it was a guy named Ham Hannah.

He said, "The guy's really good."

But they said he was real busy.

I said, "I don't care. I only live once. Get him."

So I get him to come to my room. And I think he was trying to palm me off on another doctor.

But then I got to him. I told him, "Listen, pal. This is a no-choice situation for you. If you kill me, you'll never work in this town again. Because you're killin' a living TV legend."

I said, "If you make it, I'm gonna bust your chops, because you're a really nice guy. But I'll really be appreciative."

Well, he cracks up and he starts laughin'.

Five minutes later, we're talkin' about old-time rock 'n' roll music.

He was a big rock 'n' roll fan. Needless to say, I was a big rock 'n' roll expert.

So we got along famously.

I dug this guy.

He was a cool guy. He was my idea of what a doctor should be.

And you know what? I trusted my life with him.

I said, "Ham. You gotta do me."

And he says, "I'll do you."

He says, "We'll do it Tuesday."

I said, "No problem waitin' 'til Tuesday?"

He said, "Well keep you alive."

So I had to wait from Thursday 'til Tuesday.

So Monday night football, the 49ers are playin' the Packers, and I'm sittin' in the hospital room and I'm really not that nervous.

And I got my cheesehead.

And I'm all by myself.

And the kids had already gone home.

Becka had left.

I was havin' surgery at dawn.

Eleven o'clock, they're in overtime in this game.

The door opens up.

It's Ham.

He looks in. And he goes, "How are ya?"

And I go, "Why aren't you home sleeping?"

He says, "Don't you worry about me."

I said, "No. I am worried about you. You've got a big day tomorrow. You have a very important surgery."

He says, "I'm gonna be just fine. I want to check you out."

And man, the guy comes over and he sits on my bed.

And he puts his arm around me.

And we start talkin' about the football game.

And I said, "Well, I'd kinda like to see the Packers win here because I've got a bet."

And I said, "By the way, I might add, I plan on collecting this bet."

And he just looks at me and he smiles again.

The guy was cool.

And he stays there with me until the game is over. And then he says, "All right, I'm gonna go home and get some rest. I'll see ya at 6."

Well, I didn't know, but when he got home, he got an emergency phone call and he was up half the night.

But right there at 6 o'clock in the morning, they wheel me into surgery.

I got my cheesehead on.

Whatta ya think.

I'm leavin' that behind?

No way.

As I'm goin' down the hall, there's a few people yellin', "Go-Go!"

They really were. It was funny. It was nice and light.

And then, of course, we had a very touching moment with Becka and the kids before I went into surgery.

But I told 'em, and I meant it sincerely, I said, "I'll see ya in a few hours. I'm tellin' ya the guy is cool. Everything's gonna be OK."

Becka says, "It better be."

And I said, "It's gonna be. I promise you.

"I don't break my promises."

So the next thing I know, I wake up.

Problem was, I woke up six hours too early.

They explained to me I'd have this breathing pipe down my throat, and there wasn't gonna be anyone there to take it out until 7 in the morning.

I opened up one eye, and it was 12:30 in the morning and it scared the hell out of me. I felt like I was gagging and I couldn't breathe.

That was probably the worst six hours of my life.

But Ham showed up at dawn. They took the pipe out.

I knew I was OK.

From there on in, it was a piece of cake.

And I got out of the hospital a week later and started my recuperation and all that.

I went to see Ham and I brought him an autographed picture.

And the autographed picture said, "Ham, you saved my bacon."

He cracked up.

And I said to him, "You tell me no one ever said that to you before."

Chapter Ten

He said, "I've been doing this 23 years and nobody ever said that to me."

And I said, "Well, then you had a bunch of dullards you were hackin' away on, pal."

But I said, "I really do appreciate it. I do thank you. And you won't be sorry."

He was a cool guy and a great surgeon, and tellin' you about him right now is just one tiny way I can begin to repay him.

Ham lives in Prairie Village, Kansas. And you won't find a better doc anywhere in the world.

If you need one, look him up.

Because Ham is one smoooth operator.

I am living proof, here to tell you about it.

I'll offer him up as one last example, for the time being, of the fact that I have been watched over.

I have been blessed.

More than anyone I can think of, I have so much to be grateful for.

Before I went in for surgery, someone asked me if I was worried about it. I told 'em no.

But I told 'em that I thought about going up to heaven.

And I imagined whoever's on the Pearly Gates asking me, "Do you want more years?"

I'd have said, "Yeah. Heck yeah. I'd like more years.

"But if I don't get 'em?

"I can't complain.

"I definitely got my 54 years worth."

And I totally feel that way.

But I also totally feel this, just as strongly:

The true end to this book hasn't been written yet.

My story—our story—Becka's and mine—has a great future.

There's a lot in store for us.

And I just want you to know, Becka, honey, we're gonna wind up somewhere on the Monterrey coast between Big Sur and Carmel.

We're gonna be sittin' on a rock in front of the surf.

Watchin' the sun go down.

Some beautiful music.

Holding hands and drinking a beautiful glass of wine.

Just lookin' up.

Gotta look up.

There's all kinds of great things to look up to.

Afterword

By Rebecca Bank

ear Frank,

We finished reading the last three chapters of the

first draft of your book tonight. I loved every chapter. The last three especially. The emotions they brought out in both of us were so intense. Tears, tenderness and uncontrollable laughter; thanks mostly to Elliot. You immortalized him forever. I'm sure he's smiling.

When I read the words you wrote about me, they took my breath away. You still know how to give me goose bumps. You know I believe in the meant to be's ... the things that are b'shert. Karma, and that everything happens for a reason. There are no coincidences. Well, you mentioned soul mates. Yes. Yes. Yes. I believe in soul mates, and I truly believe we have shared our lives for eons past, and eons yet to come. If I had a magic wand, I would wave it over all humanity so that each person could find their own true love. I guess I was at the right place and time when we met. Does that make me lucky or was that the hand of fate?

You know Frankie, I've had people ask me why I wasn't appalled and humiliated to have my husband so openly and explicitly write a book focusing on the details of his sex-capades. I explain that I already know your stories from front and back, sexual or just plain outrageous. Nothing about you shocks me anymore. I tell them that for many years I assumed that maybe 50% of what you told me was true, and the rest well, maybe stretched. How could one person have such a life. Over the years though, I've either met the person that matched the story, or met someone who confirmed everything you had told me, and sometimes more. I tell them that the late 50's and the 60's were "The Days", and all was possible. It was the cutting edge. Look, I say, Frank was a star of one of the top television shows of the time, he had a great personality, he dressed nice, and drove the most awesome cars. Who wouldn't want to hang around and be part of the life of such a magnanimous guy? Us Southern California baby boomers can all relate I'm sure.

Yeah, maybe not to the extremes that Frank went to. Maybe we didn't participate in the game of life quite the way he did. But we of that generation were all touched by the times, and it was fun. I believe that you are right – those were the Happier Days, things were much more carefree then.

Now to the nitty gritty. Frankie, I do take exception to some things that you brought up for the all the world to know. You just had to call me Beeky didn't you? That's the kinda thing that makes me want to box your ears. You could have at least explained how my name got from Rebecca to Beeky in the first place. Do you remember? You know I've gone by the name Becka most of my life. I think you weren't crazy about that one. You began to improvise. The "root" name was Beekstrom. From there it went to Beekus of Stromms. That's where I started referring to you as Frankus T. Bankus. From Beekus of Stromms came Strommie, Strommberg, then Strommberg Carlson, then it was on to Beekbrain to Beepy to Beeky. I guess Beeky stuck because I hated it the most. Especially when we would be in a store. We would be aisles apart and I would hear, "BEEEEEKY!" I didn't answer. Someone might actually think that was my name. So now there are times when somebody hears you call me Beeky and they pick up on it, and it makes me cringe. Someday perhaps I may get used to it. I love you Frank, you make me smile.

I have one more bone to pick with you. Then maybe I'll get some sleep. It's almost daylight now. You've been blowing ZZZ's for hours. You make me chuckle. Anyway, back to the complaint. In reference to our never ending gin rummy game. You didn't tell the folks that I'm really not that bad a player its just that you cheat and sometimes I let you win, just to keep you happy of course.

Frankie, my letter is coming to a close. Before it does though, I just want you to know that if not one book of yours sells, that's alright with me. Because I will always have a copy of the most beautiful words ever written from a husband to a wife. That is since George Burns wrote of his love for Gracie. They are soul mates too ya know.

Goodnight Frankie my love. And remember don't get your balls in an uproar!